ANTONIO MACHADO

The Authentic Voice Of Spain

ANTONIO MACHADO

The Authentic Voice Of Spain

JEREMY GORING

ISBN: Softcover   978-1-9845-9538-6
              eBook   978-1-9845-9537-9

Cover portrait of Machado (1918) by Joaquín Sorella reproduced courtesy of
the Hispanic Society of New York.

Print information available on the last page.

Rev. date: 09/01/2020

To order additional copies of this book, contact:
Xlibris
UK TFN: 0800 0148620 (Toll Free inside the UK)
UK Local: 02036 956328 (+44 20 3695 6328 from outside the UK)
www.Xlibrispublishing.co.uk
Orders@Xlibrispublishing.co.uk
814143

CONTENTS

For Rosemary, who first introduced me to Machado

Author's Preface

'Antonio Machado', wrote the distinguished English hispanist Helen Grant in 1957, 'is looked on in Spanish speaking countries today as the finest poet Spain has produced since the Golden Age.' I have to confess, however, that prior to 1993 I myself had never heard of him. It was in that year, on a visit to the province of Soria, that my wife remarked in passing that this was 'the country of Antonio Machado'. She knew about him because, many years earlier, she had read Spanish at Cambridge and had been tutored by Helen Grant as well as by another great admirer of the poet, J. B. Trend.

At first I wrongly imagined him to have been primarily a pastoral poet who had spent his entire life taking his inspiration, as John Clare had done in Northamptonshire, from a particular region of his native land. This impression was confirmed when, some years later, I read the poems by Machado included in the second edition of the *Oxford Book of Spanish Verse*: the longest one was taken from *Campos de Castilla*, with its wonderful evocation of the broad lands of Soria. It was not until 2003, when I looked him up in *Larousse 2000*, that I discovered that Machado was much more than a provincial poet. Born in Seville and living most of his life in Madrid, his Soria years had been little more than an accidental interlude. It also became clear that his poetry was far from being predominantly pastoral. According to *Larousse* he wrote 'lyrical poetry with an ethical content that expressed a profound preoccupation with the human condition, the historical and social reality of Spain, and the mystery of existence'. I was also delighted, but not surprised, to discover that, coming from a family noted for its radical views on political and religious matters, he had been a resolute opponent of Franco.

I was so interested in what I had read about the poet that in 2007, when my daughter asked me what I would like for my birthday, I requested 'a biography of Antonio Machado'. I expected to receive a slim (possibly out of date) paperback with a brief sketch of his life – the sort of book produced to provide a bit of background for students of Spanish literature. But to my surprise she sent me a stout 760-page hardback, complete with photographs, copious endnotes and a capacious bibliography: this was Ian Gibson's recently published work, *Ligero de equipaje: la vida de Antonio Machado.*

With my limited knowledge of Spanish it took me about a year to read the book, but it convinced me that there was a real need for a Machado biography in English that would appeal not only to students of Spanish literature but also to general readers in Britain and America. It has taken me ten years of quite intensive research to produce the present volume, which is based not only on material culled from Ian Gibson's magisterial work but also from a range of printed primary sources in Spanish.

Writing this book has left me indebted to a number of kind people. Foremost among them is Ian Gibson himself, who entertained me and my wife hospitably in Madrid, read the first draft of my book and made some valuable comments; a glance at my footnotes will reveal the extent of my dependence on his work. I wish, too, to acknowledge the generous assistance of Willis Barnstone, the American translator of many of Machado's poems, who commented helpfully on my efforts to do justice to Machado.

I am also indebted to a number of people in Spain who have assisted me over the years. Antonio Moreno Juste, Head of Modern and Contemporary History at Universidad Complutense, Madrid, helped me track down an obscure publication and provided me with a photocopy. The principal of the Instituto del Cardenal Cisneros, which Machado (and, over a century later, my granddaughter) attended, kindly showed me over the school and presented me with a copy of its annals. My cousin Philippa Stanford, who lives near Girona, gave me valuable information about Machado's last days in Catalonia.

I have been fortunate as well to have had help closer at hand from members of my immediate family. Without my wife Rosemary's knowledge of Spanish language and literature I could never have embarked on this biography; her English, too, is better than mine, and she has been through what I have written with a keen eye for clichés, obscurities and hyperbole. My daughter Margaret has edited the entire text with great expertise, expunging errors and advising me to provide extra information for the benefit of readers unfamiliar with Spanish history and culture; she has also prepared the Index of First Lines. Her husband José Conrado González García has taken a close interest in the project and has helped to sustain it with plentiful portions of his excellent vegan paella. My son George has helped with research, and he and our friend Alan Taylor have given valuable technical assistance with computing. And to all the other family members who have had to put up with so much talk about Machado I can only say *muchísimas gracias*.

Finally I wish to acknowledge with thanks the following copyright owners for permission to reproduce translations of Machado's poems: Copper Canyon Press for those by Willis Barnstone; the Dolphin Book Co for those by J. B. Trend; and Robert Bly for his own translations. For those translated by Alan Trueblood I am required to phrase the acknowledgment exactly as follows, 'Antonio Machado: Selected Poems, translated by Alan S. Trueblood, Cambridge, Mass: Harvard University Press, Copyright 1982 by the President and Fellows of Harvard College.' I also acknowledge with thanks permission given by University of California Press to reproduce two passages of Machado's prose translated by Ben Belitt. Except where otherwise stated, all translations from the Spanish were made by me, often with expert assistance from my wife.

Introduction

'Spain of the twentieth century', writes Willis Barnstone, the eminent American hispanist, 'was a nation of extraordinary poets, each distinctive and original. The most beloved of those poets, then and now, is Antonio Machado. He is the quietest, the least pretentious, the most subtle and amusing in aphoristic scepticism, the deepest in the spirit's labyrinths, the freshest in voice, and the plainest in clear, landscape vision.' [1] Evidence of his iconic status can be found all over Spain. In Madrid, where he spent most of his life, there is a fine memorial to him close to the metro station that bears his name. In Segovia the house in which he lived is now a museum dedicated to his memory. In Soria the classroom where he taught has been lovingly preserved and the city's principal tourist attraction is an 'Antonio Machado trail' signposted in both Spanish and English. In Baeza, where he also worked as a schoolmaster, there is a 'Machado corner' and a monument that has been a rallying-point for his admirers. And in the Museu Memorial de l'Exil at Jonquera there is a good deal of material (in several languages) about the man who was the most famous of the thousands of Spaniards who passed through Catalonia in 1938 and 1939 on their way to exile in France.

Machado is renowned as the author of poems that every Spanish child learns to recite at school. Many of these are inspired by his memories of an idyllic childhood in a garden in Seville, while others come from his best-known collection called *Campos de Castilla*, which celebrates the countryside that he came to know and love in the surroundings of Soria. Yet other poems tell of his abiding grief at the loss of his wife Leonor, so much younger than himself, who died of consumption at the age of 18. There are also the poems he addressed to the woman he fell in love with in middle age and the sonnets that he wrote in the last years of his life.

Many of these poems are reproduced in the pages of this biography, mostly in the excellent translations made by the American scholars Willis Barnstone, Robert Bly and Alan Trueblood; the book has benefited greatly from the commentaries on individual poems made by these writers and other distinguished hispanists. There are also numerous passages of Machado's less well-known prose, here translated into English for the first time. In his letters to his friends, in the articles that he wrote for newspapers, in his public speeches or in the message that he broadcast to the nation shortly before his death, we meet a rather different Machado from the one known only for his poetry. Here was a man who, throughout his life, was deeply concerned about the state of Spain – about the incompetence and irresponsibility of its politicians and the depravity and worldliness of its churchmen. His passion for truth and his hatred of injustice shines through his prose, making it clear that his sympathies were always with the poor, the powerless and the downtrodden.

Much of Machado's political and religious radicalism was inherited from his forebears. His grandfather, the first Antonio, was a member of the Revolutionary Junta of Seville set up in 1868 to work for the overthrow of the Bourbon monarchy and he was closely associated with the founders of the First Republic. His father, the second Antonio, also an ardent republican, once proudly declared that 'The Machados are in the world to fight tyranny and obscurantism'. It was therefore not surprising that in 1931, when moves were afoot to dethrone King Alfonso XIII, the third Antonio was among those pressing for the establishment of a republic. It is significant that he should have been asked to preside over the first meeting, held in Segovia, of the national republican campaign. Henceforward, so long as it lasted, he remained one of the staunchest defenders and brightest stars of Spain's short-lived Second Republic.

Most of this finds no place in *Vida de Antonio Machado y Manuel*, the first biography of the poet (which included material about his brother Manuel), written by Miguel Pérez Ferrero and published in 1950. This author, whose work is largely based upon conversations with Manuel, has much to say about Antonio's private life but nothing at all about his involvement in public affairs. In his account of the events of the years 1931 to 1936 he discusses the plays that the two brothers were writing but makes no mention of the dramatic events in which Antonio was participating off stage. In his final chapter he only refers in passing to the Civil War. '1936 ..., 1937..., 1938... Historians will write about these years of blood and fire', he says, pointing out that what he calls 'our chronicle' would not include an account of them.[2] Writing at a time when Franco was at the height of his power it would not have been prudent to do so. It was not until the Generalísimo was in his grave that Spaniards would be free to write about the great conflict that had divided the nation and the part that the Machado brothers – the one supporting the fascists and the other vigorously opposing them – had played in it.

By 1980, five years after Franco's death, the truth could at last be told. In that year the first full-length book about the poet's life and work was published. Written in French by Bernard Sesé and translated into Spanish by Soledad García Mouton, it was entitled *Antonio Machado (1875-1939): El Hombre. El Poeta. El Pensador.* The book has much more to say about the poet and the thinker than the man, small chunks of biography being sandwiched between lengthy commentaries on his writings. But it is possible for the reader to piece together the story of his life and to realise the important part that public affairs played in it. There is a chapter on the Civil War years that quotes passages of the poet's prose, although there are few extracts from his extensive contributions to the newspapers in which he expounded his views on national and international affairs.

Much fuller use of Machado's prose is made by Ian Gibson. In contrast to Sesé, the approach of this Irish-born hispanist is strictly chronological. Quotations from Machado's writings are placed firmly within the narrative of his life, so that the reader can at once see the connexion between a particular piece and the circumstances in which it was written. This is especially valuable in the case of the war years, when the pace of events was at its fastest: here there is always a need to know the exact context of a quoted passage. Readers of the sonnet 'Again our yesterday', for example, need to realise that it was composed in Valencia in 1937, at a time when the 'brother' whom the poet rebukes in the poem was living in Burgos, furthering the cause of fascism.

The present work, the first biography to be written in English, is based to a considerable extent, although not exclusively, on Ian Gibson's book and is similarly designed to offer a clear narrative of events. It is, however, less chronological and more thematic in its approach. Within a given chapter events are not always described in the order of their occurrence but in accordance with their relevance to a theme. One particular theme is actually taken right out of its temporal context and provided with a chapter to itself. This is the intriguing story of Machado's relationship with Pilar de Valderrama (the mysterious 'Guiomar' of his celebrated *canciones*), which extended over a period of seven years. It would be difficult for readers to follow the ups and downs of this prolonged clandestine affair with a married woman if they had to be continually switching their attention from it to the poet's other preoccupations.

This biography, unlike previous ones, makes use of the insights of depth psychology. Machado, who was familiar with the works of Freud, paid close attention to his dreams but left it to others to interpret them; and born on the same day as C. G. Jung, he shared with the great Swiss physician of souls a keen interest in the exploration of the unconscious and its connection with the conscious mind. In this book, where less attention is given to his evolution as a poet and more to his development as a man, Machado's life is viewed mainly from a psychotherapist's perspective. Some of his most powerful dreams are analysed and some of his buried feelings exhumed. Light is thrown on the aggressive feelings which, turned against himself, had resulted in bouts of depression that, significantly, ceased to afflict him after the outbreak of the Civil War had given him legitimate targets for his hostility.

This is the story of a writer who, as Helen Grant expressed it, 'can often transcend the limits of his age and speak to the hearts and heads of post-war generations inside and outside Spain'.[3] What she wrote in 1957 is as true today as it was then. For the benefit of people in Britain and America who are interested in Spain's history and culture Machado's story needs to be told.

I

The Three Antonios

There was a merchant of Cadiz who had three sons. The eldest, Manuel, followed his father into trade, crossed the Atlantic and grew rich in Guatemala; and the second son, Francisco, apparently did likewise. But the third son, Antonio, had other ideas: an independent-minded, idealistic young man, he wanted to remain in Spain and devote his life to changing the way things were in his country. But before he settled down he wanted to see something of the wider world.

Antonio Machado Núñez was born in 1815 into a family that had originated in Portugal and may have been connected with Félix Machado, the Marquis of Montbelo, a 17th century Lusitanian writer. He went to university to study medicine and, after the outbreak of the first Carlist War in 1833, is reported to have helped tend the wounds of soldiers fighting on the liberal side. After qualifying as a doctor he too went to Guatemala, where for two years he practised as a physician and evidently became quite prosperous. But he felt that there was more to life than making money and in 1841, after a long journey of exploration through Mexico and Central America, he sailed back to Spain. He then moved to Paris to further his medical studies and remained there for three years, becoming fluent in French and well acquainted with the country's history and politics. In 1844, after an extensive tour through Germany, Switzerland, Holland and

1

Belgium, he returned to Spain. For a time he practised medicine in Seville but, deeply distressed by the death of a young woman patient whose life he had failed to save, he decided to switch to an academic career. In 1846, following a brief period teaching at the University of Santiago de Compostela, he was appointed professor of Natural Science at the University of Seville and in the following year began to teach courses in zoology, geology and mineralogy.

Machado Nuñez now had ample opportunities to pursue his researches in the field of natural history, making a detailed study of the wildlife of Andalusia and gaining a doctorate in Natural Sciences from the Central University of Madrid. He then proceeded to publish a series of books about the region's birds, fish, reptiles and mammals. Among mammals was especially fascinated by hedgehogs which, he was surprised to discover from his nocturnal observations, bellowed like bullocks during the mating season. He loved all animals and had a great dislike of bull-fighting. 'The government would do well,' he declared on one occasion, 'to concern itself with the task of gradually extinguishing the Spaniards' unfortunate fondness for the bloody and scandalous scenes that are enacted in bull-rings. How beneficial it would be for our country's culture and civilisation if such things were to disappear!'[1] Living as he did in Seville, which boasted the biggest bull-ring in Spain, it must have taken courage to speak out in this way.

It also took courage, in a city noted for its conservatism and its fervent Catholicism, to adopt a liberal stance in political and religious matters. Strongly anti-clerical, Machado never ceased to castigate a Church that, by expelling Jews and Muslims, had helped to turn Spain into a cultural and intellectual backwater. A convinced republican, he had never put his trust in princes and in 1868 he became a member of the Revolutionary Junta of Seville which was working for the overthrow of the government of Queen Isabel II. After her deposition in the autumn of that year, he served for a time as rector of the university and as governor of the province of Seville. In an address to the university in 1873 he spoke of the need for a reform of the country's educational institutions and curricula. Machado was particularly concerned about the neglect of the sciences and urged Spaniards to follow the example of Britain and Germany by encouraging the study of natural history. Himself a pioneer palaeontologist, he had been deeply impressed by Darwin's *Origin of Species*, which had been published in Spanish in 1871. He believed that the book constituted 'a revolution in biology as far-reaching as that made in astronomy by Newton's *Principia*'. 'Fanaticism and ignorance, stemming from error and prejudice,' he insisted, 'cannot prevent Science demonstrating that everything results from the laws of the Universe, which are causal, harmonic and immutable.' [2]

Machado's conviction that the Universe was governed by laws that were essentially 'harmonic' owed less to Darwin than to the German philosopher Karl Christian Krause, whose radical ideas had been introduced into Spain by Julián Sanz del Río, the author of *Ideal de la humanidad*. This book, essentially a resumé of Krause's teachings, was published in 1860 and was received with acclamation by most Spanish intellectuals, who had hitherto known nothing about the exciting new ideas then emanating from Germany. But, as Juan López-Morillas has said; 'Spanish Krausism was more then a philosophy; it was … a certain way of concerning oneself with life and occupying oneself with it, of thinking it and living it, using reason as a compass to explore, surely and systematically, the whole of creation.'[3] Anti-clericals warmed to Krause's idea that in spiritual matters the highest authority was not the Church but the individual human conscience. His views, moreover, were in line with the republicans' conviction that there was no higher authority in the realm than that of the elected representatives of the people. But these notions were roundly condemned by the political and ecclesiastical establishment, who rightly feared that such radicalism would subvert their authority. After the 1868 revolution there were hopes that *krausismo* might become the predominant ideology of Spain, but, by the close of 1873 – with the fall of the Republic that had been inaugurated at the beginning of that year – Machado and his friends knew that there was now little chance of this happening.

Machado's unorthodox views were evidently shared by his wife, Cipriana Álvarez Durán, whom he had married in 1844. Fifteen years younger than her husband, she was the daughter of José Álvarez Guerra, a former soldier and politician who had once been exiled to France for his republicanism. Under the pseudonym of 'Un Amigo del Hombre', he wrote a four-volume work entitled *Unidad Simbólica*, in which he expressed his conviction that all the world's problems stemmed from egoism. His views were firmly grounded in the Gospels but, because he was clearly an original and independent thinker, his book was condemned by the Church as heretical. This eccentric philosopher was a man whose ideas were well 'ahead of his time'. He remained in Seville until his death in 1864, and there can be no doubt that he had a profound influence on the world-view of the Machados.

In 1846, while Machado Núñez and his wife were living in Santiago de Compostela, she gave birth to what was to be their only child, a son, whom they named Antonio. Soon afterwards they returned to Seville, where the boy grew up into manhood. Antonio Machado Álvarez was very close to his mother, his constant companion and teacher. She had inherited a passion for popular poetry and song from her uncle Agustin Durán, the first Spaniard to make a thorough study of the country's folklore and the compiler of the famous *Romancero general*, and she passed this passion on to her son. When he reached the age of 18 the young Machado entered the University of Seville, where one of his teachers, Federico de Castro, professor of metaphysics and a close friend of his father, encouraged him to make a serious study of Spanish folklore. It was Castro who inspired him to become a fervent adherent of *krausismo*: Krause's '23 Commandments', as set out in Sanz del Rio's book, henceforth became the guiding principle of his life. In due course, however, influenced by the writings of the English philosopher Herbert Spencer, Machado Álvarez came to have doubts about the first of Krause's commandments: 'Thou shalt know and love God, pray to him and sanctify him.' [4] But although he may have come to think of himself as an *agnostica* or a *positivista* rather than a *krausista*, he never abandoned his belief in those aspects of the German philosopher's teachings that urged people to love themselves, their neighbours and the whole world of Nature. His anticlericalism knew no bounds.

Some of the articles that he later contributed to journals were deemed so heretical that the mere act of reading them meant risking formal excommunication by the synod of Seville and the bishop of Jaén. He also maintained his family's links with the freemasonry that had long been part and parcel of their politics. As J. G. Brotherston has pointed out, 'he clung passionately to his masonic ideas even after their direct political relevance had been lost.'[5]

In 1867, seeking to broaden his horizons, Machado Álvarez migrated to the University of Madrid, where he joined with other republicans to found a radical review entitled *El Obrero de la Civilización*, whose contributors included Castro, Nicolás Salmerón and Francisco Giner de los Ríos. Two years later, however, following a serious illness, he returned to Seville, where he obtained his licentiate in Civil Law and, with his father's help, was instrumental in founding the *Revista Mensual de Filosofía, Literatura y Ciencias*. He himself contributed articles about popular literature under the pseudonym *Demófilo* ('Friend of the People'). He also collaborated with Castro in the publication of a book about popular culture entitled *Cuentos, leyendas y costumbres populares* and in 1872, when his old teacher moved to the University of Madrid, succeeded him in his chair. At the same time, probably because he needed to supplement his meagre academic salary, he enrolled in the local College of Advocates and worked for a time as a *juez municipal* in the district of San Vicente. At this date, it seems, he was under no pressure to earn a great deal of money, for he was still living with his parents in a house that they shared with his maternal grandmother and her handicapped unmarried son José Álvarez Durán.

That year, however, something quite unexpected happened. The young man, who seems to have been hitherto too serious-minded to think of anything but his studies, fell in love – and apparently it was love at first sight. The story of how this came about was told years later by his son, writing under the pseudonym of Juan de Mairena:

> It so happened that some dolphins lost their way
> and, carried along by the tide, had swum up the

> Guadalquivir as far as Seville. Attracted by the
> unusual spectacle, many people came from all over
> the city to the river bank; among the young men and
> women were my parents, who there saw each other
> for the first time. It was a sunny evening, and I have
> sometimes imagined being there myself.[6]

The unexpected event had evidently brought together two people who under normal circumstances would never have met socially. Had it not been for the arrival of the dolphins, it is most unlikely that Antonio Machado Álvarez would ever have had the chance to strike up conversation with a young woman like Ana Ruiz Hernández. But the relationship blossomed and, after a brief courtship, the couple became engaged.

'Antonio Machado Álvarez and Ana Ruiz', wrote Miguel Pérez Ferrero, writing in the historic present, 'are of well known and prestigious families.'[7] It seems, however, that he was totally mistaken in this assertion. Ana's father, Rafael Ruiz Pérez, had served in the Navy (probably on the lower deck) and was later stated in the census as being employed in family business in the neighbourhood of Calle Betis and Calle Vazquez de Leca. It is not known exactly what this business was, but it is likely to have been some form of retail trade. His wife, Isabel Hernández García, was described as a *vendedora de dulces* (a sweet-seller) in the same neighbourhood, which at that time was not a fashionable one. Triana lay on the west bank of the Guadalquivir, where gypsies and other socially disadvantaged people lived. Isabel, although not a native of the place, had evidently become a true *trianera*: she hardly ever left the *barrio*, even to cross the bridge to Seville, and apparently regarded a trip to the city as a novel experience. That the Machados should have agreed to their son marrying someone from such a socially inferior background bears witness to their unusual broad-mindedness and their unconditional concern for his happiness. For young Antonio himself, with his particular academic interests, it was most appropriate that he should marry into a family with whom every conversation may have provided an opportunity to advance his knowledge of the 'wisdom of the people'.

The marriage took place on 22 May 1873, when the bride was 19 and the groom 27, and it was a strictly civil affair. It would have been natural for the ceremony to have been performed in the historic parish church of Santa Ana, which was close by the Ruiz home in Triana and where Ana herself had been baptised. But, whatever the bride or her parents thought, it would probably not have affected the other party's wish that the wedding should not take place in a church. Following the revolution of 1868 civil marriages had become legal in Spain and the anticlerical Machados would have been determined to take advantage of the new dispensation. But, if it had lost control of marriages, the Church retained its monopoly in the celebration of births and so, when Ana gave birth to a son in August 1874, he was duly baptised in church. He was christened with the names of Manuel, Antonio and Rafael in a church close to the house where his parents were now living. This was clearly a year for celebrations: a few weeks after the christening the new father received his doctorate in Philosophy and Letters from the University of Seville.

Early in 1875, feeling the need for more spacious accommodation, the couple moved into the historic palace of Las Dueñas, which had recently been divided up into apartments. The palace's owner, Jacobo Luis Fitz-James Stuart y Ventimiglia, the 15th Duke of Alba, had decided to let these apartments to local people of good repute but modest means. And it was in these gracious surroundings that, on the morning of 26 July, the Machados' second son was born, a mere eleven months after the birth of their first. Two days later, in the nearby church of San Juan Bautista, he was baptised Antonio, Cipriano, José María, and Francisco de Santa Ana. All the names except the last commemorated his forbears on his father's side, while Santa Ana was chosen in honour of his mother and of the saint on whose feast day he had been born. It is surprising that, as on the occasion of Manuel's baptism, none of Antonio's godparents came from his mother's side. His godmother was his great grandmother Cipriana Durán de Vicente Yáñez, who was represented by her daughter Cipriana, the wife of Machado Núñez. In addition he had two godfathers, who were both neighbours and friends of the family in Las Dueñas – Gumersindo Díaz Pérez, a painter, and Ricardo Medrano, a local businessman.

The experience of growing up in the palace of Las Dueñas was to have a profound effect upon the infant Antonio. In 'Retrato' (Portrait) he wrote that 'my childhood memories are of a patio in Seville/ and a sunny garden where lemons are ripening.' [8] Orange, myrtle, palm and cypress trees also grew in the walled garden, where the silence was broken only by the song of blackbirds, the cooing of doves and, from time to time, the muffled peal of bells. In the intense heat of a Seville summer this garden, with its fountains flowing with cool water, was a most pleasant place to be. Given the strength of his feelings about his earliest home it is likely that when, in August 1879, shortly after his fourth birthday, his family vacated the palace, Antonio felt that he was being cast out of paradise.

If the years that the Machados spent in Las Dueñas were idyllic for Antonio, this was probably not the case for other members of the family. It was a difficult time for his father who, for reasons that are not altogether clear, was unable to pursue his beloved folklore researches. It was even more difficult for his mother, who lost two babies in quick succession – a boy, born in 1877, who only lived for a matter of weeks, and a girl who died at the age of nine months in July 1879, shortly before they moved house. We have no way of knowing how Antonio's brother Manuel felt about that particular time in his life. There are no indications in his poetry or other writings that he shared his brother's nostalgia for the days spent at Las Dueñas. For him this may have been an emotionally difficult period, since it was not he but Antonio who could bask in the assurance that he was his mother's favourite son.

In October, shortly after moving into a new house not far from their first marital home, another son, whom they named José, was born. Writing to a friend who had congratulated him on the event, his father expressed the hope that the boy would become 'a great propagandist', who would bear out his belief that 'Machados are in the world to fight tyranny and obscurantism'.[9] But at this moment he was less taken up with fighting tyranny than with promoting the study of Spanish folklore, in which task he now had an enthusiastic collaborator, Luis Montoto y Rautenstrauch, editor of the Sevillian periodical *El Español*. Montoto later wrote a vivid description of his colleague Machado's appearance at this time:

> I was always surprised by his laid-back manner and his unkempt appearance. With his cravat untied, his shirt collar unbuttoned, his trousers hitched up so high that his boots were totally exposed to view, wearing summer clothes in winter, his cloak trailing the ground when he slung it over his shoulders, his hair always tousled (but clean), talkative and high-spirited – the untidiness of his person contrasted with the elegance of his speech and the refinement of his manners. He showed affection to everyone and kept a place for his friends in the deepest recesses of his heart. He himself possessed nothing: he gave away everything.[10]

It was in one of his conversations with this friend that Machado Álvarez showed how passionately he felt about his folklore researches. 'Study the people', he said. 'Study the people who, without grammar or rhetoric, speak better than you do, because they express their thoughts fully, without adulteration or trickery; and they sing better than you do, because they say what they feel. It is the people, not the academics, who are the true conservators of the language and poetry of the nation.'[11] The man who styled himself *Demófilo* was indeed a 'lover of the people' and, being a true idealist, he believed that the study of popular culture, if carried out comparatively and internationally, would help to promote the cause of universal brotherhood.

In 1881, inspired by the news of the foundation of a Folklore Society in London, he was instrumental in setting up the Sociedad El

Folk-Lore Andaluz, which he hoped would lead to the establishment
of similar societies in other parts of the country. In the same year he
published his *Coleción de cantes flamencos*, a pioneering work that would
lead to his recognition as Spain's first *flamencólogo*. The greatness of
his enthusiasm for the subject can be gauged from the tone of a single
sentence (which in the Spanish original runs to120 words) taken from
its introduction:

> The love that we profess for our people and their
> poetry… inspires us to hope that this modest work…
> will be kindly received by men of science and
> dispose them to forgive the mistakes of one who,
> in committing them, has intended only to assemble
> the raw materials of an infant science that has come
> into being to affirm the people's right, hitherto
> unrecognised, to be considered an important element
> in the culture and civilisation of humanity. [12]

In spite of his doubts the work was well received, as were the
first issues of his journal, *El Folk-Lore Andaluz*, to which his mother
contributed popular songs and for which his father wrote an article
about the symbolic significance of dogs. He gained an even more
appreciative readership for a book published in 1883 entitled *Titín y
las primeras oraciones*, a treatise on the language of infants, based upon
his study of the linguistic development of his youngest son Joaquín.
In due course the book would be translated into English, French,
German, Italian and Portuguese, but in the short term, like his other
publications, it brought him little financial reward.

Because of his impecunious state *Demófilo* had been obliged,
shortly before Joaquín's birth in August 1881, to move with his
family into his parents' house in Calle O'Donnell. Although his
old grandmother had died, it must have been quite an overcrowded
household for, in addition to Machado Álvarez and his wife and four
children, it also included his uncle, the disabled artist José Álvarez
Durán, who had lodged with the family in Las Dueñas and in the

house they had subsequently moved to. Now, for the first time, the three Antonios were together under one roof. Plenty is known about what the first two were doing at this juncture but very little about the activities of the third who, to distinguish him from the others, ought properly to be referred to as Antonio Machado Ruiz. It is likely that the young Antonio and his brother Manuel were regularly taken over the bridge to Triana to see their maternal grandparents, who continued to live in a house close to the river. It also seems that the boys sometimes ventured further afield when their father went shooting wild birds. One of Antonio's poems was later to record the sight of Machado Álvarez standing on the banks of the Guadalquivir with the 'white smoke of his well-aimed shot' coming out of the 'blue barrel of his gun'.[13] It is also likely that, from time to time, their grandfather would have taken them on excursions into the countryside surrounding Seville to acquaint them with the animals and birds he knew so well. And it is also possible that, since there was now a rail link between Seville and Cadiz, they would on occasion have accompanied him on a visit to that city. Machado Núñez would have been keen to show them the place where he grew up and the port from which, long ago, he had sailed to Central America.

Of one particular incident in his Seville childhood Antonio long preserved a clear memory, as he recorded in his notebook in 1914:

> I do not remember exactly at what time of year it used to be the custom for people to buy children sugar canes or what my fellow countrymen call *cañas dulces*. But I do recall a sunny morning when I was 6 or 7 years old, sitting with my grandmother on a bench in the Plaza de la Magdalena with a sugar cane in my hand. Not far from us another child passed by with his mother. He also had a sugar cane. I thought to myself, 'Mine is much bigger.' I well remember how sure I was about this. However, I asked my grandmother, 'Isn't it true that my cane is bigger than that boy's one?' I had no doubt that she would agree

with me. But my grandmother replied immediately in an authoritative but affectionate tone that I shall never forget. 'On the contrary, my child, that boy's cane is much bigger than yours.' It seems that that trivial incident has had a great influence upon my life. All that I am – good and bad – whatever there is in me that is integrated or disintegrated – I owe to the memory of my sugar cane.

Having written this note I asked my mother to tell me at what time of year children in Seville suck sugar canes. 'It is at Christmas', she replied, 'the time for sweet potatoes and pears.' I also now realize that sugar canes must be sold and sucked in many places in Spain. But the Seville of my memories was not on the map or in the calendar.[14]

Twenty years later, writing under the pseudonym of Juan de Mairena, he provided another version of this anecdote:

When I was very young I was walking with my mother with a stick of sugar cane in my hand. It was Christmas time and we were in Seville. Not far away another mother was walking with her child, who also had a sugar cane. I was sure that mine was bigger than his. Oh, so very sure! Nevertheless, I asked my mother – because, even if something is evident to them, children like to have it confirmed – 'Mine's bigger, isn't it?' 'No, my son', she replied, 'Where are your eyes?' It is a question that I have been asking myself all my life. [15]

Which is the more accurate account of the occurrence? The apocryphal Mairena's account – with its penetrating question, 'Where are your eyes?' – certainly has the ring of truth, but the other one, which the poet had committed to his notebook nearer the time of the event, is probably more authentic. The earlier version of the story is more specific in terms of time and place. Antonio says that he was aged 6 or 7 – i.e. in about 1881 or 1882 – and that the incident took place not simply 'in Seville' but in the 'Plaza de la Magdalena'. Is it not more likely that it was she who was with him on this occasion – rather than his mother who, with two younger children to attend to, may not have had the time to spend sitting on a bench in the sun with one of her older ones? And in any event it does not seem to have been in her nature to administer stern rebukes; they were far more likely to have come from her mother-in-law, who was evidently a much stronger minded and more assertive person. Whatever the truth of the matter, there is no doubt that in his early years Antonio did spend a lot of time with his grandmother who, as he himself testified, helped him to learn to read. She apparently set before him her copy of the *Romancero general* and spelt out the words of the songs. She evidently not only spoke the words but also *sang* them to her grandchildren, fostering in them a love of popular verse that would prove to be lasting.

For their formal education Manuel and Antonio attended a school located in a former convent not far from their home and which was kept by a master named Antonio Sánchez Morales. Was he the old man featured in Machado's 'Memory from childhood'?

> A drab and chilling afternoon
> in winter. The schoolboys
> are studying. Monotony
> of rain across the window glass.
>
> The classroom. A placard
> shows a fugitive Cain
> and Abel dead,
> next to a scarlet stain.

In a sonorous hollow tone
the master thunders, an old man
shabby, lean and dried up,
holding a book in his hand.

And a whole children's choir
begins to chant the lesson:
'Hundred squared, ten thousand,
thousand squared, a million.'

A drab and chilling afternoon
in winter. The schoolboys
are studying. Monotony
of rain along the window glass.[16]

The Machado brothers' days in that dingy classroom, however, were numbered. Soon circumstances would dictate that they would have to leave Seville, the bright city of their birth and infancy. In 1883 Machado Núñez, who had been teaching in Seville for 36 years, was appointed to a chair in the Central University of Madrid and, since economic necessity dictated that they all had to live together, his son, daughter in law and grandsons all moved with them. There may have been some misgivings about the move, but it was clearly greatly to the children's advantage. It meant that they would be exchanging the monotonous regime of an old-style primary school for the stimulus and excitement of the most enlightened educational institution in Spain.

II

The Making of a Poet

The Institución Libre de Enseñanza – an educational establishment that was 'free' because it received no financial support from the State – was founded in 1876 by a group of professors who had been expelled the previous year from the University of Madrid. They had all been active participants in the great programme of educational reform embarked upon after the overthrow of the Bourbons in 1868 – a programme that had been abruptly terminated six years later when the monarchy was restored. Being convinced *krausistas*, these men were regarded as dangerous radicals, quite unfit to be entrusted with the education of young Spanish minds. The most celebrated members of the group were Laureano Figuerola, who had presided over the Senate in 1872, and Nicolás Salmerón, who had served briefly as President of the Republic in the following year. But the principal founder of the Institución was the group's youngest member, Francisco Giner de los Ríos, who had played no part in politics and was much less well known.

The original intention had been to establish a private university, complete with faculties of Law, Philosophy, Literature, Medicine and Pharmacy, but the courses on offer had failed to attract sufficient numbers of students. And so in 1879 the decision was taken to abandon university teaching and to concentrate exclusively on the provision of primary and secondary education, for which there was a clear demand. Within a few years, thanks largely to the endeavours of Giner de los Ríos, there were more than two hundred pupils on the roll.

The Machado family had taken a keen interest in the Institución since its foundation. Machado Álvarez was an old friend of Giner de los Ríos, whom he had first met during his stay in Madrid in 1867. When Giner de los Ríos was seeking a wife Machado Álvarez had suggested his cousin María Machado Ugarte as a possible candidate. She was the daughter of his uncle Manuel, who had made his fortune in Guatemala and had later retired to Bilbao. The prosperous merchant, however, had not been persuaded that the impecunious professor was a suitable match for his daughter. 'My father', María told him, 'does not think that I could share the vicissitudes that your profession and your ideas will cause you to experience all your life.'[1] And so Giner de los Ríos, who in any case does not seem to have been greatly attracted to the young woman, had resolved to remain a bachelor. Nevertheless, he and Machado Álvarez, who had dedicated books to the Institución and contributed articles to its *Boletín*, continued to keep in close touch.

When the Machado brothers – Manuel (aged 9), Antonio (aged 8) and José (aged 4) – enrolled there in the autumn of 1883, the school was situated in temporary accommodation in the Calle de las Infantas. Proximity to their sons' place of education had in fact been decisive in the family's choice of residence. And so it was inevitable that in 1885, following the Institución's move to permanent premises, the Machados (who had been living in the Calle del Almirante) would move too. They were fortunate in finding a new apartment at 42 (later 52) Calle de Santa Engracia, just round the corner from the school.

The Institución's new home was a low-slung two storey house in the Paseo del Obelisco (now Paseo del General Martínez Campos), with a front door leading directly on to the street and a back door opening on to a spacious garden. Adjoining it was a small building that had once been a chapel and that now housed a science laboratory. In the house itself were the classrooms, the administrative offices and the living accommodation of Giner de los Ríos, who was both headmaster of the school and (following his restoration to his chair in 1883) professor of the Philosophy of Law in the University of Madrid.

The school curriculum was closely modelled on that formulated by the great educational pioneer Friedrich Froebel, who had been a friend and disciple of Krause, and its pupils enjoyed a measure of freedom unknown in any other school in Spain. As Giner de los Ríos himself put it, the school offered 'an encyclopaedic programme, intuitive education, manual work (including gardening), informal relations between teachers and pupils, the combination of work and play with physical activities in the garden and even in the countryside.'[2] Great importance was attached to outdoor physical activities. J. B. Trend relates that, shortly before the arrival of the Machados, Giner de los Ríos had encouraged an Englishman, who was an assistant master in the school, to introduce organized games into the curriculum. 'He first persuaded the children, boys and girls alike, to play rounders, and then one day he appeared with a curious leather object which a boy called Antonio Vinent helped him to inflate. It was the first football in Spain.'[3] He might have added that it was former pupils of the school who later helped found the soccer club now known as Real Madrid.

Much of the teaching took place off the school premises. Courses in the history of art were taught in one or other of the Madrid galleries – in the physical presence of paintings and statues. Natural science classes were conducted in the countryside adjoining the city, where children could study the flora and fauna at first hand. It is likely that Manuel and Antonio, who had accompanied their grandfather on similar expeditions in Andalusia, particularly enjoyed the excursions to El Pardo, Puerto de Hierro and to the Sierra de Guadarrama beloved of Giner los Ríos. As far as we know, however, they did not take part in any of the long range excursions that so impressed a correspondent from *The Times*, who visited the school in 1884:

> The excursion organized at the Institución has been
> brought to great perfection, and the boys in the
> higher classes have visited the chief places of interest
> throughout Spain; some of the walking tours in the
> summer even cross the Pyrenees.[4]

It is clear that both boys looked back on their days at the
Institución as some of the happiest in their lives. Passing its premises
years afterwards Manuel exclaimed: 'Oh, happy days! Oh, house
blessed by the presence of St Giner de los Ríos, the adored and
adorable master!'[5] And after his death Antonio spoke of his fond
memories of his teacher. 'We children, playing in the garden of the
Institución, used to wait for the beloved master to appear. When he
did so, we ran up to him with childish shouts of joy and bore him
swiftly along towards the classroom door.' [6] How different from
Shakespeare's schoolboys 'creeping like snails unwillingly to school'!

Antonio went on to describe what it was like to be taught by
Giner de los Ríos:

> In his infant class, as in his university lecture room,
> Don Francisco always seated himself among his
> pupils and worked alongside them in a friendly
> and affectionate way... His manner of teaching
> was Socratic: the dialogue was straightforward and
> persuasive. He stimulated the minds of his pupils –
> both men and boys – in such a way that they might
> think for themselves and acquire knowledge that was
> immediate and real.[7]

'Intelligence', wrote Giner de los Ríos, 'must not be overloaded
with enormous quantities of work: pupils must be taught to regard
the possession of vast quantities of knowledge far less lightly than
knowledge of high and solid quality.' [8] It is significant that in later
years, when Antonio himself became a teacher, he too adopted

the Socratic method that Giner de los Ríos had demonstrated so effectively.

For Machado, this little man with bronzed face, white beard and 'eyes that went through you like arrows', was one of the 'great Andalusians':

> Like all great Andalusians, Don Francisco was the living antithesis of the 'tambourine' Andalusian – boastful, prone to exaggeration, loving things that were noisy and gaudy. Lacking in vanity but not in pride, knowing exactly who he was, he cared nothing for outward appearances. He possessed the simplicity and austerity of a saint; he believed in fair shares and just measurements.[9]

Indeed he had no compunction in comparing Giner de los Ríos with the greatest Spanish saints: 'Like Teresa of Avila and Ignatius Loyola,' he wrote, 'he founded a great movement, but he exercised his authority in freedom and love. Everyone in Spain who was young, vibrant and creative was drawn, as by an invisible magnet, to the strength and purity of his soul.'[10] His words would have shocked pious Spanish Catholics, who regarded Giner de los Ríos – and all *krausistas* – as dangerous heretics.

It is impossible to exaggerate the abiding influence upon Machado of the teaching of Giner de los Ríos at the Institución Libre. As Alan Trueblood pointed out, the school 'fostered the fundamental good sense and the quiet self-assurance that made Machado permanently shy of both artistic and intellectual fads, while clear-headed and unhesitant in moral commitment.' [11] But it is clear from the account given by Pérez Ferrero, who had had the benefit of hearing at first hand Manuel's and Antonio's reminiscences of the family's early years in Madrid, that what the brothers learned at home continued to be of primary importance.

The life of the family stays much the same as it has been in Seville, but Manuel and Antonio begin to participate in things more fully. By the light of an oil lamp Doña Cipriana Álvarez presides at the soirees and, when there are no visitors, she spends the time reading aloud. In her high voice she reads the romances collected by her relative, Don Agustín Durán, and the boys enjoy them so much that next day they will get hold of the book and go over their favourite passages again. At other times it is their father who takes it upon himself to read. Then attention is focused on the fascinating plot and the strange language of Bécquer's *Leyendas*, Dickens's novels or Shakespeare's plays, which Macpherson, who had translated them into Spanish, used to send to the house just as they were published.[12]

On some evenings, however, there were no readings by the fireside. The boys were sent to bed early and, as they lay awake, they listened to their parents and grandparents talking together in low tones. They could not hear exactly what was being said, but they suspected that things were serious.

At this period their father's finances were in a precarious state. Expenditure was mounting, for there were two more children to provide for – a son, Francisco, born in February 1884, and a daughter, Cipriana, born in October 1885. Meanwhile income was not increasing: the household in Calle Santa Engracia remained largely dependent on Machado Núñez's professorial salary, the modest rent his wife received from property and whatever her disabled brother José (who still lived with them) could contribute from his private means. Machado Álvarez continued to promote the study of folklore throughout Spain and to work on his *Biblioteca de las tradiciones populares españolas*, the first volumes of which had been published (with the aid of a subvention from his mother) in 1884. But all this activity brought in little or no money, and so in due course he reluctantly decided to return to the law. Openings were few, but in 1888 he was fortunate enough to obtain the post of legal editor of a new periodical, *La Justicia*, founded with the support of Nicolás Salmerón, who had been Minister of Justice under the Republic. When that arrangement came to an end in 1891 some friends offered him a job in a lawyer's office in San Juan de Puerto Rico.

Although unwilling to abandon his family and friends, economic necessity dictated that he accept the offer, and in August 1892 he embarked at Cadiz, as other members of his family had done before him, to seek his fortune in Central America. Nothing is known about his stay in Puerto Rico apart from the information that, within a few months of his arrival, he became gravely ill. When the news reached Spain his brother-in-law Manuel Ruiz, who was a ship's captain, promptly set sail for Puerto Rico and, having brought him back to Cadiz, took the sick man to the family's house in Triana, where Ana was awaiting him. There he was cared for by her other brother, a doctor, but there was nothing he could do to save his life. On 4 February 1893 Machado Álvarez died in his wife's arms, the cause of death being recorded as 'medular sclerosis'. He was 47 years old. Years later Luis Montoto described his feelings on hearing the news of his old friend's death:

> He came back to die among his own people and, by providential design, breathed his last in the place he used to visit in his dreams, the time-honoured land that he loved. This place – the haunt of potters and seamen – was the field of his folklore researches, the quarry from which he dug so many precious materials for the study of the 'wisdom of the people'.[13]

The death of Machado Álvarez was barely mentioned in the local press, but in due course an article about him was published in the *Boletín* of the Institución Libre. It was written by Joaquín Sama, an old friend from his Seville days who had subsequently been one of his sons' teachers at the school.

> He was a most congenial colleague, uncommonly
> kind-hearted, ever striving for all that is good, and
> so persevering that he was able to make an important
> contribution to the advancement of civilization and
> to the regeneration not only of this nation but of all
> humanity.[14]

How his family felt at this sorrowful time can easily be imagined. For Ana grief may have been mixed with gratitude that her husband had been spared further unhappiness and frustration – and that she, who only two years previously had given birth to a daughter who had died in infancy, would be spared any more child-bearing. Another consequence of his death was that the family, who three years earlier had exchanged their apartment in Calle Santa Engracia for one in Calle Fuencarral, had to move house yet again. Their new home was a larger flat in the same street, where Ana and her children were once again re-united – presumably for reasons of economy – with the grandparents and Uncle José, the three of whom for some time past had been living elsewhere in the city.

Meanwhile Antonio, who had left the Institución Libre in the spring of 1889 at the age of 13, spent a year at the Instituto San Isidro in Calle Toledo before moving on to the Instituto del Cardenal Cisneros, the most prestigious public secondary school in Spain, whose imposing buildings in the Calle de los Reyes contrasted sharply with the modest premises he had been familiar with in the Paseo del Obelisco. The ethos of his new school was also very different. After the relaxed regime of the Institución Libre, where there were no textbooks, no set homework and no examinations, he clearly found working for his baccalaureate very hard going. The school's chroniclers say that the course of his studies 'appeared to correspond to the prototype of the bad student, with irregular attendance and mediocre grades'. [15] In 1889-90, while at the Instituto San Isidro, he had failed his examination in Latin and Castilian but, when he took the papers again in the following year, he did achieve a *Bueno*. In 1891-2 he merely scraped a pass in Psychology, Logic and

Ethics; in 1892-3 he received the same low marks for Arithmetic and Algebra; on later occasions it was often recorded that he had not even turned up for his exams. Looking back on his school career Antonio later confessed that at this time he had 'a great aversion to everything academic'.[16] He apparently spent a lot of time in the Biblioteca Nacional reading books totally unrelated to his courses, in particular anything that dealt with drama. He and Manuel, who was also at the Instituto, went frequently to the theatre, where – thanks to their father's friendship with the great actor Rafael Calvo, one of the directors of the Teatro Español – they had the benefit of free admission.

It was through their interest in the theatre that in the summer of 1893, the brothers began to write satirical pieces for a weekly publication called *La Caricatura*, funded by Eduardo Benot, a prominent Republican and an old friend of Machado Núñez. Manuel's contributions were submitted under the pseudonym *Polilla* ('bookworm'), while Antonio's assumed name was *Cabellera* –a clown in a classical play. It is also probable, as Ian Gibson has suggested, that Antonio wrote pieces under the *nom de plume* of Yorick, the Shakespearean clown – 'a fellow of infinite jest, of most excellent fancy' – with whom years later he jokingly compared himself:

> Looking at my skull
> a new Hamlet will say:
> here is a fine fossil
> of a carnival mask.[17]

Yorick was continually complaining about the current state of Spanish drama. Spain, he wrote, lagged badly behind other countries that are 'more culturally advanced', such as England, France and Italy. Its actors needed to abandon their 'hollow, pompous and bombastic manner of speaking, their stylized gestures that are so archaic as to be grotesque, and the insufferable ranting that goes on in the course of any public performance.' [18] *Cabellera's* last contribution to the paper, dated 22 October 1893, was a piece in praise of his friend Enrique

Paradas, who possessed a quality that he himself, when he began to publish poetry, would seek to emulate:

> Enrique Paradas breathes his spirit into all his poems and therefore has insuperable repugnance and boundless contempt for those poets who, because their efforts are mechanical and crude, produce works that lack all feeling. [19]

Soon after the termination of their brief connection with *Caricatura,* the brothers parted company. Manuel, encouraged by his family to turn to more serious pursuits, moved away from Madrid to lodge with his maternal grandparents in Triana and complete his studies for his baccalaureate at the Instituto de Sevilla. The family may have hoped that the 18 year-old Antonio, separated from his elder brother for the first time ever, would also be able to abandon his bohemian lifestyle and get down to work.

The need for both Manuel and Antonio to take life more seriously was brought home to them in the summer of 1896, when their grandfather Machado Núñez, who had never fully recovered from the shock of his only son's death, took ill and died. Deprived of their principal source of financial support, the family was obliged to leave their apartment in Calle Fuencarral for a cheaper one in the same street. Joaquín, who was now 15, had to leave school and take ship to Guatemala, probably in the hope of receiving assistance from his relatives there. His departure was a source of great sadness for Antonio, who later expressed his feelings in a poem called 'The Voyager':

> It is the familiar gloomy room,
> and among us the beloved brother
> who, in the childish dream of a bright day,
> we saw depart for a distant land. [20]

Antonio, who celebrated his 21st birthday two days after his grandfather's death, continued studying for his baccalaureate and in October 1896 found himself a part-time job with a company then playing at the Teatro Español. As a *meritorio* or 'apprentice' he probably did not receive anything more than pocket money, but he evidently enjoyed the experience. He had walk-on parts in a number of plays but, according to his brother José, never spoke more than four words in any of them. He recalled, however, that Antonio worked hard to perfect these minor roles:

> During this apprenticeship he spent hours in front of the mirror, making differing gestures and facial expressions, taking the study of physiognomy very seriously. He also sought to acquire a knowledge of anatomy so that he could know precisely what muscles he had to use to convey different emotions. [21]

His contract with the company, however, came to an end in April 1897 and, although he never trod the boards again, he retained a great love of the theatre; it was probably because of his addiction to drama that he began to go to bull fights. In a letter to Manuel he congratulated him on an article he had written about three bullfighters named Bomba, Reverte and Guerra:

> Bombita, as you say, has had a great season here, showing himself to be the premier *matador* and not a bad *torero*. He was the hero of the celebrated bullfight and everyone admired him. How magnificent his two wounding thrusts were! You couldn't wish for anything better. Reverte, although he is not such a *matador*, is, if that's possible, even braver than Bombita and takes greater risks. Guerra demonstrated that he is the number one *torero* – because of his intelligent use of his cloak to tease his first bull and the skill

with which he handled his sword. But Bombita was phenomenal.[22]

To go to a bullfight would probably have been unthinkable while his animal-loving grandfather was alive; but it seems that he now felt free to taste formerly forbidden fruits. He could behave like any other Spaniard of his age and admire the grace and skill of the bullfighters, and it seems that he continued to do so for some years; in 1907 he sent his friend Juan Ramón Jiménez an essay on 'the manner of meeting God in the bullfights'.[23] But the phase does not seem to have lasted: going to *corridas* may have been one of the 'bad habits' which, in 1913, he said he had given up four years previously. While Manuel might become an enthusiastic frequenter of bull rings, it would probably have been impossible for such a sensitive and spiritually-minded man as Antonio to have gone on doing so. In later years he was scathingly critical of people who were addicted to such 'sports' and it is possible that he came to look back on his love of bullfighting, as he looked back on his youthful addiction to alcohol, as something to be ashamed of. In the 1930s, writing under the pseudonym of Juan de Mairena, he referred to his 'scant enthusiasm for bullfights' and went on to say that he suspected they had never entertained anyone, 'for the spectacle they provide is far too sombre for entertainment'. [24]

Towards the close of 1897 he was reunited with Manuel when the elder brother, having graduated – apparently after little more than a year's study – from the University of Seville, returned to Madrid. It may have been his enthusiastic account of his life there that made Antonio eager to revisit his native city. Be that as it may, the brothers were evidently there in April 1898, participating in the *fiestas*, when they heard that the United States had declared war on Spain. They would have been back in Madrid in the summer when news came through of the sinking of Spanish fleets, firstly in the Philippines and then off the coast of Cuba. This was a national catastrophe and, in the eyes of staunch republicans, it provided fresh and conclusive evidence of what they had long complained about – the corruption and ineptitude of the Spanish government. Because he shared these feelings of frustration so keenly Antonio came to be regarded as one of the so-called 'generation of '98', that amorphous collection of poets, essayists and novelists who, impatient with the conservatism of the establishment, called for the regeneration of Spain.

One of those who, in 1898, was most outspoken in his criticisms of the government was Eduardo Benot, who had held a high office under the First Republic and had been a close friend of Machado Núñez. At this period, when both Antonio and Manuel were in need of paid employment, Benot's friendship proved especially valuable. He was engaged in the preparation of an ambitious work of reference – a *Diccionario de ideas afines* – and took them on as temporary editorial assistants. It was through him that they met Nicolás Estévanez, who had been Minister for War in the Republican government and who, after the restoration of the monarchy, had spent some years in exile in France. He retained many contacts there and it was thanks to him that Manuel and Antonio were able to join the staff of the Paris publishing firm of Garnier, then in the course of preparing a two-volume *Diccionario enciclopédica de la lengua castellana*. And so it came about that, early in 1899, the brothers found themselves in the French capital, lodging in the Latin Quarter in a hotel which, prior to his death three years previously, the great poet Paul Verlaine had made his home. In this part of Paris the brothers encountered some of the famous writers in the city's cosmopolitan literary circle, including the Guatemalan Enrique Gómez Carrillo, the Galician Ramón María del Valle-Inclán and the Irish Oscar Wilde, recently released from Reading gaol. But, for Antonio, the most significant encounter was with the Nicaraguan poet Rubén Darío. 'Out of this meeting between the two poets,' wrote Gabriel Pradal Rodríguez, 'is born a friendship that transcends a purely personal relationship and comes to resemble the contact between two atavistic sensibilities.'[25]

In Paris at this time the main topic of conversation in the cafés was the notorious Dreyfus affair, with opinions sharply divided between those who despised and those who defended the unfortunate Jewish officer. On one occasion there was a street demonstration in which *dreyfusistes* were in conflict with *antidreyfusistes* and the army was brought in to restore order. In the helter-skelter following a cavalry charge Antonio, who was among the onlookers, is said to have lost the heel of one of his boots. On another occasion there was a heated discussion in a restaurant, in which the Basque novelist Pío Baroja, a friend of the Machados who was passionately pro-Dreyfus, was verbally abused by some hostile Frenchmen. In response to a man who had called Baroja's face 'hard and brutish' Antonio is reported to have declared in a solemn tone of voice: 'If at this moment someone was to come in to deliver a message to the man with the most human face of all those present, he would without hesitation give it to Baroja.'[26]

Most of the time, however, the Machados were engaged in less serious pursuits. Manuel, the cheerful extrovert, felt immediately at home in the bohemian environment of Montmartre and, in a series of articles for the Madrid daily *El País*, regaled its readers with its delights. He described his visits to the famous Café des Quatz'arts, where poets and artists congregated, flirting with models, singers and dancers; but it is likely that the introverted Antonio was unimpressed. For him what was most important about his stay in Paris was his encounter with the writings of Verlaine, whose poems, in the years immediately following his death, were on everyone's lips. He was especially moved by four of the sonnets of *Poèmes saturniens* – 'Nevermore', 'Lassitude', 'Après trois ans' and 'Mon rêve familier' – which found resonance with his often melancholy mood and nostalgia for the lost garden of childhood.

Antonio returned home in August 1899, leaving Manuel behind to enjoy himself in Paris, where he was to remain until December 1900. Back in Madrid, he resumed his protracted studies and, having acquired an extensive knowledge of the language, was able to gain a distinction in both parts of his French examination. In October 1900, having been given special dispensation by the Ministerio de Instrucción Público not to complete two courses in Gymnastics, he eventually, at the unusually advanced age of 25, obtained his baccalaureate and qualified for entry to the University of Madrid. He enrolled in the sociology classes taught by Manuel Sales y Ferré, an

old friend of his father and a professor greatly esteemed by progressive
members of the younger generation. Antonio never forgot what he
learned in his lectures, even though in later life he came to disagree
with some of the views expressed in them.

Much as he valued what he was learning at the university,
Antonio was still far more interested in what was happening in
the theatre. January 1901 saw the first performance at the Teatro
Español of a play by the distinguished novelist and dramatist Benito
Pérez Galdós. Entitled *Electra*, its theme was radically anti-clerical.
It was bitterly attacked by members of the political and ecclesiastical
establishment, and there were even skirmishes in the streets between
electristas and *antielectristas*. One result of the furore was the founding
of a weekly review called *Electra* by Francisco Villaespasa, Ramón
del Valle-Inclán, Pío Baroja and other young writers who shared
the playwright's republicanism. Another member of the editorial
committee was Manuel Machado, newly returned from Paris and
already an acclaimed poet with several publications to his name.

Up until then Antonio, who had evidently begun writing poetry
soon after his return to Madrid, had not published a single verse of it.
But *Electra* provided him with an opportunity to do so and in its issue
of 30 March 1901 two poems appeared under his name. The first
was a long one that he was later to entitle 'The Fountain'. As critics
have pointed out, this poem is a clear illustration of how strongly
its author had been influenced by the symbolism of contemporary
French poetry, especially that of Verlaine. Nevertheless, the main
source of inspiration was the poet's own childhood memories of Las
Dueñas. As Dámaso Alonso expressed it: 'When, unbeknown to
him, Machado's poetry first began to pulsate within him, there was
a patio with orange trees and a garden with cypresses and lemons'.[27]
But of more significance than anything else in the lost garden was
the fountain, symbolizing the spring, deep within him, from which
the stream of his creativity flowed.

> There are strange loves in the story
> of my long and loveless journey,

and the strangest is the fountain,
whose sadness obscures my sorrows,
whose gently smiling reflection
dispels my bitterness and gloom.
I love the old fountain,
the sun cleaves it with golden shafts,
the evening flecks it with scarlet
and the arabesque magic of silver.
Above it the sky displays
its purest lotus blue,
and near it is the bright yellow
of lemons among dark branches. [28]

Some features of this poem were long to remain characteristic of Antonio Machado's work. Unlike his brother José, he was not a painter, but he had an artist's eye for colours and in this verse he named no fewer than five in just seven lines. In the final verse, however, there are no splashes of brightness to dispel the 'bitterness and gloom': it tells of nothing but sadness, aridity and a piquant longing for love.

The second poem, which has no title, is equally suffused with melancholy and grief, but it is set within the context of a dream. It shows that from the outset Machado's dream experience is a fundamental feature of his poetic world; perhaps he is wishing to point out that, although they sometimes caused grief, it is only dreams (i.e. products of the unconscious) that are the source of true creativity. He was probably unaware of it at the time, but the publication of the two poems coincided with that of Freud's pioneering study, *The Interpretation of Dreams*. Had the father of psychoanalysis read the first poem he would probably have found in it a symbolic significance that would never have occurred to its author, in his innocence.

Antonio published two further poems in *Electra* but it ceased publication in May 1901 and for a time he had nowhere to place his work. However, in the summer of 1902, after his return from a second visit to Paris, where he had kept the wolf from the door by working as a clerk in the Guatemalan consulate, his outlook improved. His friend Villaespasa, in company with others who had been involved in the publication of *Electra*, founded a new review called *Revista Ibérica*. Its third number contained a series of Antonio's poems grouped together under the title of 'On the road', inspired by a line from a verse of the medieval Castilian poet Gonzalo de Berceo: 'All of us who walk the road are pilgrims.' The mood is one of stoical resignation in the face of the fact that human life, with all its changes, is like a journey along a road that leads inexorably from birth to death. Here again he looks back longingly and lovingly to the first stage of his own journey that began in that garden in Seville. As his brother José was later to express it: 'He was one of those poets who, throughout his life, retained in the depths of his consciousness the unsullied world-view of his infancy. That he was able to retain it seemed to him to be almost miraculous, given that, just as a river is all the time moving further away from its source, man is for ever distancing himself from his childhood.'[29]

The theme of flowing water is found in a poem published in the fourth and final issue of the *Revista Ibérica*, which appeared on 15 September 1902:

> Life today has the rhythm of rivers,
> the laughter of the waters
> that run among the rushes
> and the verdant reeds. [30]

This poem and the others that appeared in *Electra* and the *Revista Ibérica* were among those printed, some of them in a revised version, in a little book published in January 1903 which Machado called *Soledades* – the same title as that of a work by the celebrated poet Luis de Góngora, published in 1613. It is hard to hit upon a satisfactory English equivalent of the word '*soledades*'. Robert Bly, who has translated some of the poems in the collection, calls it *Times Alone*, but this does not perhaps fully convey the meaning of the Spanish. For *soledad* the dictionary offers 'solitude', 'loneliness', 'grieving' and 'mourning' – and for *soledades*, 'wilderness'. It could be argued that the title chosen for this book by a poet who spent so much time on his own, grieving for what he believed he had lost, embraces all these meanings.

Soledades, which comprised 42 poems, was divided into four parts: 'Desolation and monotony', 'On the road', 'April psalms' and 'Humour'. The title of the first part is reminiscent of the one that Verlaine gave to his *Poèmes saturniens*, which was 'Melancholia'; and it may be that the poem entitled 'Eventide' was inspired by the sonnet 'Après trois ans'. But in this poem, as in a number of others, the dominant influence appears to be Machado's childhood memories, which were always tinged with sadness. His 'April Psalms' did not speak of the joys of spring but of its sorrows: the burgeoning of the natural world could only be painful to a man deprived of love. It seems that for him, as for T. S. Eliot, April was always the 'cruellest month'.

Critics have been divided in their opinions as to the merits of Machado's first volume of verse. 'The heterogeneous collection,' writes Bernard Sesé, 'is lacking in harmony. This diversity of inspiration is a reflection of the poet's uncertainty: he often gives the impression that he is still in search of his most authentic voice.' [31] He suggested that this diversity was reflected in the variety of metres (heptasyllables, octosyllables, hendecasyllables) and strophic forms (with a preference for *silvas*). On the other hand Geoffrey Ribbans offers a more positive appraisal. 'Poetically speaking,' he writes, 'the essential fact is that Antonio evolved gradually and developed unusually slowly, long delaying, moreover, the publication of his verses: this way of working – measured, patient, even laborious – which resulted in his first book of verses, will be characteristic of him throughout his life, giving rise to the exceptional depth and thoughtfulness that we all recognize in his poetry.' [32] This fits with the poet's own assessment of his development. 'I am in a period of evolution', he wrote soon after the book's publication, 'and have not yet discovered the form in which my new poetry will be expressed.'[33]

Although only five or six hundred copies of *Soledades* were printed and the book's publication went largely unnoticed, his friends received it with acclamation. Juan Ramón Jiménez, who reviewed it in *El País*, described him as 'our great poet' and was particularly impressed by the cluster of poems in 'On the Road'. He said that 'it is a long time since anyone has written such sweet and lovely poetry as that found in these short compositions that arise mysteriously from the depths of the soul.' [34] Jiménez had himself also just published a volume of poetry and had sent a copy to Machado who, in his letter of thanks, had given expression to his strong feelings of solidarity:

> I believe in myself, I believe in you, I believe in my brother, I believe in how we have turned our backs on success, on vanity, on pedantry, and in how we work with our hearts. But I think, dearest friend, that it is necessary to put up a great fight against the despicable riffraff that are bloated with the pigswill of these times. [35]

It is clear from this that Antonio and his friends saw themselves as part of an avant garde that was making a stand against what they believed to be the decadence of contemporary Spanish literature.

Jiménez was one of a group of young poets who assembled regularly in the Machados' flat in Calle Fuencarral. José, who lived there with his brothers, later recalled the gatherings, which generated heated disagreements and so much tobacco smoke that the women in the house were obliged to open all the windows. José's account is confirmed by Rafael Cansinos-Asséns, a young writer then resident in Madrid, who later recorded his impressions of his first visit to the house:

> The Machados lived on the second floor of a large, rambling old house with a great gloomy patio where in winter, after the sun had gone off it, the cold immediately took hold. Later the sun got round to

the spacious square drawing room, with a balcony overlooking the street, which was so bathed in dazzling sunlight that, at first encounter, it was impossible to see. Everyone – that is, Villaespasa, Antonio de Zayas (Duke of Amalfi) and Ortiz de Pinedo – was already there. One of the Machados – Antonio, I think – was in his shirtsleeves, finishing shaving in front of a battered mirror fixed to the wall… The untidy room, empty of furniture apart from a few rickety chairs, with its tiled floor spattered with cigarette ends and with its walls completely bare, had all the appearance of a bohemian garret. There were so few chairs that some people had to remain standing. From within, behind a side door, came the sound of women's voices. The sun, a veritable Sunday sun, was the only adornment in that room, which resembled a students' glory hole – just the sun and the youthful good humour. [36]

Cansinos-Asséns could not remember for sure if it was Antonio who had been standing shaving in his shirtsleeves, but it almost certainly was he; for this deeply introverted man cared little about outward appearances. As had been the case with his father, people often commented upon his careless attire. At this period, according to Jiménez, he used to wear 'a very old and discoloured overcoat that had lost all but a couple of its buttons, which were always wrongly done up'. He had a cord round his waist to hold up his trousers and 'bits of string in place of cufflinks'. [37] When he came to see Jiménez in hospital the nurses were so horrified by his appearance that they were reluctant to let him in and, after he had left, set to work brushing breadcrumbs and cigarette ash off the chair he had been sitting on. Sometimes, when he visited the sick man, Antonio announced that he was going to read him a poem. On one occasion he took a dirty sheet of paper out of his pocket and, on unfolding it, was unable to read what he had written because there was a hole in the middle of it – made, without him realizing it, while he had been eating. Only someone as absent-minded as Antonio could have sat composing a poem at the dinner table and failed to notice that he had spilt gravy all over it.

At this period Machado had a particular reason for wanting to read his poems to Jiménez, for his friend was the editor of a new review called *Helios*. In the periodical's July 1903 issue there appeared four new poems of his, each with an autobiographical theme. The first was entitled 'The poet visits the patio of the house in which he was born' and describes a return, real or imaginary, to Las Dueñas:

> The languid lemon tree hangs
> a pale and dusty branch
> over the clear fountain spell
> and there at the bottom dream
> the gold fruit…
>
> It is a bright afternoon
> of almost spring,
> a tepid March afternoon,
> holding April's nearby breath.
> I am alone in the silent patio,
> looking for a candid and old illusion,
> a shadow on the white wall,
> a memory asleep
> on the fountain rim, or in the wind
> the swish of a thin dress.
>
> Into this afternoon mood floats
> a taste of absence,
> telling the soul on fire *never*
> and the heart *wait*.
>
> The taste evokes ghosts
> of dead virgin smells.

Yes, I remember you, bright happy afternoon
of almost spring,
bloomless afternoon when you brought me
the good smell of spearmint,
and good sweet basil
my mother grew in her clay pots.

Yes, I know you, bright happy afternoon
of almost spring.[38]

The memories are happy, but they are tinged with sadness. The
same mood is apparent in other poems published in *Helios* and in a
review called *Alma Española* in 1903 and 1904. But 1905 witnessed
an important change. A poem published in *El País* in March of that
year entitled 'Advice', struck a new and more positive note:

Maybe this love wanting to be
will soon learn
and be. What has passed by
will it return?
Today is remote from yesterday.
Yesterday never again! [39]

Here the poet expresses his wish to live and act in the present,
renouncing, if he can, the futile intention to recover the past. As
Ian Gibson has suggested, there are clear indications that the change
was due to the influence of one man – Don Miguel de Unamuno,
the celebrated philosopher, essayist and poet who since 1892 had
been Professor of Greek in the University of Salamanca. Machado
himself expressed this indebtedness in a letter to Unamuno in the
spring of 1904. 'There this no doubt', he wrote, 'that you, with your
cudgel, have smashed the thick crust of our vanity and drowsiness. I,
at least, would be lacking in gratitude if I did not acknowledge that
you have enabled me to leap the walls of my corral or my *huerto*.'[40]
Huerto translates into English rather prosaically as 'kitchen garden'

or 'market garden', but, as Geoffrey Gibbans has pointed out, it is 'one of Machado's fixed images to describe his soul'. He is implying that Unamuno's influence has 'enabled him to escape from his earlier Narcissism-like self-absorption'. It is undoubtedly the master's *maza* – his 'iconoclastic cudgel' – that has 'destroyed for Machado all chance of complacency either about Spain or about literature'. [41]

Machado's dialogue with Unamuno had begun the previous year after he had sent the Salamanca professor a copy of *Soledades* with an effusive inscription to the great 'sage and poet'. In response Unamuno wrote him a long letter that was later published as an article in *Helios*. He advised Machado to steer clear of *el arte por el arte* (art for art's sake), which he likened to piano music publicly performed for the purpose of showing off the pianist's skill and virtuosity. This, he said, was an 'insult to the public'. And the same applied to poets who offered people *serventesiosos*, madrigals, pastorals, *cantigas* or any other 'old junk'. He then went on to warn Machado not to make poetry his profession. 'The poet's profession,' he wrote, 'is one of the most hateful that I know and, whenever poetry is made into a profession, the poet is obliged to be what in some circles they understand by such a name: someone who simply churns out verses for almanacs.'[42]

Much of the ensuing correspondence was taken up with a discussion of the cultural differences between the Spanish and the French. Unamuno was evidently urging his young friend not to be too greatly influenced by the French, among whom *l'art pour l'art* was all the rage – and where, as a consequence, 'art' became divorced from 'life' – and to adopt an aesthetic that was authentically his own. In response Machado wrote an 'open letter' to *El País*, in which he defined his position very clearly. 'I am a contemplative man and a dreamer (everyone can see how spontaneously I write) who listens to the murmurings of the unconscious, not just for the pleasure of hearing them, but out of an incorrigible desire to give utterance to the spirit of whatever lies buried in the memory.'[43] Whatever happened he would not be unduly influenced by others but would seek to preserve his authenticity. Nevertheless, as Geoffrey Gibbans has pointed out, 'Machado's criticisms of Symbolism from 1904 onwards did not imply a total rejection of Symbolist notions but an attempt to strike a new balance between idealism and realism, to vindicate the possibility of a new direct vision and a partial return to objectivity'.[44]

Soon after writing to the press, Machado returned to the question of his differences with the French in a private letter to Unamuno:

> We must not create a world apart in which we fancifully and egoistically enjoy contemplating ourselves; we must not escape from this life in order to create a life that would be better for ourselves but of no value to others... Nothing can be more absurd than to think, as some French poets have sometimes thought, that mystery is an aesthetic element. Beauty lies not in the mystery, but in the desire to penetrate it. It is a dangerous road to take and can cause chaos within us if, in our vanity, we systematically manufacture obscurities that in reality do not and must not exist. [45]

That he himself could not 'escape from this life' but must face up to reality was brought sharply home to him in August 1904, the month that saw the death of his grandmother Cipriana Álvarez Durán. She had been the mainstay of the Machado household, which now included two individuals who were in no position to make any contribution to its finances. One was Machado's younger brother Joaquín, who had returned, sick and impoverished, from Guatemala two years earlier and was now belatedly completing his education. The other was Antonio himself, the perpetual student who had hitherto been content to earn a few pesetas by writing, but was now obliged to look for a proper job. His first idea was to apply for a post in the Bank of Spain but, in order to do that, he would have had to improve his handwriting. He did in fact go so far as to attend classes in calligraphy at a commercial college but, although he made some progress, he eventually decided against a career in banking. 'The poet of *Soledades*,' his brother José was later to comment, 'was clearly not cut out to push his pen in a bank ledger.'[46] Nor, one might add, was the author of *The Waste Land*, but sometimes financial necessity drives even poets as distinguished as T. S. Eliot to earn their livings in such a prosaic way.

Eventually, at the suggestion of Giner de los Ríos, Machado decided to follow his master's example and become a teacher. He had acquired a good working knowledge of French through his visits to Paris and his experience of France's culture, and therefore decided that this would be the subject to teach. Although, after long years of intermittent study, he had still not gained his licenciate, he was able, following a series of searching examinations extending from May 1906 to February 1907, to convince the authorities that he was fit to teach French in a secondary school. But one critical question remained unanswered: *where* was he to teach? At one stage there had been vacant posts in a fair number of provincial towns and cities but, by the time he was qualified to apply for one, only three remained: Baeza, Mahón and Soria. And almost certainly because it was the closest to home, he chose Soria.

III

Joy and Sorrow in Soria

In the early years of the 20th century, Soria, situated about 150 miles to the north-east of Madrid and accessible by train, was a city of some 7,000 people. The capital of a province where much of the land was infertile, most of the agriculture was primitive and many of the people were poor, it was one of the least favoured cities in Spain. But, as Machado's biographer Miguel Pérez Ferrero was to discover when he visited Soria, its setting was spectacular:

> Soria is situated on a bleak plateau above land that has been greened by the Duero and everything is a delicate shade of yellow. The palace of Gomara is yellow, the glowing stonework of Santo Domingo is yellow, the parched soil of the Sorian fields is yellow. To the north and north-east the city is surrounded by outcrops of grey rock, the mountain of Las Ánimas and the peaks where, according to legend, San Saturio dwelt. The Duero flows between the purple mountains and the city, around which it 'traces its crossbow curve'. On the left bank of the river are the ruins of San Juan de Duero, the most beautiful Romanesque monastery in Spain. Further downstream is San Polo. And after that is San Saturio – a hermitage carved out of the

rock, so it is said, by the saint's own hands – reached by a road flanked by black and white poplars. It is an enchanting road, beautiful, solitary and, except for the sound of running water, completely silent. .. Here the waters of the Duero are translucent and blue, and in some places create pools from which they cascade, in clouds of spray, down to the rocks below.[1]

When he came to the city itself what most impressed Pérez Ferrero were the 'noble arcades' of its *Audiencia*, which occupied one side of the Plaza Mayor, and the picturesque castle ruins set on a little hill that divided the city in two. He was less enthusiastic about the building that dominated the principal street. This was the casino, where someone was playing a tinny piano and old men sat and dozed on 'sofas upholstered in red felt'. Here, as in so many provincial Spanish cities, there was no escaping the fact that the casino was the real centre of civic life. From a cultural point of view Soria was a backwater. How many of its citizens were aware that the poet Gustavo Adolfo Bécquer, married to a local girl, had celebrated the place in his writings or that, earlier in the 19th century, the philosopher Julián Sanz del Río had been born in the neighbourhood?

As with Pérez Ferrero, so with Machado: it had not been the city but its setting that had made the greatest impression. In May 1907, when he first came there to spy out the scene, Machado recorded his impressions in a poem that said nothing about the city but much about the countryside surrounding it. For someone who had never before penetrated so far into the north of Spain, the discovery of Soria was an exciting experience that was to open new springs of creativity.

After his return to Madrid from his brief visit to Soria, Machado spent much of the summer preparing for the courses he was to teach in the autumn, but he also found time for more congenial work. Having decided to publish a new book of his poems he set about revising *Soledades*, altering the wording of some of the poems and removing others that he now regarded as too 'modernist'. To this collection he

added some that had appeared in various reviews since the publication
of *Soledades* and also a number of more recent compositions. A total of
31 poems were grouped together under the heading of *Galerías* and,
appropriately enough, the first of them (following the Introduction)
describes the poet's feelings on awakening from a dream:

> A sudden rent in the cloud, and then the rainbow
> already clear in the sky;
> a green lantern of rain and sun
> to frame the fields.
> Then I awoke. Who had muddied
> the magic windows looking on my dream?
> My heart was beating wildly.
> Astonished and dismayed.
>
> The lemon tree in blossom,
> the cypress in the garden,
> the green fields, the sun, the rain, the rainbow.
> The raindrops on your hair…
>
> And all these things were lost in memory,
> blown like a soap-bubble away on the breeze.[2]

That the word 'dream' or 'dreams' should occur no fewer than
twenty times in *Galerías* is an indication of their supreme importance
to the poet. In one poem (LXX) he calls them 'roads', suggesting
that they were pathways that people should follow if they were
to discover the truth about themselves and the universe around
them. Pascual Piqué, who described his poems as 'instruments of
understanding', said that Machado was 'one of the discoverers and
explorers of the unconscious and of its connection, disowned, in
conflict, but ultimately reconciled with the conscious mind'.[3] He
called the poet a *médico del espíritu* or 'doctor of the spirit' who, by
working through his dreams, had cured himself of ills and offered a
way for others to travel in their quest for wholeness and health. He

believed the poet had much in common with Jung, who by a strange chance had been born on the very same day, 26 July 1875. *Soledades. Galerías. Otras poemas* could be said to cover some of the same ground as *Memories, Dreams, Reflections,* the title that the great Swiss physician of souls gave to his autobiographical musings.

While some of the poems in the new collection were introspective and melancholy, others indicated a marked change of mood. As Willis Barnstone has pointed out, Machado now 'moves from the subjective and sensitive young poet, who recalls unrequited love, kitsch European melodies, and the shadow of gallows and graveyard, to being the observer and critic of a traditionalist, fraudulent Spain marked by greed and anger in the countryside and political office'.[4] Looking outward rather than inward he was also becoming a keen observer of the landscape. 'The banks of the Duero', composed after his first visit to Soria, ends with a great paean of praise:

> Poplars by the white road,
> aspens on the river bank,
> mist-clad mountains
> in the blue distance,
> on a bright and sunlit day!
> Beauteous land of Spain![5]

The man who, in order to conjure up his dreams, had previously had to shut his eyes and withdraw from the world around him has now, as Pascual Piqué observed, 'had a vision that is equivalent to a dream, to experience which he does not have to close his eyes but, on the contrary, to keep them wide open'.[6] Throughout his years in Soria he kept his eyes wide open as he wandered through the countryside surrounding the city. As Reyes Vila-Belda has pointed out, Machado had a keen eye for what she calls *lo nimio* – things that might be deemed trivial, marginal or insignificant. His observance of such things informed and inspired much of the poetry that he would write at this time. 'Poplars, elms, brambles, daisies, storks, peasants and poachers crop up repeatedly in different verses.'[7]

After settling in Soria, Machado did not at first have much time for writing verses, because he had to prepare lessons for his French classes. Little is known about how he fared as a teacher, but he was evidently thought to be competent enough to be appointed vice principal of the school in April 1908. In the academic year 1908-9 all his pupils succeeded in their examinations. Of the nine in his first class, one was graded *sobresaliente* (excellent), three were *notable* (creditable) and five simply passed; of the eight in his second class, three (including the only girl among all his pupils) were in the top category and the rest gained passes. It seems that Machado, like his old teachers at the Institución Libre, did not really believe in examinations and never actually failed anyone. Among those in his first class who were graded *notable* was a young man called Mariano Granados Aguirre, who many years later, when an exile in Mexico, recalled how privileged he had felt to be taught French by Machado. He had vivid memories of the occasion when the poet introduced his pupils to the works of Alfred de Musset and Paul Verlaine.

> We barely noticed that the grammar was difficult. Our introduction to the new language was also our introduction to new literary horizons. When Machado's voice reverberated through the silence of the classroom:
>
> > C'était dans la nuit brune
> > sur le clocher jauni
> > La lune
> > comme un point sur une i
>
> Or else:
> > Les longs sons
> > des violons…
>
> we were so deeply moved that our quiet concentration had a kind of religious aura about it.[8]

Another of his pupils, Gervasio Manrique de Lara, remembered him with great respect and affection:

> I remember when, in studying for my baccalaureate, I was a pupil in his French classes at the Institute in Soria. His benevolence was greatly appreciated. He read us passages from the books that he received from abroad, commenting on them as he read them. He did not punish anyone. Soon after his arrival in Soria he gave a reading of his verses in the *Circulo de Amistad*. Those of us from the Institute applauded him enthusiastically. But his life in the city was that of a loner.[9]

Although he had to concentrate on his work at the school, Machado soon found time to write not only poetry but also articles for the local press. In May 1908 the city's three newspapers – *Noticiera Soriana*, *El Avisador Numantino* and *Tierra Soriana* – jointly produced a special number to commemorate the Spaniards killed 100 years earlier in the struggle against Napoleon. To this Machado contributed a short article on the state of the nation following the loss of its last colonies. Its subject was 'Patriotism' and its tone was very hard-hitting. 'We are the sons of a poor and ignorant fatherland', he wrote, 'where everything is waiting to be achieved. This is all we know.' And he continued at some length in this vein.

> We know that our country is not a piece of property inherited from our forefathers; nor is it merely something to be defended against foreign invaders. We know that our country is something that needs to be continuously sustained by culture and by work. The people who neglect or abandon it are ruining, even destroying it. We know that our country is not just the ground that we tread but the soil that we till; that we have to live not only on it but for it;

that where there is no element of human endeavour there is not a country nor even a region, but merely a sterile land that no more belongs to us than it does to the vultures and eagles circling over it. Look at the stony mountains that surround this ancient and noble city: once they were densely wooded, now they are stripped bare. Do you call this your country? It is a part of the planet over which men have passed, not for the purpose of creating a country but of destroying one. You cannot call yourselves patriots just because you think that one day you would be willing to die in the defence of this barren wasteland; you will only be patriots if you come – bearing your saplings and seeds, your ploughshares and miners' picks – to transform those dark and desolate places into the country that is yet to be. [10]

His contention that the proper way to pay homage to the heroes of 1808 was to work hard for the renovation of Spain was probably not well received by everyone in Soria, but it gave pleasure to the editor of *Tierra Soriana*, José María Palacio, who was to remain Machado's most stalwart friend and supporter during his years in the city. From time to time Machado sent him poems to be printed in his paper but, in view of the conservatism of many of its readers, probably thought it best not to send any verses from his 'Portrait'. This was the newly-published poem in which Machado, mindful of the political radicalism of his grandfather and great-grandfather, had said that 'there are drops of Jacobin blood in my veins'.[11]

By a coincidence, it was with a relative of Palacio's wife that Machado had first found lodgings in Soria. Her name was Remigia Cuevas Acebes and she lived in a central location with her husband Isidoro Martínez Ruiz, who later remembered the poet as 'a great hulk of a fellow with the heart of a child – quiet and shy, but kind-hearted and delightful'. When, a few months later, the couple decided to give up the guest-house, Machado and the two other lodgers moved to another establishment in the Plaza de Teatinos (now the Calle Estudios). The owners were Remigia's sister Isabel Cuevas and her husband Ceferino Izquierdo Caballero, a retired police sergeant. According to someone who lodged in the house a few years later, the wife was a beautiful woman who possessed all the best qualities of the ladies of Soria – 'dignity, piety, kindness, courage and great charm'. But her husband was very different, being described by someone who knew him well as 'an authoritarian, bad tempered man who often got drunk' and a person that people found 'terrifying'. It was also said that his daughter Leonor 'used to put up with the ex-policeman's violent outbursts and shed her tears in silence'. [12]

When Machado first came on the scene Leonor was 13 years old and helped her mother look after her brother Sinforiano (then aged 10) and a new born baby named Antonia. Living at such close quarters with the family, the poet naturally got to know them all well and soon became strongly attracted to Leonor. As those who knew her testified, she had inherited her mother's good looks. He hair was 'chestnut brown', her skin 'pale as a lily' and her eyes 'large, wide and deep', so that at times she wore 'the look of a startled gazelle'.[13] Heliodoro Carpintero, who has made a close study of Machado's years in Soria, says that the poet, being too shy or too fearful of rejection to declare his love for Leonor openly, adopted a 'curious procedure' for paying court to her. In order to ascertain her feelings he declared his own in some verses and 'accidentally on purpose', as it were, left them lying around the house in the hope that she would read them. Once he quoted some lines from a melancholy poem about an attractive but unattainable young woman:

> And the girl that I love,
> alas! would prefer to be wed
> to a young barber.[14]

Whether or not there really was a young barber in her life, Leonor took the hint and somehow managed to let Machado know that, if she got married, she would prefer to be wed to a poet.

In the spring of 1909, a few months before Leonor reached the age of 15, which was then the legal age of marriage, Machado plucked up the courage to ask for her hand. Not daring to approach her father and mother directly, he persuaded a fellow lodger, who was a colleague at the school, to break the ice. The parents, who were at first surprised and possibly not altogether delighted by the prospect of their daughter marrying a man nearly twenty years older than she was, in due course gave their consent. Antonio's mother, whatever she may have felt about the match, also gave her approval. In deference to the demands of propriety, he then moved to another lodging house. It was Eastertide and Machado, overcome with joy, wrote 'Festival of Resurrection', a poem to celebrate the rebirth of the hope that he would no longer have to travel his road alone. Its opening stanzas express the joyful feelings that he was experiencing at that time:

> Look: the rainbow is tracing its arc
> over the fields that are turning green.
> Search for your lovers, you maidens,
> where the stream springs from the rock.
> Where the flowing water laughs and dreams,
> there the story of love is told. [15]

Not long afterwards, on 12 June, Leonor celebrated her fifteenth birthday and preparations for the wedding began in earnest. Sunday 11 July saw the first reading of the banns and a festive gathering of relatives and close friends at the bride's parents' house. On the 17th, in a mood of jubilation, Machado did something he had never done before: he gave a public recital of his poems in the local Working Men's Club. By way of introduction he talked briefly about 'the relationship between art and the people', firmly rejecting the notion that there was one kind of art for the minority and another for the masses. He then proceeded to recite six poems and, according to a report in the press, the performance was greeted by prolonged applause.

On 29 July, three days after his 34th birthday, the poet was legally married to his betrothed. Leonor's father and Antonio's mother, who had arrived from Madrid with her son José, signed the contract in the presence of the bride's uncle Gregorio Cuevas Acebes, a dental surgeon, who was acting as the *padrino*. It appears that on this occasion another of the bride's uncles admonished Machado 'not to forget that my niece is a child' – to which he replied: 'I know that and I shall not forget.'[16] The uncle clearly did not know the man he was talking to. Could there have been any risk that someone as sensitive and mature as Machado would ever be guilty of abusing the girl now committed to his care?

The religious ceremony took place next day in the church of Santa María la Mayor, which was located in the Plaza Mayor. According to a report in a local paper, the bride wore a most elegant black silk dress decorated with magnificent jewellery and a classic white veil tastefully adorned with a bunch of orange blossom, but the groom's appearance, by contrast, was strictly formal. The officiating priest was well known to Machado for, in addition to his other duties, he taught religion at his school. Other colleagues were in the congregation, swelling the ranks of the relatives and friends who, at the conclusion of the service, went on to a reception at the home of the bride's parents.

But it was not all sweetness and light. The marriage between two people of such disparate ages attracted a good deal of local attention, not all of it agreeable. In fact a group of university students, home for the vacation, tried to turn the occasion into a carnival. They created a disturbance outside the church while the wedding was in progress and, at the conclusion of the reception when the honeymoon couple left to catch their train, the station was besieged by a jeering mob. For Machado it was a humiliating conclusion to what ought to have been the happiest day of his life.

He and Leonor had planned to spend their honeymoon in Barcelona, where Manuel was then staying but, upon reaching Saragossa, they were informed that a general strike had cut the rail link to the Catalan capital. They decided instead to go north to

Pamplona and from there to Irún and Fuenterrabía, where they were free to spend the long summer days walking and talking together by the seaside, far removed – for the first time – from the unwelcome gaze of the gossipers. After that they took the train to Madrid, where they stayed for a few days with Machado's mother and other members of the family in the apartment to which they had recently moved in the *barrio* of Colón. Their sojourn in the city gave the couple an opportunity to visit the theatre, where the poet's friend Ricardo Calvo was then performing. For Leonor, who had probably never before strayed far from Soria, the honeymoon was an introduction to a whole new world.

When summer was past they returned to Soria and took possession of the two rooms that Leonor's mother had prepared for them in the family house. One was a small bedroom containing little more than a large bed and a bedside table. The other was a larger room that served both as a salon and as a study. It had a sofa, two armchairs, a huge desk and a balcony overlooking a garden that in the spring was resplendent with acacia blossom. It provided the perfect environment for Machado as he sat at his desk preparing lessons for his classes or, more to his taste, writing poetry.

That autumn he was putting the finishing touches to a long poem that had evidently been growing in his mind since he first came to Soria: entitled 'Countryside of Castile', it was published in *La Lectura* in February 1910. The poem, which was later modified and published two years later in *Campos de Castilla*, reflects the delight of a man who had only just discovered the Castilian countryside. Raised in Andalusia, he had subsequently experienced little of Spain apart from Madrid, a city dating only from the 16th century, and was unacquainted with the ancient kingdom of Castile In coming to Soria, whose castle had once defended the kingdom against invaders from the east, he was mindful of Castile's former pre-eminence and prosperity. But now this glory was a thing of the past, since so much of the region lay in ruins.

Noble, sad Castilian land!
Country of high plateaus, of rocks and empty spaces,
of crumbling cities, roads without stopping places,
of fields untouched by plough or shade or spring,
of boors that gape but cannot dance or sing,
who still, when hearth fires fail, can only flee
down the long river valleys to the sea.[17]

While Machado was right about the emigration of the peasantry from the countryside, he was wrong about the absence of popular culture. For the poet, unlike his folk-loving father, had not spent much time in places where people still danced and sang.

When he ventured into the Sorian countryside it seems that Machado did not want to meet people but to get away from them. He and Leonor loved to leave the noise and bustle of the city and walk along the quiet tree-lined road by the river from San Polo to the sanctuary of San Saturio – a walk that inspired some of his most beautiful poems. Sometimes they went further afield and climbed to the summit of Santa Ana, the rocky hill where, on a clear day, they had a magnificent view of the surrounding countryside. To the east, they could see the Moncayo, Bécquer's favourite mountain; and to the north-east the imposing Sierra de Urbión, from whose steep slopes the infant Duero sprang.

Machado longed to trace the river back to its beginning, and one day, as Pérez Ferrero relates, he achieved his ambition:

> In September 1910 Antonio wants to see the source of the Duero, to listen to the magical murmurings of its waters as they spring from the earth. Leonor does not accompany him on this excursion. She will stay at home for a few days, anxiously awaiting his return. Antonio goes with some friends. They travel from Soria to Cidones in the postal van. From Cidones to Vinuesa they follow the road on foot. And from Vinuesa, where they stop to organize the expedition,

they go on horseback to Covaleda, a village in the
pine-covered mountains that is inhabited almost
entirely by old people. On leaving Covaleda they
encounter a storm that, for a time, causes them some
anxiety. Drenched to the skin, they reach the summit
of Mount Urbión. There is not a cloud in the sky
above. They stand entranced, barely noticing how
wet and tired they are. It seems to them that they are
on top of the world. Then they descend to Vinuesa
via the Laguna Negra and the Revinuesa valley. [18]

Not long after his return from this expedition the new school
term began and Machado was invited to take part in a celebration
to mark the tenth anniversary of the death of a distinguished son of
Soria, Antonio Pérez de la Mata. Philosopher, priest, psychologist,
teacher and author of many books, he was a leading *krausista* and
a man that Machado had much admired. In his commemorative
address the poet gave forceful expression to his conviction that the
only thing that could save Spain was a proper appreciation of culture:

In a country that is poor and ignorant … where
most people do nothing more than what is necessary
to earn their living or, worse still, to prevent their
neighbours earning theirs; in a nation that is almost
illiterate, where science, philosophy and art are either
dismissed as being superfluous or condemned for
being corruptive; in a people who have no desire
for regeneration nor any respect for the tradition of
their forefathers; in this Spain, so beloved and so
unhappy, that scorns culture and turns its back on
its fruits, tell me: is not the courage of the man who,
with his whole heart and mind, embraces some lofty
ideal, comparable to that of Hercules, whose Atlas-
like shoulders could bear the weight of mountains? [19]

Machado, who had begun his address by assuring his hearers that it was his patriotism that led him to criticize his fellow countrymen, went on to say that Spain was suffering from a lack of faith and an excess of intolerance. People had no wish to understand their opponents' arguments 'because, in the depth of our stupidity, we suspect that, if we manage to do so, the *casus belli* will disappear.' War, he suggested, was the very thing that the Spaniard, 'a quarrelsome cock with sharp claws', was always expecting and wanting. 'He prefers to fight rather than to understand, and he hardly ever employs the weapons of culture, which are the weapons of love.' Having reminded his hearers about what he called the 'bloody and brutal crimes' that had recently been committed in the towns and villages of Soria, he went on to refer to what the Pope had recently described as a 'crisis of kindness'; in no other country, he suggested, was this crisis as acute as it was in Spain. In praising Pope Pius X for his 1907 encyclical *Pascendi*, Machado would certainly have pleased his largely Catholic audience.

At the conclusion of his lecture Machado addressed his remarks directly to the students in his audience.

> You are contributing to the homage that today we are rendering to the memory of Antonio Pérez de la Mata, and your presence could be the highest honour that is paid to him. And I say *could be*, and not *is*, because you represent an uncertain future. Your *tomorrow* might perhaps be a return to a dead and corrupt past. So that you may represent the dawn of a bright and fruitful day it is essential that you are prepared to work and study to make, by your efforts, an addition to the treasure that past generations have bequeathed to you. Tomorrow you will be men, and this means that you will enter fully into life and, since life is a fight, you will be fighters. In your engagements you will employ only the weapons of knowledge, which are the strongest, and the weapons of culture, which

are the weapons of love. Treat people with respect, because Christ's teaching requires that you love your neighbor and respect is a form of love; but above people are spiritual values and the things to which people owe allegiance: above the magistrate, Justice; above the professor, Education; above the priest, Religion; above the doctor, Science. Have nothing to do with a bogus culture that cannot pass through the sieve of your intelligence. Do not believe that God has placed your heads on your shoulders as an ornamental cap-stone. Use your brains in the way they were meant to be used! Avoid the spiritual laziness that fills the mind with murderous suspicions. Hold yourselves in readiness for work and for action, like the string of a crossbow at its maximum tension. Never accept the challenges of opportunists and schemers because, if you fight them, you will have to employ crude weapons and, although you may triumph, you will be downgraded spiritually, descending from the status of a man to that of a wild beast. [20]

He went to say that the students must learn to distinguish truth from falsehood and never judge people by outward appearances. 'A man who is despised for his shabby attire,' he went on, 'may be a learned man, a hero or a saint – while a doctor's cap can cover the skull of an imbecile.'[21] The students must have enjoyed it, but it is likely that the speech, which was subsequently reproduced in the local press, did not go down too well in the more conservative quarters of the city.

There is in fact definite evidence that some of Machado's other utterances at this period did upset people in Soria. In January 1911 a poem of his entitled 'In the land of the Duero', which had been published in *La Lectura*, was reprinted in *Tierra Soriana*. In it the poet referred to a matter that he had touched upon in his recent lecture – the 'bestial crimes' currently being committed throughout the countryside of Soria.[22] That a 'foreigner' should be saying such things caused great offence to some readers, one of whom was moved to compose a malicious parody of the poem and have it published in *Noticiera de Soria*.

> There are no men in our country towns
> capable of vice or bestial crimes;
> for under their ugly outer gowns
> are souls quite free from evil designs. [23]

The crude parody, however, infuriated José María Palacio, who promptly took up his pen in Machado's defence.

Luckily for Antonio and Leonor, they were at the time not in Soria but in Madrid, where they were staying with Ana Ruiz. Her apartment must have felt quite overcrowded, for, in addition to José, Joaquín and Francisco, the household now included Manuel and his wife Eulalia Cáceres, the cousin and long-standing fiancée that he had married six months previously. Everyone was jubilant, because Manuel had just published a volume of sonnets that drew high praise from Antonio. But he and Leonor did not stay long in Madrid, for they were on their way to Paris, where he was due to spend a sabbatical year furthering his knowledge of French language and literature. When they eventually reached the city they took up residence in the same hotel, situated in the heart of the Latin Quarter, where the two brothers had stayed in 1899.

In February Antonio wrote to the government body that had given him a grant to say that he was refreshing his knowledge of medieval French philology and attending Joseph Bédier's lectures on medieval poetry. A month later he reported that he was embarking on the preparation of a Historical Grammar of the French Language that was 'more logical and orderly than what we have in Spain'.[24] But he did not disclose to those who were funding his stay in Paris that what he was most enjoying were the extra-curricular lectures of Henri Bergson. The eminent philosopher's latest book, *L'évolution créatrice*, had made him such a cult figure that the hall where he lectured – the biggest in the College of France – was always overflowing with hearers, many of whom were women. Machado warmed to Bergson's belief that it was the *élan vital* and not a deterministic natural selection that was at the heart of evolution – and that it was intuition rather than logical analysis that revealed the world of process and change. As he later recorded in his notebook, he was impressed by the lecturer's 'lively eyes' and 'handsome head' but described him, rather surprisingly, as a 'cold man'. He also said that, although Bergson's words were 'perfect', they 'added nothing to what he had written'.[25]

Because he was now obliged to devote most of his energies to working on his Historical Grammar, Machado was unable to spend as much time as he had on his previous visits sitting and chatting in cafés. He did manage to renew his acquaintance with the poet Rubén Darío, who was living in Paris with his partner Francisca Sánchez and had just been appointed literary director of a new review. For the most part, however, not having his gregarious brother Manuel around to help him make new contacts, his social life was fairly limited. Moreover, now that he was no longer a bachelor, he always had to consider the needs of his wife.

Almost nothing is known about how Leonor spent her days in Paris. It is likely that, with Antonio so often absent, she sat alone in her hotel room with very little to do. Not knowing much French, she would have found it difficult to communicate with other people. Perhaps feeling lonely and homesick, the 16 year old girl may have confided in her mother, but, in the absence of surviving correspondence, this remains conjectural. It may be that in due course her suppressed unhappiness found physical expression in sickness, for on 14 July she began to vomit blood. Beside himself with anxiety, Machado rushed out to look for a doctor but, because it was a day of national celebration and everyone was out in the streets, he was unable to find one. Next day, after a sleepless night, he took Leonor to a hospital where the nurses were used to caring for sick foreigners. In due course, as he had probably feared and expected, she was diagnosed as having tuberculosis. After six weeks in hospital the doctors advised Machado to take his wife home, where it was hoped that the pure mountain air would assist her recovery.

Early in September, having borrowed money for the fare from Darío, the couple took the train to Madrid, where they stayed for a few days with Ana Ruiz before going back to Soria. After her return home Leonor's health appears to have improved slightly, but her condition deteriorated with the onset of winter, which in Soria is notoriously cold. When eagerly awaited spring eventually arrived Machado rented a little house on the outskirts of the city, where the invalid could sit in the garden and breathe in pure air. Mariano Granados, who often visited the house, recalled seeing the poet pushing Leonor in her wheelchair. He described 'her sickly complexion and her fragile beauty' and 'the childish, slightly frightened, look on her face, now darkened by deep rings under her eyes'.[26]

Fortunately for Antonio he had plenty to do to take his mind off his anxiety about her illness. Having given up his grant he had returned to school to continue teaching the language and literature with which he was now much better acquainted. He also found time to do what he most needed to do at this critical juncture – to express his feelings in poetry. A poem published in February 1912 in *La Lectura* had no title, but each verse began with the words: 'Last night while I was sleeping':

> Last night while I was sleeping
> I dreamed – blessed illusion! –
> a fountain flowed
> inside my heart.
> Water, tell me by what hidden
> channel you came to me,
> with a spring of new life
> I never drank?
>
> Last night while I was sleeping
> I dreamed – blessed illusion! –

I had a beehive
inside my heart,
and from my old bitterness
the gold bees
were contriving white combs
and sweet honey.

Last night while I was sleeping
I dreamed – blessed illusion! –
a fiery sun glowed
inside my heart.
It was fiery, giving off heat
from a red fireplace.
It was the sun throwing out light
and made one weep.

Last night while I was sleeping
I dreamed – blessed illusion! –
that it was God I held
inside my heart.[27]

Alan Trueblood says that 'this poem, expressive of aspiration to faith but not of its possession, is nourished on Machado's reading of the Bible and the Spanish mystics.' The imagery of the first verse is reminiscent of that of St John's gospel, where Jesus is recorded as saying: 'The water that I shall give him shall be in him a well of water springing up into everlasting life.' The language of the second verse has similarities with that of St Teresa of Avila, who said that 'humility always toils like the bee in the hive', and also of Fray Luis de Granada, who talked about the soul 'toiling like a bee in the cork of its honeycomb'. And as for the third verse, its imagery has been seen to have something in common with that of Blessed John of Avila, who told how someone may be so filled with divine fire that he or she becomes an 'oven of love', and of St John of the Cross, who spoke of the ways in which the divine light may affect human sight.

[28] Is this evidence that, at this sorrowful time, Machado was turning for comfort and guidance to the writings of Spain's greatest saints – to Teresa, the 'fiery soul', and John of the Cross, the 'flaming spirit', whom he was later to address in one of his 'Proverbs and Songs'?[29]

What the poem clearly indicates is that Machado was continuing to pay close attention to his dreams. As Antoni Pascual Piqué suggested, this dream compensated for the one-sided attitude of his conscious mind and provided him with that 'spark of joy and illumination' that he needed in order to survive. 'At a very difficult moment, in despair over his wife's suffering, Machado had what was perhaps the happiest and grandest dream of his life, showing him what was really happening – the birth within him of something essential if he were to continue with his search.'[30]

There are signs that the poet was also finding some relief from his sadness by keeping busy. At this period he was certainly spending a good deal of time preparing the collection of poems that was eventually published in April under the title of *Campos de Castilla*. The book encapsulates the whole gamut of Machado's thoughts and feelings about his experiences during his years in Soria. As Federico de Onís expressed it, it was 'like a reflection of his interior life, of his humble emotions, of his secret dreams, and his transcendental meditations: pure lyricism, whose supreme worth lies in what reverberates through everything that enters into him – landscapes and people, the present and the historical, the anecdotal and the eternal.' [31] The principal poem was the one called 'Countryside of Soria' that he had been writing and revising for years. The best known passage is the one where the poet addresses the once proud city of Soria:

Soria, cold *pure town*,
Soria, Estremadura's crown,
with a castle's ruined flanks
overhanging the Duero's banks,
town walls eaten by time,
houses black with grime! [32]

Campos de Castilla also contains a number of short poems called 'proverbs and songs' and one very long one, running to over 700 lines, entitled 'The Land of Alvargonzález'. This poem had its origin in a short story that Machado had written soon after his return from the 1910 expedition in search of the source of the Duero and was inspired by what he had heard of evil happenings in the lands through which he had passed. It told the gruesome tale of a countryman murdered by his sons as he lay sleeping by a mountain spring.

> Over the naked fields
> the full moon looms
> stained with purplish red,
> an enormous globe.
> The sons of Alvargonzález
> are walking silently
> and see their father asleep
> next to the bright spring.
>
> The father's face
> is creased by a scowl between
> his eyebrows: a dark gash
> like the imprint of an axe.
> He's dreaming of his sons,
> that his sons have raised knives,
> and when he wakes he sees
> what he dreamt is right.
>
> Beside the bright spring
> the father lies dead.
> He has four stab wounds
> between his chest and ribs;
> his blood is pouring out;
> a hatchet blow on his neck.
> The bright running water
> tells the crime of the fields

while the two murderers flee
into the beechwood grove.
They carry the body down
to Laguna Negra below
the Duero river. Behind them
they leave a bloody trail.
In the bottomless lake
that surrenders no secrets,
they tie a stone to his feet,
bequeathing him a grave.[33]

The poem was in some respects reminiscent of the ballads in the *Romancero general* that Machado's grandmother had read to him as a child, but he was at pains to point to an essential difference between them: 'My ballads', he wrote, 'do not emanate from epics, but from the people who compose them and the land where they are sung; my ballads are about ordinary human beings – in the countryside of Castile and in the First Book of Moses, called *Genesis*.'[34] It seems that, by adopting the ballad form, he was able to achieve a measure of detachment from his subject matter. As Arthur Terry observed, 'the ballad, because of its dramatic nature, entails a kind of objectivity which is hardly possible in the lyric.'[35] 'In his approach to the reality of things, of people, of landscapes', wrote Helen Grant in her commentary on the poem, 'Machado seems to be seeking in them not only the reflection of his own feelings ... but the authentic and unique essence of things and their place in the scheme of the cosmos.' [36]

The people featured in 'The Land of Alvargonzález' were those whom Machado had read about in reports of crimes committed in the villages and countryside of Soria – the very same people he had referred to in his lecture at the commemoration of Pérez de la Mata. Some of the most brutal crimes occurred within families, where even parricide and fratricide were not unknown. The poet was horrified to hear of contemporary examples of the kind of envy and jealousy which, in the *Genesis* story, had caused Cain to kill Abel. As Pedro

Salinas pointed out, the poem reveals the poet's preoccupation with the dark side of human nature. 'What Machado is writing about', he said, 'is not *a* crime, but *the* crime, which stems from humanity's inherent capacity for evil … What he wanted to show in his portrayal of man were the terrible things that were always happening, not physically but spiritually: the man who kills what he creates and, as an appropriate punishment, destroys himself in so doing; the notion that, in killing someone else, we sooner or later also kill ourselves.'[37]

Campos de Castilla sold well and had good reviews, but success did little to raise its author's spirits. As spring turned to summer Leonor's condition continued to worsen and in July Machado planned to take her to see a specialist in Madrid and wrote to his mother to let her know. The letter provides a clear indication of how he was feeling at this time:

> It would be pointless for me to try to conceal from you how greatly I am suffering; but you must bear in mind that with great calamities comes great resignation. Because I have the consolation of being able to consecrate myself to caring for her – and fulfilling what love and duty impose on me – I cannot be subject to acute and uncontrollable feelings of grief, but only to a sorrowful acceptance of what is irremediable. I say this because I believe that, as well as your natural sadness on account of Leonor's illness, you are also very worried because you imagine that my state of mind is close to despair. No. My sorrow is great, but my feelings are not uncontrollable. I have not lost all hope for a relative, if not complete, recovery.
>
> My health, moreover, could not be better. To suffer mentally is certainly injurious, but what is much more harmful to health is an unstructured life, which mine long ago ceased to be; today, because of the needs of

the invalid, my life is more structured than it has ever been. My life is governed by the clock, and I only get a break when I take a breath of fresh air. Although it may seem strange to you, my health has never been so good. So then, dearest mama, don't worry about my situation; the terrible blow was the one I received in Paris, which came, just when we were so happy together, like a bolt from the blue. Our minds, in the end, are infinitely adaptable, and the very tasks that misfortune imposes on us are simply so many ways of alleviating and mitigating grief. You know this better than I do, because your life has been one of continuous suffering on behalf of those you love. Besides, happiness is simply a matter of egoism and unawareness. Things are always happening to cause us to suffer, but the only grief that does not defile us is that which we endure on behalf of others.[38]

But Machado's hopes for his wife's recovery proved to be without foundation: a few days later things took a turn for the worse. On 30 July Ana Ruiz came up post-haste from Madrid and on the following day Leonor received the *viaticum*. On 1 August, at ten o'clock at night, she died.

Machado later wrote a poem describing how he felt:

> One summer night –
> my balcony door stood open
> and the front door also –
> death entered my house.
> He approached her bed –
> not even noticing me –
> and with very fine hands
> broke something delicate.

Death crossed the room
a second time. What did you do?
He did not answer.
I saw no change in her,
but my heart felt heavy.
I knew what he broke:
It was the thread between us![39]

The funeral took place next day in the church of Santa María la Mayor where, almost exactly three years before, the couple had been married. The same priest officiated, but this time there were no disrespectful murmurings in the congregation. A large crowd accompanied the coffin to the cemetery of El Espino. The event was fully reported in *El Porvenir Castellano*, which also carried a remarkable piece by José María Palacio:

> Rarely have we more reason to say, as we do now, that grief paralyses our spirits and makes it very difficult for us to put into words the truth and depth of our feelings.
>
> The much-loved wife of our intimate friend, Don Antonio Machado, has died. Doña Leonor Izquierda de Machado, so young, so good, so beautiful, so worthy of a man with such a generous heart and such a shining intelligence, has died. Poor Leonor!

He then proceeded to address Machado directly:

> In truth, beloved Machado, it is absurd, incomprehensible and cruel, but death is, as it were, obstinate and unshakeable.

Think again about those profound verses, saturated with irony and scorn, by your brother Manuel who, like yourself, is an excellent poet:

> May life take pains to kill me
> now that I don't take pains to live!

But no, it is not life that kills, although life shows how painful it is to live, especially for you in your present circumstances, where a young life has been cut short and so many hopes and affections have been shattered. Why, my God, has life to be so bitter?

Your poetic and artistic soul trembled in the presence of goodness and beauty, and with your lyre full of epithalamiums and your heart bursting with generosity and noble affections, you were prepared – on what you called the happiest day and the saddest night of your life – to make a sacred commitment that you, my dearest friend, would wish to last for ever, but which a treacherous and tenacious illness has changed, in a truly absurd manner, to bitter sadness and to an affliction which, when it is as intense as yours, overwhelms you and drives you to despair.

Palacio continued in similar vein for several more paragraphs, encouraging the poet not to brood over the past but to look hopefully towards the future, and concluded by saying: 'Grief sanctifies great souls; in the face of grief they have to be strong.' [40] Machado never forgot these words and years later paid tribute to 'Palacio, *buen amigo*' in one of his loveliest poems.

A week after the funeral Machado and his mother said farewell to Soria. When they arrived at the station to catch the night train, was the poet recalling the summer evening just three years before when he and Leonor had set off for their honeymoon? Was he thinking about the jeering crowds that had gathered there and turned the happiest day into one of the saddest nights of his life? Back in Madrid the poet, who could not bear the thought of being in Soria without Leonor, decided to seek employment elsewhere. He would have liked to have found a teaching post in Madrid, but Giner de los Ríos told him bluntly that he had no chance of getting one and advised him to seek another post in the provinces. Shortly afterwards he heard that there was a vacancy at Baeza, one of the places that five years earlier he had rejected in favour of Soria. Although fourteen other candidates were in the field, he was more experienced than they were and his application was successful. There was, however, another factor in his favour. The director headmaster of the secondary school at Baeza was Leopoldo Urquía, a *krausista*, whose family had been friendly with the Machados when they lived in Seville.

And so it was that, one day in late October 1912, Antonio found himself at Atocha station waiting to board a train to Baeza, some 200 miles away to the south.

IV

Seven Long Years in the South

Baeza, like Soria, is a city set on a hill. It stands on a ridge 2,500 feet above sea level and, except when visibility is obscured by mist, commands fine views over a wide stretch of Andalusia. It is an ancient city, first fortified by the Romans, long occupied by the Moors and eventually, in the early 13th century, 'reconquered' by Christians. It came to prominence in the 16th century, when the nobility built fine palaces there and a university, second only in fame to that at Salamanca, was established. In the following century the city's fortunes faded with the decline of the once flourishing textile industry and with the departure of the aristocracy to more fashionable locations. By 1824, when the university finally closed its doors, Baeza had become – socially, economically, culturally and in almost every other way – a backwater.

This was certainly how it seemed to Machado when he first set foot there in 1912. Although the city, with its 15,000 inhabitants, was twice the size of Soria, it could not boast half its attractions. Soon after his arrival he recorded his impressions in a letter to his friend Palacio:

> This place is almost illiterate. Soria is Athens compared
> with this city, where no-one ever reads a newspaper.
> Suffice it to say, apart from that, the people here

are good, hospitable and kind. The only things
that interest them are politics and sport; there is no
appreciation of spirituality or culture. When it comes
to spirituality little Soria is, in my judgment, vastly
superior to this city… There is no local newspaper,
no library, no bookshop, nor even a stand where you
can pick up a Madrid newspaper. [1]

His insistence that the city lacked spirituality is significant. It was
said that few citizens of Baeza, which was bursting with churches
and convents, were without a son or daughter in a religious order,
but this meant nothing to Machado: his anticlerical ancestry ensured
that he had never equated religion with spirituality.

Because of his negative feelings about organized religion, many
Catholics labelled Machado an atheist – and this view has persisted.
What his actual beliefs were at this time are clear from 'Profession of
Faith', a poem written not long before his arrival in Baeza:

God is not the sea. He is of the sea,
he glitters like moon on water, or comes in sight
like a white sail appearing;
the sea is where he wakes up and falls asleep.
He created the sea and is born of the sea,
like clouds and storms:
the Creator he, and his creature makes him;
his breath is spirit and by the spirit he breathes.
You will I make, my God, as you made me,
and that I may give you the soul you've given me,
I will create you within me. May the pure stream
of loving-kindness that flows forever
flow in my heart. Oh, Lord, seal up
the clouded springs of unloving faith. [2]

This poem, it has sometimes been suggested, indicates that
Machado was a pantheist – one who believes that God is everything

and everything is God. But it would be more accurate to describe him as a panentheist – one who believes that the world exists in God but that God is not exhausted by the world. For Machado God was transcendent as well as immanent. With Krause he believed in one 'beyond whom nothing is nor has reality and in whom all finite beings are grounded'. [3]

Such elevated thoughts were probably not foremost in Machado's mind when he arrived in Baeza. He first had to find somewhere to lay his head. To begin with he put up at the Comercio hotel, but not long afterwards was able to rent an apartment in what is now the Pasaje de Cardenal Benavides. In due course he was joined by his mother, always concerned about his welfare and now, following his bereavement, especially so. She immediately took a great liking to the Urquía family and loved to share with them her memories of Seville, a city as special to them as it was to the Machados. Their younger daughter Francisca later remembered Doña Ana as a sociable and talkative woman – someone she liked to accompany when she went for a walk. This little girl was precociously brilliant and, although only nine years old, was soon enrolled in Machado's French class, where she was the sole female pupil. 'Don Antonio,' she recalled, 'used to sit by my side and give me his special attention I liked being with him. I heard my father say that he was Spain's premier poet and I was proud to be so close to him that I could touch him.'[4]

Spain's 'premier poet' continued to be productive during his first months in Baeza and a sequence of fifteen of his 'songs and proverbs' was published in *La Lectura*. Though living in the south, his heart was clearly still in the north and the mood was often melancholy:

> There in the highlands
> where the Duero traces
> its crossbow curve
> around Soria, among the leaden ridges
> and stains of wasted live oaks,
> my heart is vagabonding in daydreams…

Leonor, do you see the river poplars
with their firm branches?
Look at the Moncayo blue and white. Give me
your hand, and let us stroll.
Through these fields of my countryside,
embroidered with dusty olive groves,
I go walking alone,
sad, tired, pensive, old.[5]

At times, however, his mood was less sombre and he was able to compose verses that were humorous in tone. On one occasion he contributed a poem called 'Men of Spain' to *El Porvenir Castellano*, the journal that he had helped Palacio to found during his time in Soria. It describes the kind of man that was often to be encountered in the provincial towns and cities of Spain, where social life centred on the casino. This typical Spaniard was an elderly man with 'withered skin, grey hair and eyes blurred with melancholy' who on Sundays dressed up in a velveteen jacket and 'buttoned up' trousers and wore a smart *cordobés* – a hat resembling a boater – on his head. His head was 'as empty as the world he inhabited' and he talked about nothing but the exploits of matadors, murderers, brigands and thugs. In politics he was reactionary, gloomily predicting that liberals would return to power, 'as surely as storks return to their bell-towers'.[6]

It is likely that the 'men of Spain' that he wrote about were those he met in the *tertulia* or 'conversation circle' that gathered each evening in the dispensary of a pharmacy close to his home. The difference between them and the men he had been used to meeting in Madrid made the poet think increasingly in terms of 'the two Spains'. This polarization was apparent in a poem entitled 'The Ephemeral Tomorrow', published in *La Lectura* in May 1913 – a brilliant example of Machado's wit at its most satirical.

The Spain of the brass band and tambourine,
bull-ring and sacristy,

that deifies Frascuelo and the Virgin –
the mocking spirit but unquestioning mind –
must have its marble and its festivals,
its infallible future, its great poet.
The barren yesterday begets a morrow
empty, and (if we're lucky) transient.
He'll be an owlish youth, a good-for-nothing,
hangman in the fashion of a dancer;
mimic the manners of French royalists,
touched with the ribald unbelief of Paris,
but in the style of Spain: the specialist
in vice accessible to everyone.
That under side of Spain which prays and yawns –
old trot, card-sharper, sad-faced, quarrelsome;
that Spain which prays and charges-in, head first
whenever it deigns to use its head at all.

It will still have a numerous progeny
of men who love traditions they call sacred,
holy wafers and holy offices;
and apostolic beards will still be seen,
while bright bald pates will shine on other skulls
so venerable and so orthodox.
The barren yesterday begets a morrow
empty and (if we're lucky) transient,
the shadow of a feckless parasite,
a hangman in the fashion of a dancer,
a vacuous yesterday, an addled morrow.
Like the sick overhang of a drunken belly
full of inferior wine, when a red sun totters,
crowning the granite peaks with turbid heel-taps,
there'll be tomorrow's indigestion, written
in the pragmatic, pleasant afternoon.
But another Spain is coming,
the Spain of mallet and chisel,

with that eternal youth which only comes
from the solid past of our people.

A Spain implacable yet redeeming,
a Spain that now is dawning,
with a torch in the hand of the avenger,
a Spain of fury but of an idea. [7]

As Geoffrey Gibbans has pointed out, *maza* (here translated as
'mallet') is the word that Machado had used earlier when speaking
of Unamuno's 'iconoclastic cudgel'. [8]

There was a need for such cudgels because, as Machado saw
it, the emergence of 'another Spain' was being obstructed by the
clergy, who were in control of the country's educational system and
were implacable enemies of progress. To counter their influence, as
he stated in an article in the Madrid paper *El Liberal*, there was an
urgent need for good teachers to be sent into rural schools. At the
same time guidance should be sought from those whom he called the
'investigators of the popular soul' – the scholars who had undertaken
research into the nation's folklore. Here he shows himself to be a true
son of *Démofilo*. For him, as for his father, folklore was (as, writing as
Juan de Mairena, he was later to express it) 'not a reminiscent study
of ancient cultures' but 'the viable and creative culture of a people
from whom he had much to learn if he was to improve his teaching
of the privileged classes'.[9] It was in a spirit of filial piety that at this
time he was planning to prepare a collection of 'songs and proverbs'
set within the context of the countryside of Andalusia. He wrote
to Juan Ramon Jiménez to tell him that he intended to publish the
poems in the autumn of 1913, but in the event nothing came of the
project. Perhaps one reason for this was that his mind was still too
full of memories of that other countryside through which, in happier
times, he had walked hand in hand with Leonor.

After his wife's death Machado long remained stricken with grief.
As he told Ramon Jiménez, he had at one time been so distraught
that he had contemplated suicide, but the success of *Campos de Castilla*

had saved him from this fate. 'God knows!' he wrote, 'this was not out of vanity, but because I thought that, if my creativity could be of some use to the world, I had no right to annihilate it.'[10] But, as those aware of his deep bond with his mother have pointed out, he was almost certainly also deterred by the belief that, if he killed himself, she too would not long survive. As it was, with mother and son living together in Baeza, the two were able to provide each other with much needed emotional support. Spending Holy Week 1913 in Seville, meeting relatives and re-visiting old haunts, would probably have been, for both of them, a therapeutic experience.

After his return to Baeza he appears to have been in a less melancholy mood. A poem he wrote in late April is indicative of more positive feelings:

> Palacio, good friend,
> is spring
> already dressing the branches of the poplars
> by the river and the roads? On the highland
> by the upper Duero, spring is late
> yet beautiful and gentle when it comes!
> Do the old elms
> have a few new leaves?
> The acacia trees must still be bare
> and the mountains of the sierra full of snow.
> O peak of the Moncayo white and rose,
> there in the sky of Aragon, how lovely!
> Are brambles in flower
> among the grey cliffs,
> and white daisies
> in the slender grass?
> On those belfries
> by now the storks must be turning up.
> There must be green wheatfields,
> and brown mules in the seeded furrows,
> and peasants who plant the late crops

with April rains. By now the bees
are sipping thyme and rosemary.
Are plum trees in flower? Are there still violets?
Stealthy hunters with partridge decoys
under their long capes
must be around. Palacio, good friend,
are there nightingales on the riverbanks?
With the first lilies
and first roses in the orchards,
on a blue afternoon, go climb Espino,
up to high Espino where her earth lies. [11]

Such a keen observation of the natural world is rare at this time among Spanish poets, but then few of them had field naturalists for grandfathers or teachers who took them rambling through the *campos*. Machado's depiction of the countryside in spring – the resurgence of life among the trees, flowers, animals, birds and bees – bears some resemblance to that of his English contemporary Edward Thomas, who at that very time was at work on *In Pursuit of Spring*, the book that marked his transition from prose-writer to poet.

That spring saw the reawakening in Machado of his interest in philosophy. Shortly after penning the poem for Palacio he wrote to another friend, José Ortega y Gasset, now professor of metaphysics in the University of Madrid, to say that he had gone back to reading philosophy, 'the only subject that really excites me'. In addition to Plato, Leibniz and Kant, 'the most poetic of thinkers', he was also immersing himself in the work of 'those new philosophers who are laying the foundations of a new metaphysics', especially Henri Bergson.[12] But 'One Day's Poem', composed at this time, suggests that his admiration for the French existentialist was waning:

Henri Bergson: *The Immediate
Data of Consciousness.* Could this be
another of those French snares?
This Bergson is a rascal,

wouldn't you say, Master Unamuno?
He can't perform
like that Immanuel,
the immortal handspring. [13]

The tone is one of good humoured mockery, but it conceals a serious point. 'Bergson, for all his concern with free will,' wrote Arthur Terry, 'has nothing to say on the question of God or immortality; Kant, on the other hand, denies the rational proofs of God but goes on to postulate a God who is "known" only by faith.' [14]

If his attitude to Bergson is ambivalent there is no doubt about his contempt for some other French writers, whom he describes in his letter to Ortega as 'that *troupe* of pedants who claim to represent the cream of the intellectual life of France'. Here he was referring to 'neo-catholics' such as Charles Maurras and other members of the right-wing organization called Action Française, whose chauvinistic antisemitism had become manifest at the time of the Dreyfus affair. Machado said he was afraid that the 'terrible reaction' that this would produce in France might cause a 'backlash' in neighbouring Spain.[15]

In the same month he was provided with an opportunity to give wider vent to his feelings when, out of the blue, he received an invitation to contribute an autobiographical piece to an anthology being prepared for publication. The book was never in fact published, but the text of what Machado wrote survives and provides a fascinating glimpse of how things stood with him at this time.

> I love Spain dearly, but my opinion of the country is completely negative. Everything Spanish both delights me and annoys me. My mood is one of resignation rather than rebelliousness; but from time to time, when I am feeling momentarily optimistic, I have aggressive impulses of which, almost invariably, I later feel ashamed. I look inwards rather than outwards and recognize the injustice of criticizing in my neighbour what I am aware of in myself. My

thinking is generally directed towards the resolution
of what Kant calls *the conflict of transcendent ideas* and I
seek in poetry a relief from this unrewarding task. I
have a profound belief in a spiritual reality that is set
against the world of the senses. After I have written
it I feel a great aversion to everything I write and
my greatest torture is correcting the proofs of my
compositions. This explains why all my books are
riddled with errors.

My great passion is travelling. I am well acquainted
with parts of High Castile, Aragon and Andalusia. I
am not very sociable, but I retain a great affection for
people. In my youth my life was disorderly: I drank
a lot, although I never became an alcoholic. Four
years ago I underwent a radical change and gave up
all my bad habits. I have never been a womanizer and
I detest pornography. I adored my wife and I do not
think I shall marry again. I think that the toughness
of Spanish women is unsurpassable and that the
decadence of Spain is largely due to the predominance
of women, who are much more formidable than
the men. I am disgusted by a political system under
which, because of the excessive influence of the
city, the countryside suffers degradation. I detest the
worldly clergy who, I believe, are contributing to
this degradation. Generally speaking I like to mix
with ordinary people rather than with aristocrats,
and I prefer the country to the town. It seems to me
that the difficulties we encounter as a nation are due
to our spiritual weakness; but I believe that we must
fight for a better future and find a faith that we do
not now possess. It is more useful to speak the truth
and condemn the present than, out of prudence, to
preserve the present at the cost of the future. To put

up with things just because they are useful seems to me to be ridiculous and dangerous. Now is the time to fight the Catholic Church and proclaim the people's right to freedom of belief, for I am convinced that Spain will die of spiritual asphyxia if this iron yoke is not broken. The only obstacles are hypocrisy and timidity. This is not a matter of culture – it is possible to be very cultured and at the same time respectful of the fictitious and immoral – but of conscience. Conscience comes before literacy and bread. I admire Costa, but Unamuno is my master.[16]

Joaquín Costa, the old friend of his father who had been one of his teachers at the Institución Libre, was a fine man and a fearless thinker, but he belonged to an earlier generation. It was understandable that the man that Machado continued to regard as his 'master' should be Miguel de Unamuno, who in 1913 published his great philosophical treatise, *The Tragic Sense of Life in Men and Peoples*. It was to Unamuno that he wrote when he felt the need to share his thoughts and feelings about the state of things in Spain. In June he returned to the subject of 'neo-catholicism' that he had recently written about to Ortega and he squarely blamed the Church for the ignorance of the people. He reported that in the priest-ridden city of Baeza barely 30% of the population could read and almost the only publications for sale were prayer books and ecclesiastical periodicals. The Church, which was 'spiritually rotten but organizationally formidable', did nothing to reform the coarse habits of the people. 'Moreover', he wrote, 'the countryman, resigned to his fate, works and suffers in conditions so deplorable that they are equivalent to suicide.'

He concluded his letter to Unamuno with some touching words about his own sufferings:

The death of my wife left my spirit in tatters. My wife was an angelic creature whom death cruelly cut down. I adored her, but greater than adoration is compassion. It would have been a thousand times better if I, not she, had died. I would have surrendered a thousand lives to save hers. I do not think that there is anything extraordinary in my having such feelings. There is something immortal in us that wants to die whenever someone else dies. Perhaps that was why God came into the world. I find consolation in thinking so. Sometimes I am hopeful. It is also absurd to have a negative faith. However, the blow was terrible and I do not think I have recovered from it. While I fought alongside her against the irremediable I was sustained by the knowledge that I was suffering much more than she was, since she, at the last, did not think about dying and her sickness caused her no sadness. Well, nowadays I feel her to be more alive than dead and sometimes I firmly believe that she will be restored to me.[17]

It is not clear what Machado meant by that final sentence. Was it Leonor or was it Love that would be restored to him? Was he hoping that one day he might find another woman upon whom he could fix his affections and so satisfy his longing to love and be loved?

It seems that at this period the only woman in his life was his mother. Ana Ruiz apparently continued to live with him in Baeza for some years. In December 1915 she was not listed in the Madrid census, where the Machados were recorded as living in an apartment at 99, Calle de Fuencarral. The head of the family was named as Manuel Machado, by occupation an archivist in the Biblioteca Nacional, and the household included six others. These were his wife Eulalia Cáceres, her sister Carmen and their aged father, Manuel's brothers José ('painter') and Joaquín ('student'), and a servant. (Francisco had left home to become a prison officer in El Puerto de Santa María.) But a year or so later Ana Ruiz was evidently back in Madrid, living with José and Joaquín in an apartment in Calle General Arrando, only a ten minute walk away from the one now occupied by Manuel and Eulalia. The new arrangement meant that there was ample accommodation for Antonio when he came to Madrid in his long vacations: he had a large bedroom that doubled as a study where he could be on his own and, if he felt like it, work throughout the night.

Machado liked staying up late to write if he did not have to go to work in the morning. In his summer vacation in 1913 he was composing a poem inspired by reading *Castilla*, a recently published book by 'Azorín' – the pseudonym of the novelist and essayist José Martínez Ruiz. The two men were almost exact contemporaries and a dozen years earlier they had both been contributors to the militantly anticlerical periodical *Electra*. Since then, however, Azorín had become rather more conservative in his views and Machado seems to have been looking for an opportunity to remind him that the Church remained an obstacle to the regeneration of Spain. The point he evidently wished to emphasize was that anticlericalism was not essentially anti-Christian. The poem made it clear that, in spite of his loathing for 'apostolic juntas', 'catholic ladies' and 'garrulous clergy', he was, like Azorín, a firm believer in God. [18]

Machado sent the poem to Juan Ramon Jiménez for inclusion among the 'elegies' in a new collection that he was planning to produce. In an accompanying letter he said that he had some reservations about the quality of the poem. 'You may find elements of crudity in this composition,' he wrote. 'I have within me an unavoidable destructiveness and imperfections that debase my spirit, causing me to get carried away and to write superficially.'[19] The proposed collection never materialized, but the poem was published later that year in *El Porvenir Castellana* and eventually reproduced in *Poesías completas (1899-1917)*. However, in November 1913 Juan Ramon Jiménez took the poem with him to a gathering held in Azorín's honour at Aranjuez and read it aloud to those present. Machado himself was not there. He had been invited but, to his regret, the venue was too far from Baeza for him to be able to attend it. Had he done so he could have observed for himself whether Azorín was paying attention when these words were addressed to him:

Oh, thou, *Azorín*, listen: all Spain is longing
for a resurgence, for a new beginning!
Must we be numbed in a Spain facing death
and stifled in a Spain that's gasping for breath?
To rescue the new epiphany
we must now come together
with torches in hand to greet the new day.
Listen! Can't you hear the dawn cocks crowing? [20]

It would be interesting to know Azorín's reaction to this poem. Would he have felt, as he did when he read *Campos de Castilla*, that 'in these verses we feel that the whole spirit of the poet is vibrating'.[21] Would he have realized what Machado was saying to him between the lines – that it was the Church that was primarily responsible for preventing Spain's resurgence?

His continuing preoccupation with the problems besetting Spain is revealed in an especially vivid dream that he had in May 1914 and recorded in minute detail in his notebook. (From the handwriting in the facsimile it appears to have been written in a hurry not long after he woke up.) This 'nightmare', as he called it, unfolded dramatically like scenes in a play. In the first scene he was lying in a prison cell, having been condemned to death, when he was woken up by a tap on the door. In came 'a little, jovial old man with a parcel under his arm', who looked like a barber and turned out to be an executioner; the parcel, it transpired, contained the device he had invented for dispatching criminals efficiently. In the second scene the 'I' in the dream appears to have been in a law court, where he was accused of killing a ticket inspector (on a Barcelona train) by throwing him out on to the track. He told the judges, whose 'good humour' surprised him, that he had no memory of the incident and, when members of the jury were asked for their verdict, they said (three times over) that he was guilty and (thrice again) that he was not. In the third scene the executioner reappeared, insisting that he would be obliged to hang the criminal in his cell because otherwise regulations required that he would have to do so in a theatre with the audience present;

but this was not possible because the priests were reselling the tickets. Hearing this, the dreamer knew that he was doomed. At this point a great crowd of people approached and women's voices could be heard asking: 'Is this where they are going to hang an innocent man?' The hangman opened the big heavy door and into the cell came a motley collection of 'townsmen, workers, women, soldiers and children' – and, of course, a clergyman. Many brought chairs so that they could watch the spectacle more comfortably. Some planned to have lunch. One man was selling oranges. Then a clergyman and a townsman spoke up, complaining that things were not like they used to be in the old days when hangmen had 'served an apprenticeship as bull-fighters' and knew how to execute people with dignity, as God demanded. The executioner said nothing. He wanted to point out the advantages of using the apparatus that he had invented, which was much more scientific. 'Hurray for science!' someone shouted. 'Hurray for Christ!' another responded. At this point the townsman intervened:

> Shut up, you riffraff! … Silence in the name of the King! (Pause) The executioner has a royal warrant to try out the apparatus that he has invented. Naturally, the criminal has the right to request the last rites of our sacred religion before he is executed, but he can dispense with them if he wishes. Our august monarch wishes to show his beloved people that he is tolerant and responsive to the new rhythm of the times …

Following the execution, which is not described, there is a brief encounter, on the banks of the Styx, between the dead man and Charon, the grim boatman of the underworld:

> *Charon*: Who brought you to this river bank, you
> unhappy man?
>
> 'A barber hanged me, but I don't know why.'

Charon: 'They all say that! Wait here and you will
        embark.'

'They all say that! … And I thought I had died
in an original way.'

At the foot of the page Machado wrote: 'This is an almost exact
transcript of a dream. Nothing in it has been made up. It ought to
be studied. It cannot be published without exegesis and analysis – a
very difficult undertaking and perhaps not interesting enough to
compensate for the hard work involved. A document is not a work
of art.' [22]

Machado's document may not have been 'a work of art' but it
reads like the work of a playwright – a precursor of the tragicomedies
for which he and Manuel were later to become famous. But what
precisely was the meaning of this drama that had welled up out of
the poet's unconscious? He subtitled the document 'Spain in the near
future' and probably thought it had a prophetic message. There is
certainly much in the dream about institutions that he thought (or
hoped) to be on the point of collapse. There is profound antipathy
towards the Catholic Church and its priests, and a firm rejection
of its sacraments. There is contempt for a monarchy that prides
itself on thinking it is ruling in the interests of the people. There
is abhorrence of a judicial system under which innocent people
are often condemned and sometimes executed. There is ridicule of
the bourgeoisie, who are pompously loyal to the establishment and
arrogantly contemptuous of people they regard as their inferiors.
There is dislike of the whole lifestyle of a people for whom dignity
and decorum are all important and who look upon matadors as
models of good manners. How much better Spain would be without
such archaic attitudes and institutions!

At a deeper level, however, the dream is less about the future
state of Spain than the current state of the dreamer. It is, after all, a
dream about death dreamed by a man who not so long before had
contemplated killing himself. It is noticeable that the people who

feature most prominently in it are, like himself, male. Women are said to be present, but they take no part in the proceedings; in fact they insist that the prisoner is innocent and oppose his execution. Perhaps they represent Machado's well-developed 'feminine side' that could not bear his country's overwhelmingly 'macho' culture. What the ticket inspector represents is far from clear. What caused the dreamer to become so angry with him that he threw him out of the train? Since this was the Barcelona train, did it have anything to do with Machado's feelings of frustration at being prevented from reaching that city on his honeymoon? Does the savage action indicate that this gentle, mild-mannered poet had a 'shadow side' that could be aggressive and even violent? And did his disappointment on discovering, when he reached the Styx, that the manner of his death had not been in any way unusual have something to do with his belief – often held by a man who is his mother's favourite – that he was in some way 'special'?

Whether or not Machado, deep down, felt himself to be 'special', other people evidently did think so. Amongst these were the principal of the Institute at Baeza and Machado's students there. Those he taught clearly recognized that he was in quite a different category from other teachers they encountered. One of his pupils, Rafael Láinez Alcalá, recalled how impressed he was by the original way in which Machado taught French poetry, insisting that they learned great chunks of it by heart. He was also taken with the poet's unusual appearance. He used to wear a wing collar, a black cravat with a huge knot and a flabby black hat seated at an odd angle on his untidy head of hair. His clothes were speckled with ash from his 'inevitable cigarettes' – so that it was not surprising that he acquired the nickname of Antonio *Manchado*, an adjective that can be translated as 'stained', 'soiled', 'marked' or 'speckled'. Láinez also recalled that the poet walked with a slight limp and often supported himself with 'a strong rustic stick'. [23]

Throughout his time in Baeza, walking continued to be, as it had been in Soria, Machado's principal outdoor activity. Sometimes he was accompanied by a member of his *tertulia* called Cristóbal Torres, with whom, in spite of – or perhaps because of – their political disagreements, he had developed a close friendship. More often than not, however, he seems to have walked alone – not something that many Spaniards would have deliberately chosen to do. His favourite route was along the Camino San Antonio, an ancient highway that ran, girded by olive groves, from Baeza to Ubeda, a distance of nine kilometres. This little city was famed for the beauty of its Renaissance architecture, but it seems that for Machado this was not its main attraction. People apparently used to say that he went there primarily to buy matches, of which he always needed plentiful supplies, but, since these were easily obtainable in Baeza, the rumour must have been false. It was also suggested, rather more tentatively, that he went there to visit a prostitute – an unlikely explanation for the peregrinations of a poet who, as he himself expressed it in his autobiographical note quoted above, had never been much of a *mujeriego* or womanizer. In Baeza, as in Soria, the main reason for his frequent excursions was probably his need to escape from the claustrophobic atmosphere of a small provincial city and to get exercise for his limbs and fresh air into his lungs. Like Coleridge, Wordsworth, Edward Thomas and other English poets, it was in walking through the countryside that he found inspiration for his muse.

Sometimes Machado's travels took him further afield. On one occasion he and a colleague from the Institute and two others went on an expedition to the Aznaitín, a mountain that, on a clear day, was visible from the walls of Baeza. It is not known whether the climbers reached its peak, but coming down the mountain proved so difficult that at one point the poet was reportedly obliged to slide down the slope on his bottom. On another occasion he went, possibly with his brother Joaquín and a friend of theirs, on a journey in search of the source of the Guadalquivir. Just as in Soria he had searched for the source of the Duero, so now he was eager to find the *fuente* from which Seville's great river sprang. Since he was wont to compare the course of a person's life with that of a river – and, as some of his poems show, had a nostalgic longing for the *fuentes* that

played in the garden of his childhood – there may have been some
deep significance in his desire to get back to the beginning of things.

The first stage of the journey of exploration is commemorated
in a poem entitled 'The Olive Trees':

> Two leagues from Ubeda
> in the blazing sun, Pero Gil's Tower
> (name of a dismal Spanish town). The coach
> jogs on past olives grey and dusty.
> Over there, the staunch old castle.
> Beggars and urchins in the square,
> a swarm of rags and tatters.
> On we go past the portal
> of Mercy Convent.
> White walls, dark cypress trees,
> melancholy that smarts
> like an iron grindstone
> rasping the heart. Piety walled up
> to tower over this refuse heap.
> Now, brothers, this house of God, you tell me:
> what does this house of God contain?
> And that pale youth
> watching us astonished,
> taking us in with his mouth, you'd say,
> he'll be the local idiot,
> of whom they simply say: that's Luke,
> Blas or Ginés – town fool, you know.
> On we go. Olive groves. The trees
> are flowering. Our two beasts,
> run down, scraggly, slowly pull us
> toward Peal. So rich this countryside.
> Earth does its share; the sun toils too.
> The land is where man belongs:
> he procreates, he sows, he tills,
> and by his toil yokes earth to heaven.

We cloud the springs of life,
the pristine sun,
with our unhappy eyes,
our bitter prayers,
our idle hands,
our thinking.
In sin we are conceived,
in pain we live. God stays away!
This piety that towers
over this sordid village, over this refuse heap,
this house of God – you tell us, blessed
cannons of Von Kluck: What does it contain?[24]

Alexander Von Kluck was the general who commanded the German forces at the battle of the Marne in September 1914. The allusion to his cannons, writes Alan Trueblood, the poem's translator, 'sweeps away the earlier personal pain, the pessimism regarding Spanish society and the mounting existential "nausea" in a final surge of Machado's "Jacobin blood", which sees only total destruction and rebuilding as a remedy for the ills of Spanish society.'[25]

After leaving Peal, where Machado's poem ends, the travellers are thought to have taken the shorter route – via El Chorro and Puerto Lorente – to their destination in the densely wooded Cañada de las Fuentes. Soon after reaching it a storm blew up, similar to the one Machado had encountered years before on Urbión, and the party was forced to take refuge in a workmen's hut. Pérez Ferrero, to whom many years later he evidently gave an account of the excursion, states that it was for the poet a deeply moving experience 'because it reminded him of the ones that he had made to the mountains of Soria.'[26]

Pérez Ferrero also mentioned a later expedition that Machado and a number of unidentified companions made to the Sierra de Quesada to see the famous shrine of Tíscar. It is located among huge rocks at the foot of a crag called the Peña Negra and it houses the image of the Virgin of the Sierra, the patroness of Quesada. The visit inspired Machado to write a poem:

> In the Quesada mountains
> is a giant eagle,
> greenish, black and gold,
> wings always outstretched..
> It's stone, it never tires.[27]

The 'giant eagle' is formed by the outlines of three contiguous peaks known as Pico Rayal, Navilla Alta and Aguilón del Loco. That Machado should have written about this is typical of the man who, although one of a party that had come to see the shrine, chose to turn his back on it and admire the view before him. What he beheld in his mind's eye – a great bird of prey with outstretched wings, sculpted by Nature out of the rocky terrain – was far more impressive than the tawdry image of the holy patroness of Quesada. It is in fact likely that many of the people who have since made the pilgrimage to this lonely place have come not to venerate the Virgin of the Sierra but to see the plaque that commemorates the poet's visit and his first sighting of the 'giant eagle'.

These expeditions to scenes of peace and beauty took place at a time when almost every other European nation was embroiled in the violence and ugliness of war. The 1914–18 war deeply troubled Machado's spirit. 'This war,' he said in a letter to Unamuno soon after its outbreak, 'seems to me to be as tragic and terrible as it is lacking in noble ideals. After it is over we shall have to rectify concepts and feelings that appear to us to be sacred, but which are in reality criminal and inhumane; I am beginning to doubt the sanctity of patriotism.'[28] He regretted that his country remained neutral and regarded the prevailing Spanish attitude to the conflict as shameful. 'We have treated the war as a spectacle, as if it were a bull-fight', he protested in another letter to Unamuno, 'we are shouting and screaming in the front seats, but one day, unless God prevents it, we ourselves will be pitched into the ring.'[29] The analogy is striking but not wholly appropriate, since the spectators at a bull-fight presumably always want the matador to win. It might have been more accurate to compare the conflict to a football match, with the onlookers supporting rival teams. At this time Spanish conservatives generally supported the Germans, while the liberals backed the British and the French.

Before the outbreak of war Machado had often spoken disparagingly of the French and their culture. In an article in *La Lectura* in the summer of 1913 he had written:

> It is evident that at present French literature and philosophy is characterized by a total lack of originality, by wretchedly reactionary tendencies and by a fraudulence that would be comical if was not combined with apocalyptic terror. Those of us who have lived in France for any length of time in recent years know that this great nation is today so spiritually exhausted that only fear has the power to hold it together. Nowadays this fear goes by the name of 'patriotism', 'nationalism', 'catholicism', 'classicism', etc, etc.

He went on to remark that, although in the last two centuries Spain had acquired 'three quarters of its culture' from France, it now received 'only products of *desasimilación*' — a word that he appears to have invented to carry the meaning of 'disintegration' or 'decomposition'. These 'products' comprised 'every manner of thing that was putrid and corrupt: sensuality, anarchism, pornography, decadence and aristocratic pomposity'.[30]

The Great War, however, led Machado to revise his opinions. The poet who, as a boy, had felt his spine tingle on first hearing the singing of the *Marseillaise* and, as a young man, had become aware that 'Jacobin blood' flowed in his veins, was now moved by more positive feelings toward France. In an article published in *La Nota* (Buenos Aires) in July 1916 he stated his conviction that she was fighting not only to defend her own territory but on behalf of all humanity. Those Spaniards who were backing Germany, he wrote, 'do not represent the clear conscience of Spain but, more likely, the subconscious, the psychological zone of base instincts, perhaps the traditional inertia that, obstinately and insistently, obstructs the flow of all that is vital and liberating.' [31] It was therefore only natural that, when Unamuno, Ortega y Gasset, Valle-Inclán and other liberals produced a manifesto urging Spain to support the Allies, Machado should have been among the signatories. He and Manuel also signed a petition drawn up by the Liga Antigermanófila, an association that had been formed to fight Spain's 'enemies within' – those who were using the opportunity provided by the war to 'deter the Spanish people from taking the only course of action that will promote their interests, guarantee their liberties and ensure their national security'.[32]

It was around this time, when he was deeply concerned about the war and wanting to understand more about its causes, that he decided to embark on a systematic study of the writings of the great philosophers, even teaching himself Greek in order to be able to read the earliest ones in the original language. 'His philosophical reading', writes Bernard Sesé, 'probably prompted him to undertake, in the light of his own destiny, a more rigorous consideration of the great questions that preoccupy people: the meaning of life, destiny, death and, further on, the existence of God. Henceforth his writings take on a more serious tone.'[33]

1915, the year in which Machado began to learn Greek, saw the death of the Socratic teacher who had first aroused his interest in the Hellenic world. The news of the passing of Francisco Giner de los Ríos, who died in February at the age of 75, filled him with a feeling of great sadness and inspired one of his loveliest poems.

> At the time the master disappeared
> the morning light
> said to me: 'For three days
> my brother Francisco has not worked..

Has he died?'...All we know
is that he has gone off on a clear road,
telling us this: Show
your grief for me in work and hope.
Be good, forget the rest, be
what I have been among you: a soul.
Live, life goes on,
the dead go on dying, the shadows go by;
the man who abandons still has and the man who has
lived is alive.
Make noise, anvils; be silent, you church bells!

So the brother of the morning light,
the old happy man with a holy life,
leaving the sun of his work,
went off toward a purer light.
...Oh yes, my friends, carry
his body to the mountain!
to the blue hills
of the Guadarrama!
There I know deep ravines
with green pines where the wind sings.
His heart can rest
under an ordinary oak
in the thyme fields, where the golden
butterflies are fluttering......
One day the master there
imagined a new blossoming of Spain.[34]

The mourners did not carry Giner's body to the mountains, but buried it in the Civil Cemetery in Madrid, where the bodies of so many of those associated with the Institución Libre had been laid to rest. Machado himself was unable to be present at the funeral, but Ortega y Gasset and others of his friends were there to mourn the passing of a man whom many regarded as a saint.

Another death that deeply saddened Machado was that of Rubén Darío, who died in Nicaragua just a year later, in February 1916. Darío, who was only 49, had long suffered from cirrhosis of the liver – a consequence of the *alcoholismo* that Machado himself, once a heavy drinker, was thankful to have avoided. He had great esteem and affection for the man who had inspired him with his poetry and given him moral and financial support in his time of need. Machado had been flattered when the Nicaraguan had portrayed him in a poem:

> Mysterious and silent
> he came and he left us.
> You could hardly meet his gaze,
> it was so profound.
> He spoke with a touch
> of timidity and loftiness,
> and you could almost see the light
> of his thoughts, burning.
> He was luminous and deep
> as a man of good faith.
> He might have been a pastor of lions
> and, at the same time, of lambs.
> He scattered thunderstorms
> or carried a honeycomb.
> The wonders of life,
> of love and pleasures
> he sang in deepest poems
> whose secret was his own.
> Mounted on a rare Pegasus
> one day he went off to the impossible.
> I pray to my gods for Antonio.
> May they always save him. Amen. [35]

Machado's response to his friend's death was to write a poem beginning with the question: 'If all the world's harmony was in your poetry/where have you gone, Darío, in search of it?' [36] The poem was duly published in *España* alongside a tribute from Darío's great friend from his Paris days, Amado Nervo.

It may be that Darío's passing revived Machado's grief at the premature death, on a February day over twenty years before, of *Demófilo*. In March he wrote a poem commemorating the father who, in his childhood, he used to watch shooting wildfowl on the riverbank, working in his study or relaxing in the garden of Las Dueñas. The poem was not published, but some of its language was later incorporated in a sonnet:

> This light of Seville … The great house once again
> where I was born, filled with fountain sounds.
> My father in his study. High forehead,
> touch of beard, the moustache drooping.
> My father, still young. He reads and writes,
> leafs through his books and muses. He gets up,
> goes towards the garden door and walks about.
> Sometimes he talks out loud, sometimes he sings.
>
> And then his large eyes with the restless look
> seem to be wandering in a void,
> unable to settle anywhere.
>
> They slip off from his yesterday to look through time
> to his tomorrow and, Father, there they light
> so pityingly on my grey head.[37]

A few months later Machado's melancholy mood was lifted by the arrival in Baeza of a party of students from the University of Granada, led by the professor of Literature and the Arts, Martín Domínguez Berrueta. As the poet was aware, this man's approach to education had been much influenced by the Institución Libre. 'Berrueta', he wrote approvingly, 'travels through Spain with his pupils; instead of a classroom he teaches them in trains, in *coches de posta* and in the streets of old cities, where they acquire a feeling for local culture and he, with his knowledge and skill as a teacher, awakens their lively curiosity.'[38] On this occasion they had come to experience at first hand the beauty of Baeza's Renaissance architecture. They called on Machado, whose school term had just ended, and received a very cordial reception. When invited to read some of his poems he responded very positively and, on the evening of 16 June, the students assembled to hear them. 'In Baeza', the group's chronicler later reported, 'the celebrated Machado, unexpectedly departing from his customary quiet and modest mode of living, agreed to Señor Berrueta's request and, in a most intimate and informal fashion, read a selection of his poems – some of them unpublished – and, little by little, every word that he spoke began to stir the souls of those listening.' Another listener later recalled that, in addition to his own verse, Machado read some poems by Rubén Darío in a 'resonant voice' that indicated the intensity of his feelings.[39]

Among the students in that privileged audience was an 18 year old named Federico García who, because his father's surname was one of the commonest in Spain, was always known by his mother's name of Lorca. He was already quite well known in Granada as a pianist and composer, and during his stay in Baeza he performed at a concert in the Casino de Artesanas. But now, inspired by Darío and Machado, he was beginning to write verse and when, in the spring of the following year, he returned to Baeza with Berrueta's group, he was already making his name as a poet. On this visit he and Machado both took part in a performance in the Casino, with the older man reading passages from 'La Tierra de Alvargonzález' and the younger playing the music of popular songs on the piano. Perhaps Lorca felt too intimidated by Machado's presence to read any of his own poems, but, if he did have any such inhibitions, they were soon to be swept away with the publication of his first collection, *Impresiones y paisajes*. Early in 1918 he wrote to his friend Lorenzo Martínez Fuset to say that he planned to take some copies of the book to Baeza to present to Machado and other friends and acquaintances in the city. Fuset wrote back to say that he had spoken to Machado. 'This man's modesty knows no bounds', he wrote. 'When I showed him your letter he said it would be inappropriate for you to make such a journey just to see him; however, he would be very happy to see you and urged me to ensure that you sent him the book.' Machado also told him that Lorca must not confine his creativity to Granada, but see to it that his first successes occur 'in places where the triumph makes a greater impact and brings more rewards.'[40]

In 1916, when he first met Lorca, Machado was busy correcting the proofs of a new collection of poems called *Páginas escogidas* that he hoped would have a good reception and bring him some financial rewards. The book comprised 54 poems from *Soledades. Galerías. Otras poemas,* a selection from *Campos de Castilla* (including the whole of 'La Tierra de Alvargonzález') and five poems that had been published in periodicals between 1913 and 1916. In his introduction to the volume he explained that he had omitted some of the poems composed at a time when he was under the influence of the French symbolists. He was now writing verse in a more intimate, introspective vein.

> I thought that the poetic element was not the word in its phonic value, nor colour, nor line, nor a complex of sensations, but in a deep pulsing of the spirit: what the soul supplies, if it does supply anything; or what it says, if it says anything, when aroused to response by contact with the world.[41]

He then went on to try to explain how and why this change had come about:

> Five years in and around Soria, which is now sacred ground to me – there I married and there I lost my wife, whom I adored – drew me, my vision and my feelings into what was deeply Castilian. Moreover, my set of ideas had changed very much. We are victims, I thought, of a double hallucination. If we look outward and concentrate on entering things, our external world begins to lose solidity; and if

we conclude that it exists not in and for itself, but exists because of us, it ends by dissolving. However, if, moved by our private reality, we turn our eyes inward, then the world pushes in on us, and it is our interior world, our being, that disappears. What to do then? Weave the thread given to us, dream our dream and live; it is the only way we can achieve the miracle of growth. A man attentive to himself and trying to overhear himself drowns the only voice he could hear – his own; but other voices confuse him. Are we then doomed to be merely observers? But when we see, reason is present, and reason analyzes and dissolves. The reason will soon bring the whole theatre down and, finally, our shadow alone will be projected against the background. As for the poet, I thought that his job was to create new poems out of what is eternally human – spirited stories that have their own life, even though they came from him. I considered the old narrative *romance* the supreme expression of poetry, and I wanted to write a new book of them. *La Tierra de Alvargonzález* was born of this longing.[42]

In July 1917, only two months after the publication of *Páginas escogidas*, a much larger collection of Machado's poems came off the press. Entitled *Poesías completas (1899-1917)*, the book included almost all the verse he had ever written. There were in total 152 poems, a fair number of which had not appeared in the earlier selection. The additional material included the parts of *Campos de Castilla* not to be found in *Páginas escogidas* and poems written since 1912, the most notable of which were those belonging to what came to be known as the 'Leonor cycle'. But what was to become perhaps the best known of the new poems was one in the group called 'Proverbs and Songs':

Walker, your footsteps
are the road, and nothing more.
Walker, there is no road,
the road is made by walking.

Walking you make the road,
and turning to look behind
you see the path you never
again will step upon.
Walker, there is no road,
only foam trails on the sea.[43]

The poem may have been inspired by memories of exploratory
expeditions through the countryside of Soria or Andalusia, when
the walkers, having left the road, had to make their own pathway
through the undergrowth. As he expressed it in the opening lines of
a poem written long before he ever set foot in Baeza: 'I have walked
many roads/and opened many paths.'[44] The symbolic significance is
powerful and profound. On his journey through life Machado would
forever be opening new paths – blazing new trails of thoughts and
feelings that others less insightful could later follow.

That he was in many respects a man 'ahead of his time' is clear from
a letter that he sent to Unamuno in January 1918. While in Madrid
for the Christmas vacation Machado had attended a conference that
the Basque philosopher had called to consider the current state of
Spain and, after his return to Baeza, he wanted to continue the
dialogue. In his letter he spoke of something that had been much on
his mind since the outbreak of the Great War – the dire consequences
of man's inhumanity to man. He said that the problem, as he saw it,
was that, in spite of Christ's teaching, the hatred that had caused Cain
to kill Abel persisted – so much so in fact that *cainismo* now governed
the relations between nations. He believed that the only country
that was free from it was Russia where, since the 1917 revolution,
'nobler and more universal sentiments' prevailed. He was thinking
particularly of the teachings of Tolstoy, a translation of whose book

What I believe had long been available in Spain Machado shared Tolstoy's passionate conviction that the essence of Christianity was not to be found in the doctrines of the Church but in the teachings of Christ about love and forgiveness. The great Russian's writings were music to the ears of the poet who had always affirmed that the brotherhood of man was not a remote ideal but, since all men are the sons of a 'common father', a present reality. '*Tolstoísmo* will save Europe', he declared, 'if Europe ever does find salvation.'

He then embarked on a long consideration of a question that was of perennial concern to him – the meaning of Christ's teaching about brotherhood.

> If envy is hating our neighbour on account of our love for ourselves, what of brotherhood? In my judgment, if we were to say that we love our neighbour because we love ourselves, we would be misunderstanding the spirit of Christianity; then brotherhood would be an indirect form of each person loving himself. Brotherhood seems, rather, to be the love we have for our neighbour because of our love for our common father. My brother is not a creation of mine nor any part of myself; to love him I have to direct my love towards him and not towards myself; he is equal to me, but he is other than I; our resemblance does not come from us but from the father that begot us. I have no right to turn my neighbour into a mirror so that I can see and adore myself; this narcissism is antichristian; my brother is indeed a mirror, having a reality as complete as mine, but he is other than myself and I must love him with total self-forgetfulness. To love is not a pleasure but a sacrifice. Christ would not have decreed that love is an unending duty if he had thought that a man could use his neighbour's soul as a mirror in which to comb his beard or trim his moustache. With the great love that you feel for

yourself – so I understand Jesus as saying – love your
brother who is equal to you but is not you; you will
recognize him as a brother; but what you have in
common is kinship with God himself, who is your
father.[45]

It is perhaps surprising that Machado could write with such
confidence and authority to such a distinguished professor as
Unamuno when he himself was at the time still an undergraduate,
struggling to complete his first degree. In 1915 he had enrolled as an
external student in the Faculty of Philosophy and Literature at the
Central University of Madrid and at the end of the academic year
had passed his examinations in Spanish Literature, Logic and History
with distinction. In the academic year 1916-17 he achieved similar
results with his papers in Latin, Greek and Literary Theory. What
now remained were examinations in Psychology, Anthropology
and the History of Philosophy – all of which he passed with flying
colours in the summer of 1918. And so, at the unusually advanced age
of 43, Machado finally gained his licentiate – the Spanish equivalent
of a British B.A. No sooner had he done so than he decided to add
to his academic qualifications by obtaining a doctorate in Philosophy.
For someone who had for so long been steeping himself in the work
of Plato, Leibniz and Kant, this was not an insuperable task. Machado
wrote to Ortega y Gasset, who was already regarded as one of Spain's
foremost philosophers, to ask him to act as his examiner and he was
delighted when he agreed to do so. Being examined by someone
eight years younger than himself must have been rather unnerving,
but Machado survived the experience and in September 1919 gained
his Ph.D. with distinction. The man who seemed for so long to have
been running the race at the speed of a tortoise ended up completing
the course like a hare. Had any other student of the university ever
proceeded from a licentiate to a doctorate so quickly?

While he had been concentrating so hard on the study of
philosophy he had not given as much attention as he had previously to
the writing of poetry, and he may as a consequence have experienced

a measure of internal conflict. There is certainly a hint of this in a short poem published in 1917:

> Reason says:
> Let's seek the truth.
> The heart replies: What's the use?
> We already have the truth.
> Reason: Ah, to have truth
> in one's grasp!
> The heart: What's the use?
> Truth is in hoping.
> Says reason: You lie.
> Comes the heart's reply:
> It's you that are lying, reason,
> saying things you don't believe.
> Reason: Between you and me
> there can be no understanding, heart.
> The heart: As to that, we'll see.[46]

This sounds like a conversation between Machado the philosopher, striving with his intellect to discover the truth about God, man and the universe, and Machado, the poet who intuitively already knows it. But at this period of his life he had to give first place to philosophy if he was to acquire the academic qualifications he needed to get a better job.

For a long time he had been looking for a way of escaping from Baeza, which he called his *rincón moruno* – his 'Moorish corner'. Early in 1915 he had told Jiménez that he would like to return to Madrid. 'I have been in exile for eight years and I am weary of this provincial life, which in the end drains one of all creativity. I often think of abandoning my post and going there [to Madrid] to earn my living by my pen, but this again would mean penury.'[47] At the close of 1918 he wrote in similar vein to Federico de Onís: 'The moral climate of this place does not suit me; while I have been here my output has been meagre.'[48] Although his Baeza years had not in fact been totally unproductive, Antonio clearly felt he would have been much more creative if he, like Manuel, had been living in Madrid. So desperate was he to get back to the capital that in April 1918 he had toyed with the idea of teaching Italian in some institution there. In the spring of the following year, having finally accepted that a move to Madrid was out of the question, he was considering applying for teaching posts in Zaragoza, Orense, León, Palencia, Salamanca and Lugo. Eventually, in October 1919, he succeeded in obtaining a post in Segovia, a city that had the advantage of being so close to Madrid that it only took three hours to get there by train.

V

In and out of Segovia

Segovia, situated 90 kilometres to the north of Madrid, is one of the most ancient and illustrious cities in Spain. Founded by the Celts, fortified by the Romans, occupied for centuries by the Arabs, it became in the later Middle Ages the seat of the kings of Castile. They held court in the Alcázar, the splendid 'castle palace' that stands on a rocky promontory linked to its hinterland by the great Roman aqueduct for which the city is famed. The city's prosperity peaked in the 16th century, when its magnificent cathedral – Spain's last great Gothic church – was built. But thereafter its fortunes waned. When Philip II transformed Madrid, once little more than a village, into the capital of all Iberia, Segovia ceased to have much political importance. And by the 17th century its economy, like that of Baeza, had declined sharply following the collapse of its once flourishing textile industry. By the beginning of the 20th century, according to Pérez Ferrero, the city was virtually defunct.

> Segovia is asleep, dreaming of a history full of events that are famed throughout Spain, of illustrious names and of relics that neither time nor men have managed to destroy. It preserves the vestiges of remote centuries, the imperishable signs of its past greatness. Its streets and alleys bear the names of saints

and heroes or romantic appellations that are a legacy
of the melancholy and sentimental taste of the 19th
century… It has been compared with Bruges, now
said to be 'dead'; but these sorts of Castilian cities are
not really sleeping deeply. All is quiet, but inside the
houses, in their inner rooms, in the patios, beneath
the arcades, in the dark corners of the odd-shaped
plazas, a vital spirit is stirring among the inhabitants,
which, although hidden behind drab exteriors, is
evident in the fire burning in their eyes.[1]

Segovia may have seemed to be moribund, but it was much
less of a backwater than Baeza. For one thing, it was home to two
newspapers, both of which carried reports of Machado's arrival. On
26 November 1919 *El Adelantado de Segovia* expressed the hope that
'the gifted poet will discover springs of inspiration' in the city. [2] On
the same day *La Tierra de Segovia* announced that 'Antonio Machado,
the poet of Castile, is returning to Castile' and stated its conviction
that his stay in the city would awaken deep feelings in 'the Castilian
soul of this Andalusian poet'.[3] There was clearly an expectation that
Segovia, like Soria, would inspire Machado to write poetry that
would bring lasting fame to the place. It was probably this that had
led the paper to devote the entire front page of its next issue to an
encomium of the poet. It reproduced two of his poems and carried
an article by José Tudela, an old friend of Machado's now living in
Segovia, entitled 'The Poet of Castile' – and, for good measure,
a piece by another writer expressing the wish that the newcomer
would take possession of the city's heart. But it was not to be.
Although Machado liked Segovia, he never really came to love it,
partly perhaps because he found its architecture so much more austere
than that of Soria.

Apparently, however, Machado found little austerity in the city's
people. Luisa Torrego, the proprietress of the guest house where he
lodged in the Calle de los Desamparados, was evidently a kindly
woman, the warmth of whose personality helped to compensate for

the physical coldness of her establishment. Mariano Grau, one of his students, recalled that in winter the house was so cold that, as the poet jokingly remarked, he was often obliged to open the balcony window to let in the air in the street which was warmer than that in the room. He provided a vivid description of Machado's lodgings:

> I recall his appearance in that Franciscan room, which was filled almost to the brim with books, periodicals and papers – books on the chairs, on the table, on the floor, on the chest of drawers, in the corners, right up to the very edge of the bed. Books, many of whose frayed pages bore the marks of his impatient handling; and also books that the poet had no intention of ever opening, which had come to him from every part of Spain with dedications that were sometimes fervent and extravagant.[4]

He went on to say that Machado used to sit at a *camilla*, a table with a heater underneath it which in this case functioned very inefficiently; but he later acquired an oil stove – a gift from his brother Manuel – that gave out more heat but smoked so badly that it threatened to asphyxiate him. On one occasion, as another lodger recalled, the malfunctioning appliance caused such a conflagration that Machado, his face blackened, was obliged to rush from the room. Little wonder that in cold weather he preferred to take his books to a café rather than risk reading in his room.

Machado needed to keep up with his studies because he had many lectures to prepare. His arrival in Segovia had coincided with the setting up, within the Institute to which he had been appointed, of a 'Universidad Popular', which offered educational opportunities for young people of limited means. The courses, which covered a range of subjects with an emphasis on their practical application, were free of charge and were held in the evenings out of working hours. They commenced early in February 1920 and Machado committed himself to teaching a course in Spanish literature and one in French, which included a section on the writing of commercial letters. In undertaking this work he was doubtless mindful that both his father and his grandfather had emphasized the importance of making education freely available to the masses.

A rare glimpse of how his young students at the Institute regarded him is provided by the account that one ex-pupil gave to José Luis Cano:

> The appearance of Don Antonio was imposing. He had large and prominent feet, which he dragged a little as he walked along in his black boots with their rounded toecaps... He was quite unkempt: his suits, always of a dark colour, were rather crumpled and his trousers were a bit long, with patches at the knees. He was accustomed to wearing a double-breasted jacket with huge pockets bulging with useless bits of paper, the *Heraldo de Madrid* and quarter pound packets of tobacco. When in class he used to roll cigarettes, scattering a great quantity of tobacco on the table, which then spilled over on to the floor. He wore a shirt-front and a wing collar, a long corvette and big shiny starched cuffs, beneath which in winter a long-sleeved 'brioche-stitch' vest was visible. He always wore a floppy trilby hat of a kind then in fashion... In class he was extremely affable. Every day he chose one of us to read aloud. Henceforward the classroom was transformed. Fear and anxiety at the prospect of having to read was succeeded by a mood of euphoria among those not selected to do so and, while the chosen student managed as well as he could in front of Don Antonio, the rest of us began to exchange trivialities in the way that children all over the world enjoy doing, as well as pelting each other with little balls made from bits of breakfast rolls and pinching one another 'on the sly', ever struggling with the

terrible desire – which came over us from I know
not where – to burst out laughing. Without warning
a fight would break out between two or more pupils.
That was too much. Don Antonio would bang the
table and shout 'Silence!' And after a pause he would
say, 'If I catch one of you I will throw him out of the
window.' For a few minutes the classroom was as still
as a pool of oil and the pupil would continue with
his reading.[5]

Machado, as Rubén Landa Vaz, one of his colleagues, recalled,
'did not enjoy teaching French to beginners and enjoyed examining
it even less.' Having spent so long as a boy at the Institución Libre
he retained an aversion to the examination system and never took
his work as an examiner too seriously. On one occasion, as the same
colleague related, he had to examine a student who sought special
permission to be admitted to the baccalaureate course and had to
show a good standard of general knowledge.

Don Antonio sat at the corner of the table and
proceeded to ask the following or similar questions:
'Do you know that the river Tajo passes through
Toledo and flows into the Atlantic? It is clear that
you do. And likewise that the multiplication table
is also called Pythagorean? Very well. And you will
also know that the Catholic Monarchs were Isabel and
Ferdinand? You may go now.[6]

Landa reported that no other member of the examination board
had anything to say and the student's request was granted.

The Institute where Landa and Machado taught was located in
the Plaza de Díaz Sanz beside the first arches of the Roman aqueduct.
To reach it from his lodgings the poet had to walk a fair distance, but
he was evidently glad of the exercise. In fact it became his custom
to take a long walk each evening through the city and its suburbs,

usually in the company of a few friends. On one occasion he was joined by a young American writer, John Dos Passos, who had come to Segovia in the hopes of meeting the author of *Campos de Castilla*. He and Machado met in the casino, where they sat together watching a game of billiards and talking about Walt Whitman and Emily Dickinson. 'There was,' he observed, 'no trace of worldliness about him: long ago he had accepted the pain and ignominy of being what he was, a poet, a man who had given up all hope of reward to live for the delicately imagined mood, the counterpoint of words, the accurately recording ear.' After a time they were joined by two other men and left the casino for a stroll round the city by moonlight. 'It was unbelievably beautiful', Dos Passos recalled. 'I remember how pleased Machado was with the names of the streets and the churches. *San Millan de las Brujas* – Saint Millan of the Witches – delighted him particularly.'[7]

Those who went regularly on these evening walks belonged to a *tertulia* composed mainly of Machado's colleagues in the Universidad Popular. Among them was Blas Zambrano, a man a year younger than himself who since 1909 had been teaching grammar in the Escuela Normal.de Maestros and who was to become his closest friend in Segovia. Years later Machado had this to say about him:

> Don Blas Zambrano was a teacher by profession and, and above all – although he himself did not seem to realize it – by vocation. It is noticeable that the finest men are not accustomed to boast about being either *called* or *chosen*. Among his friends were many young men who had never trod the boards of the classrooms in the Escuela Normal, where Don Blas performed his official duties, but who preferred his approach to that of their former teachers in the institutes, schools or universities where they had studied. None of them called himself a pupil of Don Blas – if anyone had been one in the literal sense of the word he did not appear to remember it – but they all recognized him

as their master, to the point of declaring that, in their
spiritual development, they owed everything to him
and almost nothing to their former teachers.[8]

One who knew them well said that both were burly men who
swayed as they walked and, as a consequence, were both nicknamed
charlot (Charlie Chaplin) by their pupils. Another member of the
tertulia recalled that the two were alike in that they walked slowly
with the aid of a stick and wore starched shirt-fronts, wing collars
and large cravats. The two men clearly saw eye to eye on many issues.
They were instrumental in establishing a local branch of the League
of the Rights of Man, an organization founded in France at the
beginning of the century and introduced into Spain by Unamuno.
Machado was elected president of the Segovia section.

Another man with whom the poet became very friendly was
Emiliano Barral, a gifted young sculptor. Impressed by Machado's
noble head, he asked if he would sit for him; and, possibly with
some reluctance, the poet agreed. The sessions which followed were
doubly creative, for they resulted in a fine piece of sculpture and a
delightful poem:

> Your chisel chopped me
> out of a roseate stone
> holding a cold dawn
> eternally spellbound.
> And the sour melancholy
> of dreamed-about grandeur
> so Spanish (a fantasy
> dressing up my laziness)
> emerged from that rock
> that is my mirror. The face
> came line by line, plane by plane,
> my mouth of little thirst,
> and under the arc of a hazy brow
> two eyes with a far-off gaze

that I wish were mine
as they are in your sculpture:
eyes dug out of hard stone,
in stone, so as not to see.[9]

While Machado valued the companionship of the members of the *tertulia*, he was not as dependent on his friends as he had been in Baeza. Now that he was so much closer to Madrid, he went back there every weekend to stay with his mother and his brothers José and Joaquín in their flat in General Arrando. Every Saturday he caught the midday train to the capital, arriving at the Estación del Norte some four hours later. On the journey he was sustained by the generous hamper of food that Doña Luisa always provided, but it was not a very comfortable trip. As in the journey described in a poem entitled 'On the train', he had to sit 'always on a wooden seat/ in a third-class carriage'.[10]

Being back in Madrid at weekends he was able to read the periodicals that in Baeza had been difficult to obtain. One of them was a weekly called *La Internacional*, which in February 1920 invited writers to contribute articles in answer to two questions put by Tolstoy: 'What is art?' and 'What must we do?' Among those who contributed to the discussion were Unamuno, Juan Ramón Jiménez, Valle-Inclán and the two Machado brothers. In his answer to the first of Tolstoy's questions Antonio wrote that art must be free from the restraints of religious or moral imperatives and must result from 'an integrated activity to which all the activities of the spirit, in greater or lesser measure, make a contribution'. In answer to the second one he said that the artist, while attentive to external influences, must always be true to himself. 'My next book', he said, 'will in large measure consist of verses that do not try to conform to a style that is currently popular... but of poetry that contains whatever I have in common with the spirit of the songs and thoughts of the people. So I shall continue to travel my road without any change of direction.' He said he was following in the footsteps of Lope de Vega, whose popular compositions always contained 'a concentration of elemental ingredients – a confluence of rhythm, dance and song'. But he pointed out that Lope's works, for all that, were 'completely original' – so much so in fact that 'he invents his own folklore'.[11]

Machado at this time was not actually writing many poems; it seems that in the course of 1920 he wrote only two. One entitled 'Olive tree by the roadside' was dedicated to the memory of his lately deceased friend Cristóbal Torres. The other was written in response to an account of an incident that he had read about in a newspaper. According to this report a strike in Zaragoza had badly affected the city's street lighting. When four municipal employees arrived to carry out repairs, a man had shot them at point blank range with an automatic pistol. He killed two and a third later died of his wounds. The assassin, a 28 year old working man from Asturias with the (possibly pseudonymous) name of Inocencio Domingo de la Fuente, was detained in the kitchen of a porter's lodge. When the police brought him out into the street the crowd tried to lynch him. At the police station there were four other detainees, all of them trade unionists who had allegedly given moral support to the assassin, and a fifth – a youth who had apparently been arrested merely because he had brought him something to eat. Meanwhile right-wing elements in the city assembled in force and tried to launch an attack on the trade union headquarters. The situation became so serious that the city was declared to be in a state of war. Machado was shocked by the brutality and commemorated it in a poem entitled 'The fifth detainee and the unscrupulous use of force'. Here he expressed his antipathy towards the mob that had turned on the trade unionists and his admiration for the unknown youth who had had compassion on the assassin.

> Through a deserted street, a man
> in a blue shirt, with an ill shaven face,
> an innocent look and a light heart,
> is quickening his pace.
> In his right hand he carries a bag
> wrapped in a white handkerchief.

He turns a corner.
'Where are you going?'
'I am bringing
a little food for that boy.' [12]

Machado's misgivings about miscarriages of justice were also demonstrated in a piece he published soon afterwards in *El Sol*. It was called 'By mistake', but it is not known whether the story recalled an actual incident or was a product of the poet's imagination. It may have been a dream.

Two poor men who were eating in a wayside tavern were shot dead by the police. It was a mistake that the forces of order regretted but could not rectify. But the dead men could not have been satisfied with the way in which they were remembered by the living, because that night – a clear moonlit one – they knocked on my door. And before that they must have knocked on many others. Perhaps no-one heard them. Alternatively they may have been asked why they had so thoughtlessly woken up a poor third-year *modernista*. The fact is that the dead men – ghosts, if you like – went up to my bedroom, and there I could have a close look at them. They were two rather stiff figures, resembling illustrations torn out of an old ballad collection. They inclined their heads. Perhaps they wished to apologize for the untimely hour. 'Oh, no', I said to them; 'I am happy to receive you at any hour, because I know why you have come. You are seeking some respect for your memory.' They shook their heads. 'No? Then it is because you have children and you want them to show that respect.' Both spectral heads remained bowed. It was as if they wanted to say, 'Yes… but that's not it.' I began to get worried, because conversation was becoming impossible. 'Then', I went on, 'you wish for something more... for example, *justice*.' My two ghosts nodded their heads. 'You are asking for a lot', I said to them, 'or perhaps for too little, because in Spain justice is merely a mockery.' I took up my pen and wrote this verse:

> The rich man says to the poor man:
> you can have charity and gratitude.
> Justice? No, you can have justices –
> policemen to protect my property.

And I added, 'Take this, my sons, and let them publish it for you in the papers.'[13]

Now that he was spending so much time in Madrid, reading the papers and talking with friends in one or other of his favourite cafés, Machado was more keenly aware of – and more concerned about – the current state of Spain. He was severely critical of the government, which in the first decade of the century had embarked on a disastrous war in Morocco. In September 1921 he gave vent to his feelings in a long letter to Unamuno. 'My proximity to Madrid and my longer stays in the capital,' he wrote, 'have given me, in exchange for other advantages, less confidence about the future of Spain.' He thought that, although the country was wealthier, riches had brought 'an increase in bestiality, egoism and materialism'. There had been a noticeable decline in standards of public morality. 'It seems,' he said, 'that none of our politicians knows his duty. Those repugnant Spanish left-wingers, always at the palace with their begging-bowls...' They had broken with 'our noble political tradition' and had undone 'the educational work of Pi y Margall, Salmerón and other worthy republicans'. Machado then went on to express his anger in a memorable paragraph of polemical prose:

Instead of deepening the moat that might drown
the abominable Spain of the Regency and of this
petty king – and at the same time proclaiming
republicanism, strengthening it, purifying it and
enriching it with new life – they decided to throw
a drawbridge across it to the antechamber of the
throne of mercy. They were too naïve or perhaps too
foolish and vain, because they seem to have thought
that, once they were inside the cauldron, they could
sanitize the rotten mixture of which they themselves
were going to form a part. What a great mistake! I
believe it is necessary to resuscitate republicanism,
clearing out the old embers and making a fire with
new kindling.[14]

That Machado remained preoccupied with political and social
affairs is apparent from the jottings he made in his notebook in
January 1922 to mark the beginning of a new year.

A great decrease in wealth. The profits of war that
the belligerents gained by theft and exploitation are
disappearing as quickly as they came.

The war in Morocco has brought sorrow to many
homes. Less concern about having a good time. The
theatres have had a bad Christmas and face a financially
disastrous January. The projects of Cambó – the
'Catalan crow' – were approved and the financial
vampirism that is devouring Spain was satisfied.
Parliament was dissolved and will not function while
there are no budgets to approve.

Machado had disapproved strongly of the decision of General
Dámaso Berenguer, who had been appointed High Commissioner
in Morocco in 1920, to take military action against the tribesmen

who continued to resist the Spanish incursion into their country – an action that backfired badly and led in 1921 to the death of 12,000 soldiers at the disastrous battle of Annual. It is not so clear why he should have been so hostile to the proposals put forward by the Catalan industrialist, Francesc Cambó, to improve the economic situation by such measures as the investment of public funds in hydro-electric schemes and the nationalization of the railways. It was probably not so much the programme itself as the corruption associated with its implementation that aroused the poet's wrath. He may also have dismissed Cambó as a wealthy capitalist who saw everything in terms of profit and loss and had no concern for the welfare of Spaniards, whom the poet called 'the most wretched people in Europe'.

Machado then went on to say why he thought Spain was in this unenviable situation:

> The individuals who constitute the cadre surrounding
> the monarchy are all the old politicians, that is to say,
> all the politicians, since there is not one among them
> who is youthful, healthy or energetic. A succession of
> groups and cliques known by a variety of names await
> their turn in front of the palace gates, begging bowls
> in hand. All are keenly aware of how old they are and
> believe that the ruin of Spain is irremediable, but all
> hope once again to fulfil their ignoble ambitions or
> else (in the case of those who have not yet reached
> the top of the greasy pole) that the hour may come for
> donning the longed for livery. *Et après eux le déluge*.[15]

In February the poet had an opportunity to share some of his thoughts and feelings about the current state of Spain at a conference that he organized in Segovia on the subject of 'Present day problems'; and he persuaded Unamuno to address the gathering. Machado introduced him to the great company that had assembled in the city's Juan Bravo theatre with these words:

Don Miguel de Unamuno, who in these troubled
times is the most eminent representative of the Spanish
intelligentsia and of the conscience of Spain, is about
to address you. To welcome this great thinker I, in
the name of my colleagues in the Universidad Popular
of Segovia and of this gathering of men of goodwill,
wish to say how grateful we are to him for wishing to
come to speak to us. And I will say no more because
I know you cannot wait to listen to him.[16]

In April 1922 a rather smaller company gathered in the Casa de
las Picas in Segovia for a conference at which Machado himself was
the principal speaker. The subject was one of his favourite topics: the
literature of modern Russia. What, he asked, was so special about the
writings of Dostoevsky, Turgenev and Tolstoy that many Spaniards
were now reading, usually in very bad translations? The answer, he
suggested, was 'universality', and it did not come, as so many ideas
did, from the Greeks, whose society was dependent on slave labour,
but from quite a different source: 'It is called human brotherhood,
and it was the great revelation of Christ.'

The heart of man, Christ tells us, with his longing for
immortality, with his yearning for moral perfection,
with his thirst for love that is never satiated, also
beholds a road leading endlessly ahead towards the
supreme unattainable perfection of the Father. And
this longing, this thirst that you, o man, discover only
by looking into your own heart, is felt by all men.

For a novelist like Tolstoy, whom he described as the 'synthesis
of the Russian soul', the principal source of inspiration was the New
Testament. 'It was said that the Russian has chosen a book, the
Gospel, held it close to his heart and with it, and only with it, tries
to change the course of history.' He concluded his address, which
at times sounded more like a sermon than a lecture, by contrasting

the spirit of Russia with that of western nations that have achieved a
high level of material prosperity.

> These peoples are now suffering from a serious amnesia
> and are forgetting about the sorrows of humanity.
> Their civilization is becoming superficial, they have a
> love for things that are useful and pleasurable, they are
> oblivious to the third dimension of the human soul,
> the religious depth of life and the tragic sense of it,
> and, as the great Unamuno says, they set fundamental
> problems aside and, without knowing it, they block
> the inner springs of their very civilization.

He closed his oration with words that would long ring in the ears
of some of his hearers: 'Russian literature has been a loud and vibrant
alarm clock that wakes us up and banishes our epicurean dream.'[17]
Machado's optimism regarding Russia was in marked contrast
to his pessimism about Spain, where so many important issues were
not allowed to be discussed. In August 1922 he made the following
entry in his notebook:

> The religious question is the great *taboo* among our
> people. We have all convinced ourselves that such
> a question must never be mentioned. The political
> question, regarding our form of government, is
> another *taboo*, although of lesser importance, since
> only a few pedants declare it inessential. (Our position
> with regard to the European war was yet another
> *taboo*. Don't talk to me about the war!) The same
> applies to the social question. The day is not far off
> when, with a 'God forbid! God forbid!' from the
> men of good taste, this nightmare will shake the
> conscience of Spain. [18]

His dissatisfaction with the government was in fact shared by many others, on the right as well as the left of the political spectrum, and in September 1923 matters came to head, with General Miguel Primo de Rivera staging a coup d'état and setting up a military dictatorship. This was not the kind of constitutional change that Machado had wanted or envisaged. 'Spain is on her hands and knees,' he wrote in *Los Complimentarios*. 'Will she get up again? She will probably find the posture comfortable and keep to it for a long time.' [19] He was to be proved right, for Primo de Rivera's tyrannical regime was to last for seven years, during which time anyone who dared to promote republicanism was likely to be persecuted. The poet, who seems to have kept a fairly low profile, escaped censure, but Unamuno was deprived of his Salamanca chair and obliged to go into exile, first in the Canary Islands and later in France. Machado was outraged. The banishment of the man he looked up to as his 'master' was clear evidence that 'Spain was the most stupid country on the planet'.[20]

Machado's comments on the current situation were at this stage largely confined to his notebooks, letters and conversations with his friends. His published writings were for the most part restricted to his poetry, of which a new volume, entitled *Nuevas Canciones*, appeared in April 1924. It was, as Machado informed José Tudela, 'a simple miscellany of lyrical poetry scattered in newspapers and reviews, in which I don't think I have added much that is essential to my work'. [21] Antonio Sánchez Barbudo thought that the collection was marred by signs of 'decadence', but went on to say that 'even in the midst of decadence there appear brilliant sparkles of emotion, of intuition, of beauty – and here and there, now and again, splendid poems'. [22] One of the poems he probably approved of was a brand-new composition called 'The eyes':

> When his beloved died
> he thought he'd just grow old,
> shutting himself in the house
> alone, with memories and the mirror

that she had looked in one bright day.
Like gold in the miser's chest,
he thought he'd keep all yesterday
in the clear mirror intact.
For him time's flow would cease.

But after a year had passed,
he began to wonder about her eyes:
Were they brown or black? Or green? ...Or grey?
What were they like? Good God! I can't recall...
One day in spring he left the house
and took his double mourning down the street
in silence, his heart tight shut ...
In the dim hollow of a window
he caught a flash of eyes. He lowered his
and walked right on... Like those! [23]

Convinced that the 'beloved' referred to was Leonor – and not the 'unknown woman of Baeza' that some thought Machado had fallen for in 1914 – Geoffrey Ribbans has commented on the difference between the reference to her here and in the 'agonised poems written within about a year of her death'. In them, he says, the poet 'addresses her as if she were present', but now he refers to her in the third person. He is in 'double mourning' because he has lost not only his wife but also the memory of her.[24] The glimpse of a pair of eyes, similar perhaps to those that Pérez Ferrero saw shining in a drab Segovian street, may have helped at long last to assuage his grief for the loss of Leonor. Now perhaps he may be able to fall in love again.

On its publication *Nuevas Canciones* produced mixed reactions from the critics. One thought the poems were 'brilliant and difficult', while another praised their 'lyricism and logic'. On the other hand there was a reviewer who objected to the 'sententious tone' of the collection and another who thought it displayed an 'indifference to melody'. But the strangest review was written by Enrique Díez-Canedo, who was himself a poet, and was published in *El Sol* with

the title 'Antonio Machado, Japanese poet'. The reviewer said that
Machado, whose Andalusian characteristics had been modified by
a 'Castilian austerity', had now adopted an 'oriental style' that was
'more tenuous' and 'more insubstantial'. He suggested that some
poems bore a resemblance to Japanese haiku – with three lines and
seventeen syllables.[25]

Not long afterwards Machado himself wrote a review in *Revista
de Occidente* of a new collection of verse by the Andalusian poet,
José Moreno Villa. This provided him with an opportunity to stand
back and consider at some length the current state of the poet's art.
Modern poets, he suggested, could be divided into two opposing
camps: on the one hand there were the *conceptistas*, who stood 'at the
margin of all human emotion' and devote themselves to the creation
of ingenious images; on the other were those who, disregarding all
objectivity, write poetry that is merely a 'product of the half-awake
world of dreams'. He commended Moreno Villa for not belonging
to either camp, saying that his work was distinctive for its 'balance
and equilibrium'. [26] Machado was clearly glad to welcome him into
the company of those who tried to be responsive both to the outer
world of the senses and to the inner world of the spirit. For his part
Moreno Villa was delighted with the review. 'In this essay,' he said,
'there are many penetrating observations of a kind that only Antonio
Machado, poet and philosopher, is capable of making.'[27]

By this date the philosopher-poet was also coming to be known
as a playwright. Early in 1925 a performance of a play that he and
Manuel had written had been staged at the Español theatre in
Madrid. It was a translation of Victor Hugo's *Hernani* that they had
prepared back in 1902 but which had never been performed. Had
the authorities realized that the play's hero was an unruly Spanish
bandit and that its first performance in Paris had led to violent
clashes between opposing factions in the audience, they might have
considered banning the production. But in the event the Madrid
playgoers received the performance with acclamation, as is clear from
a glowing review in the *Heraldo de Madrid*:

When, at the close of the play's penultimate act, in
response to the insistent demands of the delighted
audience, the Machado brothers – two of the most
cultured and distinguished poets in Spain today – came
on stage, the loud and incessant applause that they
received and the enthusiasm that this demonstrated
were a genuine expression of the admiration that the
public feel for the brilliance of the poetry with which
both brothers have enriched Spain. [28]

This dramatic success led the producer of *Hernani* to ask the
brothers for a play of their own composition for the company to
perform. Accordingly they went back to working on a play that
they had begun writing seven years previously, which was entitled
Desdichas de la fortuna o Julianillo Valcárcel. By the beginning of June
they had written the first act of what Antonio described in his
notebook as 'a five act tragicomedy in verse'. It was based on the life
of the bastard son of the Conde-Duque de Olivares, the celebrated
17th century Spanish statesman, who had been cast into prison and
had subsequently died of despair The young man, named in the play
as Julián or Julianillo, was in love with a woman that the authors
called Leonor, possibly as a tribute to the memory of Antonio's long
deceased wife. It is uncertain whether setting the play in the court of
Philip IV, famed for its cruelty and corruption, had anything to do
with the Machados' antipathy to the current Spanish regime. What
is quite likely is that, in telling the sad story of Julianillo, Antonio
had himself in mind. It is significant that the play's hero suffers from
the melancholic hypochondria that its author once described as his
usual state. 'Antonio', his mother was wont to say, 'has never had the
happiness that it is proper for young people to enjoy.' [29]

The play was first performed at the Princesa theatre in February
1926 before a highly appreciative audience and was very favourably
reviewed in the press. *ABC* praised the work's versification and said
that it represented a continuation of the great tradition of classical
Spanish drama. 'In a single battle', wrote a reviewer in *La Libertad*,

'Manuel and Antonio Machado, whose literary reputation is of the highest order, have surpassed the achievements of the great generals. From a theatrical point of view their tragicomedy is perfect and demonstrates a real understanding of the nature of drama.'[30] It might have been expected that such a successful play would run to the end of the month scheduled for its performance, but in the event it was terminated after twenty nights. The Machados, however, were happy about the play's reception and decide to embark at once on another one.

Meanwhile Antonio was putting the finishing touches to a collection of poems entitled *Cancionero apócrifo* that was eventually published in the summer of 1926 in two issues of the *Reviste de Occidente*. It was 'apocryphal' because it purported to be the work of Abel Martín, a pseudonym that Machado may have adopted in order to enable him to express ideas that might have upset his readers. Some, for example, could have been shocked by the sonnet 'To the great Zero' – an irreverent parody of the first chapter of Genesis that is said to reflect the poet's interest in the philosophy of Heidegger's *Sein und Zeit*, recently translated into Spanish as *Ser y Tiempo*.

> When the I AM THAT I AM made nothing
> and rested, which rest it certainly deserved,
> night now accompanied day, and man
> had his friend in the absence of the woman.
>
> Let there be shadow! Human thinking broke out.
> And the universal egg rose, empty,
> pale, chill and not yet heavy with matter,
> full of unweighable mist, in his hand.
>
> Take the numerical zero, the sphere with nothing in it:
> it has to be seen, if you have to see it, standing.
> Since the wild animal's back now is your shoulder,

and since the miracle of not-being is finished,
start then, poet, a song, at the edge of it all
to death, to silence, and to what does not return.[31]

Along with the poems there was a commentary that provided information about the imaginary Martín's life and thought. He was said to have been born in Seville in 1840 and to have died in Madrid in 1898, to have been the author of an important philosophical treatise showing evidence of his interest in the work of Leibniz, and to have published a collection of poems entitled *Los complementarios* in 1884. His poetry was evidently preoccupied with 'the problem of love'. 'That Abel Martín was an extremely erotic man', wrote Machado, 'we know from the testimony of many who knew him, and also from his own poems, in which there are numerous expressions, more or less hyperbolical, of a passionate veneration of women.' [32] Machado pointed out that Martín's eroticism differed from that of Plato, which had its origin in 'the contemplation of a beautiful body' be it male or female. 'The Martínian Eros is aroused only by the contemplation of the female body and precisely on account of the awareness that it possesses an irreducible difference. For Abel Martín it is not beauty that inspires love, but the metaphysical longing for that which is essentially other.'[33]

Together with Abel Martín the poet adopted a second pseudonym, which made its first appearance in the *Revista de Occidente* at the conclusion of the second part of *Cancierio apócrifo*. Here Machado announced that on another occasion he would publish the 'anecdotal history' of Abel Martín that had been written by a character called Juan de Mairena. 'To Juan de Mairena', he wrote, 'we owe a penetrating critique of the work of Abel Martín, rebutting the many contradictions and the sensualist bias that vitiate the master's ideology.'[34] He gave the impression that the work would soon be appearing in the pages of the *Revista*, but this did not happen. In fact Juan did not put in an appearance until 1928 – in the second edition of Machado's *Poesías completas*. Here he was described as a poet, a philosopher, and the inventor of a *máquina de cantar*, which was evidently a machine for creating poetry. He was said to have been born in Seville in 1865 and to have died in a place called Casariego de Tapia in 1909. Besides the *Vida de Abel Martín* he had allegedly published an *Arte poética*, a collection of poems called *Coplas mecánicas* and a metaphysical treatise, *La siete reverses*.

Why Machado chose to attribute so much of his prose to these two pseudonymous authors is a question that has often been asked. Bernard Sesé suggests that the reasons were both literary and psychological. From the literary point of view 'the two personages give unity to what runs the risk of being merely disjointed dialogue, to give more life and colour to the expression of ideas and more credibility and spontaneity to the contra- dictions or the ambiguity of theories.' From a psychological perspective it enabled the author to 'conceal himself behind his creatures' and 'makes it possible for him to change his personality and express new and diverse aspects of himself'. [35] There are times when Mairena appears to have a positive disdain for Machado, even going so far as to describe him as 'a Sevillian poetaster who had strayed into the Sorian uplands'. The deeper significance of this strange duality was indicated by Segundo Serrano Poncela, who says that the poet was 'projecting his loneliness upon an "other" of distinctly gregarious and volatile habits – an identity, unlike himself, in harmony with the here and now – with the friends, admirers, discipleship, public fame which were never vouchsafed to the poet.' [36]

A probable reason for the delay in the appearance of Mairena's work was Machado's preoccupation with another fictitious character called Juan de Mañara, the hero of a play that he and Manuel began to work on in the summer and autumn of 1926. *Juan de Mañara*, a drama in three acts, was based on the lives of two celebrated Sevillians – the mythical Don Juan celebrated in Zorrilla's famous play and the historical Miguel de Mañara, a man who, after a dissolute youth, went on to devote his life to charitable works. The play, with its scenes of passionate encounters between Juan and his beloved Beatriz, has all the ingredients of a classic love story, but it can also be seen as a piece of political and social commentary. Beatriz's family – the

Montiels – are reactionary landowners and, in the Madrid of 1926, as Ian Gibson suggests, the possibility of an allusion to the dictator Miguel Primo de Rivera was inescapable. Moreover, from the lips of the family's 'personal priest', as well as from its leading members, come a series of platitudinous remarks about modern youth, 'athletic, gymnastic, sporty', and other current topics. The satirical intentions are obvious: these people, so proud of their lineage, of their nuns and of their adventurers, stand for the sterile self-satisfaction of the Spanish ruling class.

Juan de Mañara was performed in the Reina Victoria theatre in March of the next year and, as a writer in *La Libertad* reported, it had a rapturous reception:

> The first act sees a continuous upsurge of enthusiasm. Measured so exactly that it never at any moment loses its tempo, the performance of the love scene between Beatriz and Juan sets the audience on fire and causes such an outburst of applause that the authors are obliged momentarily to interrupt the proceedings and come on stage…
>
> At the conclusion of the first act the applause is again so loud and unanimous that they have to lower and raise the curtain six times in homage to the authors and performers…
>
> In the last two acts the curtain is raised and lowered at various times, as the public's appreciation becomes more and more apparent.
>
> And afterwards, in the corridors, in the vestibule and in the seats where they have been sitting, members of the public are, according to their inclination, discussing, extolling or interpreting the great work

that Manuel and Antonio Machado have brought to fruition.[37]

The play ran for 48 nights, which in a city such as Madrid, with its numerous theatres, represented a considerable success.

March 1927 was a wonderful month for Antonio. Seven days after the first performance of *Juan de Mañara* he was elected a member of the Spanish Royal Academy. This had nothing to do with his recent success as a playwright, but was an acknowledgement that he was now one of the country's most celebrated poets. His friends were delighted, but he himself appears to have regarded his election as a thing of little consequence. When Unamuno wrote from exile in France to congratulate him, Machado replied: 'It is not an honour that I ever wished for; I almost dare to say that it is one that I hoped never to receive. But God gives handkerchiefs to those who don't have noses.' He went on to say that there was little to boast about in such a miserable country as Spain had become under Primo de Rivera; but he was glad to have gone to the first performance of Unamuno's play *Todo un hombre*, which he thought to be 'the finest to be put on in the theatre in recent years'. He had also read his book *Agonía del cristianismo* which, in Jean Cassou's translation, had been well received throughout Europe. 'I am not surprised', he wrote. 'Unamuno is saving Spain from oblivion, while Spain … No, Spain does not forget it.'[38]

A few months later Antonio and Manuel embarked on the writing of another play, which they entitled *Las adelfas*. Adelfa – oleander – is an evergreen shrub growing throughout Andalusia and, according to local folklore, is an emblem of unrequited or unhappy love. The heroine is a young widow named Araceli, duchess of Tormes, whose husband Alberto has died six years previously either by suicide or as the result of an accident. Because the memory of his death continues to disturb her sleep with bad dreams, she decides to consult a young doctor called Carlos Menos, who had been one of her closest childhood friends. He is in fact her *hermano de leche* – meaning that, as infants, they had shared the same wet nurse. In the course of a lengthy dialogue at the beginning of the play he is able, through his acquaintance with what he calls 'the new science of psychoanalysis', to help her to understand the meaning of her dreams and so eases her mental affliction. He himself, it turns out, has long been deeply in love with her, but is too reticent to tell her so, while she views their relationship as simply that of sister and brother. Now feeling free to do so, she falls in love with another man who, appropriately enough, is called Salvador. He becomes her 'saviour' in more senses than one: while his love saves her from her misery, his wealth (acquired as a 'captain of industry') saves her from the penury that had made her decide to sell her estate.

Since the theme of unrequited or unhappy love is one that runs through so much of his poetry it is generally thought that the play was more the work of Antonio than of Manuel. As an introvert he was the one who was more interested in the realm of the unconscious. Who but he could have invented a word like *erotimática* to describe the 'new art' that, according to Carlos, can plumb the depths of the soul? The young doctor believes that in these usually inaccessible 'zones' repose unfulfilled desires and 'murky and unpleasant fantasies'. Inside every human being, he says, there is a 'sick world of disappointments and destitution'. He continues at some length in this vein, describing all the dark material buried in the unconscious and concluding with the ringing declaration: 'Our mission is to bring it out into the light'.[39] This suggests that Machado was well aware of Freud's teaching that healing comes when material that has long lain repressed in the depths of the unconscious is brought out into the open.

It is likely that Machado became well acquainted with psychoanalytical theory after the publication in 1922 of a Spanish translation of Freud's complete works. He may have discussed such matters with Ortega y Gasset, who contributed an introduction to the first volume of the works. And he would certainly have read the numerous articles about psychoanalysis that had recently been appearing in the *Revista de Occidente*. Be that as it may, he recognized that Freudian ideas were far too radical to be generally acceptable; and this may have been why *Las adelfas* was not first staged in Madrid but in Barcelona, where people were generally more receptive to new ideas. Antonio in fact had a high opinion of the Catalan capital. When a journalist asked him for his impressions of the place, which he said he was visiting for the first time, he replied that Barcelona was 'a magnificent city, Spain's number one, without a shadow of doubt', adding that 'Barcelona seems much more like Paris or Seville than Madrid'. He concluded with this observation: 'It can be said that Madrid is a capital, while Barcelona is truly a city.' [40]

The arrival of the two famous poets aroused considerable interest in the city, especially after a piece they had written about their play appeared in a local newspaper. Here they explained what the *adelfas* symbolised, pointing out that the *adélfico* represented a morbid attempt to relive the past. They made it clear that the purpose of the play was to emphasize that it was more important to live in the present than *a retrotiempo A retrotiempo* appears to be a term that Antonio invented to describe the regressed state in which he himself, habitually preoccupied with archaic emotions, had tended to live. The value of psychoanalysis, the brothers suggested in this article, lay in its ability to liberate people from traumatic past experiences and enable them to live life to the full.

The first performance of the play took place in the Eldorado theatre on 15 April 1928 before a highly appreciative audience. The first act was interrupted by bursts of clapping and at its conclusion there were loud calls for the authors to come on stage. The second act was received even more enthusiastically, with the curtain having to be raised repeatedly. At the finale there was thunderous applause and the two authors were greeted with prolonged ovations. The press reviews were apparently favourable, although one critic did query the suitability of writing a play of this kind in verse. Had the theatre not been booked by another company *Las adelfas* might have run for more than four nights but, as it was, the brothers were well satisfied with their success. They were delighted that it was also going to be performed in Vigo, La Coruña, Gijón and finally in Madrid.

The play eventually reached the capital in October and, on the day before its first performance, a man from *La Libertad* interviewed the authors in a café in the Calle de Toledo. Antonio had come straight from Segovia and the reporter commented on the 'melancholy and childish' expression on his face. 'In the person of Don Antonio'; he wrote, 'there is an air of exhaustion, of a man who is walking in his sleep, blindly "searching for God among the clouds", finding his bearings by the promptings of his heart.' Manuel, it is clear, was very different. 'This poet is nimble, lively, elegant, and, as we watch him walking, we don't know whether he is on his way to a fashionable social gathering or to some low dive where there are dark eyed women, swirling red flounces and the faltering sobs of the bourdons – a confused medley of singing and weeping. We don't know why, but he reminds us of that gypsy bullfighter called Rafael Gómez, when he makes his bow with his feet together and his body stiffly bent, like a "dandy" dressed up as a matador. During the interview Antonio, with his distracted air, says little. He keeps silent, he smiles, he hardly speaks a word, he gives his opinion timidly.' The journalist added that Manuel later said to him: 'It's the same in rehearsals. He never says anything. It never occurs to him to correct an actor.'[41] It was perhaps because the quiet Antonio and the garrulous Manuel were so different that the two worked so well together.

The play was duly performed in the Centro theatre, but it was evidently not as well received as it had been in Barcelona. The Machados were called on to the stage at the end of each act, but two reviewers thought the public were applauding them as established poets rather than as the authors of this particular play. A reviewer in the *Heraldo de Madrid* said it had been a mistake to write the play in verse, while another critic thought the theme too 'European' for a Madrid audience. Unsurprisingly, the most adverse appraisal was that of a writer in *El Debate*, Spain's most influential Catholic newspaper. 'There is nothing immoral about the play,' he said reassuringly, 'but, as we often see, the openness with which it treats adultery, the cynicism of the adulteress and her frank confession, without shame or repentance, make her unbecoming and dangerous.'[42] As it turned out, however, most people who went to see it were evidently not upset by the moral tone of the comedy, which ran for 28 nights.

Because his time was now so much taken up with writing plays Antonio was evidently not composing many poems. One of the few that he wrote in 1928 was an exceptionally long one called 'Recollections of dreaming, fever and dozing' [43]which Luis Rosales thought to be 'one of the most important, surprising and strange pieces' that he ever wrote. [44]

It is significant that the later verses of the poem reproduce features of the dream that Machado recorded in his 'document' of May 1914 under the title of 'Spain in the near future', where there are many indications of his hostility to the political and ecclesiastical establishment – and of a judicial system that condoned the condemnation of the innocent.

The 'Rap Rap! Who's knocking?' and the reference to 'Mr Executioner' recalls the 1914 nightmare that began with a knock on the door and the entry of a man who looked like a barber but turned out to be an executioner, ready to hang a man that many thought to be innocent. In the poem, as in the dream, following his execution the condemned man descends to the underworld, where he meets Charon. While the dream had ended with a brief and inconclusive encounter with the sinister boatman, the poem continues with a conducted tour through the urban landscape of the underworld which, with its 'cypress gardens' and 'round orange trees', has similarities with that of Machado's native Seville. But when he goes on to speak of the 'Square of the Greatest Disillusion' and the 'Square of Old Woman Spinning' we have moved beyond what he terms 'Memory Street' into the kind of terrain described by Dante.

'The poet's description and characterization of the Inferno as the final stage of his posthumous journey', wrote Rosales, 'is one of the poem's most successful inventions, and perhaps even one of the most original and profound examples of Machado's intuitive thinking.' As we accompany him on his journey Machado 'is going to make us live his whole life, from birth to old age, alongside him.' It is highly significant that, although the *plazoleta* of the Greatest Disillusion has not previously been mentioned, the poem says *'back we come'* to it. Disillusion is not a stopping place in real life, but it is in this itinerary:

'It interrupts the perambulation; it obstructs the flow of life.' This little *plaza* is a place of great importance: the poet 'wants us to take a good look at it'. But it is not the final stopping place. After traversing the 'long street of love' we arrive eventually at the *plaza* of the 'Old Woman Spinning'. 'The spinner is death, the little sister of our mortal flesh; it's our life that she is spinning.' [45] For the man who has been described as 'a poet of death' to have concluded the poem in this way probably gave him a measure of satisfaction. While most people feared death and wanted to keep away from it, Machado, as his friend Juan Ramón Jiménez expressed it, 'apprehended it in itself, yielded to it in large measure; possibly, more than a man who was born, he was a man reborn.'[46]

The poem remained unpublished until November 1931, when it appeared in the *Revista de Occidente* under the pseudonym of Abel Martín. In the meantime the earlier poems attributed to Martín had been included in the second edition of Machado's *Poesías completas*, which was published in April 1928. The book, which ran to nearly 400 pages and contained a photograph of the author, reproduced all the poems that he had written between 1899 and 1925. It received a laudatory review in *La Libertad*, where the contributions of Martín and Mairena were described as a delightful mixture of 'irony and truth'. The reviewer said that the two apocryphal writers performed a valuable task because, in the course of their dialogue with each other, they went some way towards 'uncovering the secret of their creator's poetry'.[47]

It would be some time, however, before people would uncover what, in the summer of 1928, was to become the most sensational secret of the poet's life.

VI

The Courtly Lover

One day at the beginning of June 1928 a handsome, fashionably dressed, dark haired woman arrived in Segovia with a letter of introduction to Machado. She was Pilar de Valderrama, an accomplished poet, who had recently published a volume of verse entitled *Huerto cerrado* that had been well received by the critics. The wife of a rich man named Rafael Martínez Romarate, she was 39 years old and the mother of three teenage children. She lived in Madrid in a large house overlooking the Parque del Oeste with a terrace commanding a fine view of the Sierra de Guadarrama. Although she was wealthy, had many friends and a busy social life, she was not happy. She still mourned the loss of a much-loved father, who had died when she was young, and her marriage was on the rocks. A few months before her visit to Segovia her husband had confessed to a two-year affair with a young woman who subsequently committed suicide in dramatic fashion by throwing herself out of a window in the Calle de Alcalá. Pilar had always known that her husband was something of a Don Juan, but this marked a turning-point in her life. What was she to do? Her first impulse was to flee from the house and never return but, after talking things over with her mother, she decided to take a trip to Segovia 'in search of peace of mind'.

When she reached the city it was raining and very cold. Unable to make contact with Machado, she returned to Madrid, to discover that her husband had left for France. Because of this she thought it safe to go back to Segovia and make another attempt to meet the poet. This time she was successful and she met him by appointment in the vestibule of the Comercio hotel. Years later she recorded her impression of that first encounter:

> I cannot describe the feeling I had when I met him and shook his hand. Here was the much admired poet that was standing before me; he was in a dishevelled state, it is true, but with a very kind face, a broad and shining forehead – in short, a fine head on a tall, ungainly and unattractive body.
>
> I don't know what happened to him, but I noticed that on seeing me he remained silent, as though spellbound; he did not stop staring at me and hardly said anything – except to tell me how much he regretted being so busy with examinations that he would not be able to accompany me or attend to me as much he would have liked. He added that in two days' time his court case was coming to an end and he would not be able to avoid going to Madrid, which he regretted; but he would be pleased to see me and be at my service.[1]

Machado was delighted to accept her invitation to have supper with her at the hotel the following evening, but in the event he hardly spoke or ate anything and did nothing except gaze at her. After supper they decided go for a walk along the esplanade leading to the Alcázar. It was a lovely warm evening and the sky was studded with stars. As they walked, she told him – without going into precise details – that life was very difficult for her. For Machado it was pure bliss to have such an attractive woman walking and talking at his side. He never forgot that walk. It was one of those moments in his life when his spirit ascended to the stars. As they parted he asked for her address, so that he could send her a copy of the recently published second edition of his *Poesías completas*. She replied that, because of the state of her health, she could not say when she would be back in Madrid. He then promised to write to her as soon as he knew her whereabouts. And he duly kept to his word.

In the course of that summer the two met secretly in a public garden adjoining the Moncloa palace, where they sat on a low stone wall surrounding a fountain that Machado christened the *banco de los enamorados* – the 'lovers' seat' – but the risk of their being recognized was too great, and soon Valderrama decided to end their encounters. By the autumn, one of the few chances Machado had of seeing her was when, having arrived from Segovia at the Estación del Norte, he would go into the nearby Parque del Oeste, from where he had a good view of her house. Here he would lurk for a time in the shrubberies, hoping to catch a glimpse of his beloved if she came out on the balcony; sometimes he was lucky, but often he was not. Later that autumn, however, the situation changed for the better, when Valderrama agreed to meet him at weekends in a café at Cuatro Caminos (the Franco-Español, in the Camino de Aceiteros, now Avenida de la Reina Victoria). This was then a predominantly working class district on the outskirts of Madrid, where there would be little risk of bumping into anyone they knew. In his letters to her he called it *nuestro rincón* – 'our corner', 'our nook' or 'our retreat'. In her memoirs she recalled that the café had uncomfortable chairs and a marble topped table, and that the clientele invariably consisted of *empleados* and *obreros* and their wives. These were clearly not the kinds of people that she was used to meeting socially.

From the beginning of 1929 onwards, when Machado, who was now teaching only on the first three days of the week, returned to Madrid on Wednesday evenings, the couple were able to meet more frequently. It became their custom to go to the café on Friday evenings and also on Saturdays, either in the morning or the evening. If it happened that Valderrama was unable to be there she would telephone the café and leave a message with the proprietor. In the meantime they kept in touch by letter. She wrote to him at his

lodgings in Segovia, while he communicated with her via one of
her three trusted friends – Hortensia Peinador, María Estremera and
Marta Valdés – or else via the offices of the *Mensajería Continental* in
Madrid. Valderrama estimated that, in the course of their seven year
relationship, Machado wrote her about 240 letters, all but about 40
of which she eventually destroyed. In the letters that survived she
took the precaution of inking out passages that she thought to be
imprudent, but with the subsequent fading of the ink some of the
obliterated words have since become legible. However, of the many
letters that she sent to him not a single one remains in existence.

The first of Machado's surviving letters to the woman he called
mi diosa – 'my goddess' – was written in Madrid in January 1929. It is
in two parts: the first was penned on Friday the 11th and the second
on Saturday the 12th.

Friday

I am beginning the letter that I shall post, alas! in
Segovia on Sunday. Because my holidays, inevitably,
are over, I shall be returning to my nook in Los
Desamparados. Now there will certainly be no sound
from the Eresma because, so I am told, the poor little
river is frozen over. But at night my goddess – will
she remember? – will come to see her poet. I shall
try to ensure that the room is not too cold; although
my goddess is so good and has so much warmth in
her soul that neither the cold nor the wind will worry
her when she goes to be with her poet. In the *Leyenda
Áurea* – haven't you read it? – a collection of the lives
of the saints, there is no account of any saint as good
as you are to your poet, Pilar of my soul, in sitting
with him on the lovers' seat or in our chilly café.
The best part of the story gets lost in the secret of
our lives. But God, who sees everything, will take it
into account. When I think about you, Pilar, above

all when I think about what you are doing for me, I believe again in God.

At noon tomorrow I shall go to our café in the hope of seeing you, always with the intention of being good and with the aim, which I have not yet achieved, of kneeling down before you.

I passed through the Parque. I did not see my goddess. The balcony window blinds were drawn. That means, I thought, that my queen will not appear. 'Go back, poor Antonio, because you will certainly not see her today.'

I am very sad, Pilar. But tomorrow is a great day; I shall see my glory!

Saturday

I return from our café, where I waited for you until two o'clock, and at home I find your letter, which was brought – at one o'clock, I think – by Hortensia Peinador. My goddess is ill, but does not want to alarm her poet. I want to believe that there is nothing amiss. Stay quietly in bed, my life, because the weather is certainly very bad and the 'flu is everywhere. I was so worried about the cold in our café that today I asked for a little oil stove to be put in our corner.
It was burning until I left. You will see, another time, how well it warms things up.

Tomorrow is Sunday and I am going to Segovia – how I shall be grieving! – not because I think your illness to be a cause for concern, for I am sure it is not – but because I have not been able to see you. I am hoping that my queen will write to me there to tell me that all is well. But don't worry about writing to me or strain yourself in doing so. Stay well wrapped-up in bed, because your poet is standing there – at your bedside – giving you the warmth of his heart. Do not doubt for a moment that I am with you, that I am always accompanying you; and if I don't say anything to you it is because – as you know – when I am at your side I hardly ever speak: I merely gaze at you. Apart from that I only know how to weep or to kiss your hand, my goddess. I want to learn how to tell you stories that amuse you, as mothers do to children. Because of my sex and my lack of the 'Mother' and 'Old Nurse' cards in the 'Lovers' pack, I have not yet learned this, but I shall learn how to tell them to you.

Your illness does not surprise me; I too have had a rather feverish night, and in my case it was all to do with the 'flu, although luckily it was benign. I recommend you to have plenty of blankets so that you sweat a bit, and take some punch with a little glass of brandy. It is a sure remedy. Afterwards do not go out unless it is sunny and you have fully recovered. Take good care of your little body, my goddess, because, although you are primarily soul, it is also of God's making and certainly one of those that he made when he was in a good mood and at pains to do his work well. Also make sure you sleep well, my precious, but without taking sedatives, which are only temporary remedies and, in the end, stir things up. Close those eyes of yours – so precious, so indescribable – and with a firm will to sleep, thinking about your poet, you will sleep. And the two of us will meet, perfectly transfigured, in your dreams. I shall be a venerable patriarch and you will be a child in his arms. If you do not agree, dream about me as you wish, my goddess.

I shall leave this letter in Madrid with Hortensia Peinador. From Segovia – where I am going only in the hope of getting your letter – I shall write to you via our *Continental*, so that you may collect it when you can. Don't worry. I shall be in Madrid, as always, on Wednesday night. So that, from then until Sunday, if you want to do so, you can write to me at home. You understand?

Don't forget anything I have told you. I don't want to tire you out. I am going out to post this letter after I have discovered what Hortensia's number is – I don't remember if it is 13 or 33. What a dreadful memory!

Farewell, my queen and glory, your poet's heart, pounding for you – and only for you – is keeping you company.

Farewell, do you feel everything I am sending you?

Until this very moment

Antonio

Going through your letters again I have found Hortensia's address (Plaza de Salmerón 13)

Goddess, my precious; a thousand and a thousand and a thousand…. And again, my heart.[2]

On the following Wednesday evening, when he was going by taxi to Segovia station, Machado seized the opportunity to read some 'words full of affection' that Valderrama had just sent him. He wrote immediately to express his delight: 'I have felt that you were by my side, Pilar, my life. And I have heard what you are saying to me. And now I am returning to Madrid full of pride, because for me the warmth of your *"tu sabes?"* is truly life-giving.' And then he added: 'How happy I am when I think about what you are saying to me! Will it be true?'[3] *Sabes?* – 'you know?' – was to occur so often in their correspondence that it became a kind of code word. The implication was that there were things that he knew and she knew but that no-one else knew – things that would for ever be kept secret between them. In a letter written at the end of January Machado suggested that the lovers occupied a *tercer mundo* – a 'third world' of their own to which no-one else could gain admittance:

> On Sunday at twelve I felt you were so close to me. And your *Sabes?* set my heart on fire. And what a delightful fire it is that comes from you! And how rapturous, insane and wanton that *tercer mundo* is! Afterwards I went out to post the letter and to go over the places that I told you about. And then I returned to dream about you all night. You may not wish to know… On Monday I did not go to my class because, after so much dreaming, I had to sleep a little. Do you understand?[4]

It seems that Valderrama understood only too well what he was getting at and, fearful lest anyone should set eyes on such a suffusion of sensuality, she inked the whole paragraph out. She suspected that Machado wanted their relationship to be physical, but she was evidently determined to keep it merely spiritual. When, in one of his early letters, the poet sent her 'countless kisses', she promptly deleted them.

At this period Machado's mood oscillated between elation and despair. When he received a letter from his beloved, he was overjoyed; when the post brought nothing, he was dejected. He was also upset because Valderrama had asked him not to go into the park opposite her house, probably for fear that her husband might see him lurking there. The only hope he now had of catching a glimpse of her was on Sunday mornings when she went to mass in the church of San Ginés in the Calle de Arenal. If he spied her as she went in, he was happy; if he did not, he was miserable. When she asked him for a poem for inclusion in *Esencias*, a book that she was planning to produce, he took it as a signal that all was going well. When she told him one day that she had reason to believe that he had been talking to another woman, he was clearly delighted by what he hopefully interpreted as evidence of jealousy.

> I am pleased to know that you are a little upset, my sweet one, because it is a sign that you love me; but don't worry, Pilar. It is towards you and only you that all – yes, all! – my loving feelings can flow. The secret is simply that I do not possess any more love than this. For some time now I have seen this clearly. My other loves have only been dreams, through which I caught a glimpse of the real woman, the goddess. Since this one came on the scene all the others have disappeared. Only the memory of my wife remains with me, because death and devotion have consecrated it. [5]

Little is known about how the affair proceeded between February and July 1929, because no letters survive from this period. While Antonio and Manuel were working on a new play called *La Lola se va a los Puertos*, Pilar and her husband for their part were preparing to put on a dramatic performance of a work by Jacinto Benavente. Staged in the little theatre they had built in their house, it was performed on 28 April by a group of young people including the couple's three children. It goes without saying that Machado was not among those invited to join the audience, but he would doubtless have had a full report of the proceedings when he and Valderrama next met in the café at Cuatro Caminos.

How often they met there that summer is a matter of conjecture, but they certainly did so on one memorable evening in mid-August. On this occasion, when Machado arrived at the café he discovered that the place was overcrowded and that the proprietor, not wanting to inconvenience such valued regular customers, had provided them with alternative accommodation upstairs. So when Valderrama eventually arrived she was in for an unpleasant surprise: 'The waiter ushered me upstairs', she later recalled, 'and in a little room on the first floor there was Antonio waiting for me. On opening the door I saw a table, a divan and the poet, who greeted me joyfully. I did not even sit down and, in spite of his insistence that I should stay for a few moments, I bade him farewell until another day and walked out.'[6] Poor Machado was very upset and, as he informed Valderrama, his anxiety manifested itself in his dreams. 'I have had dreams – good and bad – and in one of them – the bad one (and I will tell you the good one afterwards) you scolded me very cruelly and I was weeping very bitterly; and as a punishment you left me in a dark room and walked out, shutting the door behind you and saying to me from afar: 'Here you stay, my poet, and I do not love you.' It was evident to someone as familiar as he was with the literature of psychoanalysis that the dream was bringing to the surface long buried memories of some childhood trauma. 'In this dream,' he told Valderrama, 'you are the beloved maternal figure, whose punitive actions are seen to signify an absence of affection.' And before proceeding to tell her about the second dream he made a statement that could have been lifted directly from Freud's *Interpretation of Dreams*: 'One frequently dreams of what one does not even dare to think. Because of this our dreams are complementary to our waking life and he who does not remember his dreams does not know himself.' He then proceeded to recount the second dream, which he called 'the good one':

> I simply dreamed that, after a brief courtship, I married you: Do you want me to tell it to you? But it will be difficult for me to remember all of it; because the dream's cinematic reel turned too quickly and some

parts of it were obscure, although others, by contrast, were clearer and more intimate than in real life. It was one of those old cities of my exile – Segovia, Soria… – some indeterminate Castilian city, and it was one morning in spring shortly after dawn. You were on your way from church, wearing a black cloak and a black mantilla, and with a mass book in your hand. I was following you, reciting some verses which I cannot remember and which you were listening to, from time to time turning your face towards me… Afterwards there was a river bank and we were walking together between the poplars and, finally, there was a church that I remember very well – that of Santa María la Mayor in Soria, where I was married. There we knelt down together after the ceremony. There was a great crowd of people and the sound of an organ. The dream was mixed up with authentic memories of my wedding, but with this difference: on this occasion my mood was one of overflowing happiness – the complete opposite of what it was at my actual wedding. Then the ceremony was for me a veritable martyrdom. And now I was going out with you on my arm, full of pride and joy. It may be said that, obliged as I am to keep our love a secret, in the dream I was getting my own back by proclaiming it to the entire world. Such are the compensatory absurdities of the dream, thanks to which we inhabit another world that is more agreeable to us than this one. I don't want to tell you the rest of the dream. It was too happy, even for a dream.

Machado went on to beg Valderrama not to punish him by her absence and to forgive him. 'I will be good', he wrote, 'every bit as good as you wish. I promise it, my life.' In future she would do the talking and he would simply listen to her, 'spellbound'. 'You have no idea how your voice enchants me and helps calm me down. Also read me anything you have written. My love is very great, Pilar, very deep and very true. I could not live without seeing you or at least without the hope of seeing you. Do you understand? It is true that your presence drives me crazy; but I will put on a straitjacket.

Ay! If you could see how much I suffer just by thinking that you might be upset…'[7]

Fired by his passionate feelings Machado composed a series of poems, which were published in the September 1929 issue of the *Revista de Occidente* under the title of 'Songs for Guiomar'. There have been various suggestions as to why he chose this particular name. It may have been inspired by one of the stories in the *Romancero general* that Machado had heard his grandmother read to him when he was a child – a story that told of the elderly Emperor Charlemagne's love for the Infanta Guiomar. Alternatively it may have been borrowed from the writings of Cervantes, where the name occurs quite frequently. But a more likely candidate, as Ian Gibson has suggested, might be Guiomar de Manuel, who has a street named after her in Seville and who was a benefactress of the nuns of the convent of Las Dueñas. It was this convent which gave its name to the nearby palace, where the poet was born. In the 'Songs for Guiomar', however, unlike so many of his earlier poems, 'the garden' referred to (in the second song) is not that of the author's childhood; its location 'high over the river' indicates Segovia.

> In a garden I dreamt of you,
> Guiomar, high over the river,
> a garden of a time locked up
> behind a cold iron grating.
>
> An unusual bird is singing
> softly in the lotus tree
> by the living and holy water.
> All thirst and all fountain.

In that garden, Guiomar,
a mutual garden that our two hearts
simultaneously contrive,
our hours fuse and grow. The grapes
of a dream – we are together –
we squeeze into a clean glass
and forget our double tale.

(One: Woman and man,
although a gazelle and lion,
come together to drink.
The other: Love can't be
so lucky as to have
two solitudes in one,
not even of a man and woman.) [8]

'These verses', writes Bernard Sesé, 'exhibit a renewal and rejuvenation of his inspiration: new images, brighter colours and a mood of great happiness, an onrush of amorous fervour.' Machado, he suggests, is no longer an adolescent. 'This is the love of a man who has almost reached his declining years, of a heart full of seriousness, of a poet whose interior world now has its essential contours.'[9] Now Machado is not looking back nostalgically to a remembered past but rather forward hopefully to an imagined future, in which he and his beloved can be forever together. The poem is as full of wish-fulfilment as its author's dreams, but its topography is firmly rooted in reality. The lovers' idyllic train ride (in the third song) through the 'granite mountains' appears to follow the route of Machado's weekly journey between Madrid and Segovia. From what other railway line can the traveller catch a glimpse, as the sun sets, of 'the gold of Guadarrama'? When the poem speaks of 'a goddess and her lover' fleeing away together, readers would have had no difficulty in discovering the identity of the lover, but who, apart from the three ladies of Madrid who were privy to the plot, could have guessed that of the goddess? Was she a real person, people might ask themselves, or just a figment of the poet's amorous imagination?

Concealing Valderrama's identity became slightly more difficult after the publication in the spring of 1930 of her *Esencias. Poemas en prosa y verso*. The book actually included a little poem of Machado's own composition:

> I know not what I think
> I know not what I say,
> for now my voice is not my voice
> nor are my thoughts my own. [10]

Although its true authorship was not acknowledged, discerning readers might have noted the poem's similarities with some of Machado's earlier writing. But if so, they are more likely to have suspected Pilar of plagiarism than of anything more morally opprobrious. Few would have imagined that, because two of the poems were set in Segovia, the author had actually been there to visit the city's celebrated poet.

In any event readers of *Esencias* were at first few in number because sales were very slow. On 24 April, in the first of his letters that survive from that year, Machado told Valderrama that he had searched in vain for the volume in the Madrid bookshops. At the time of writing, when she was confined to bed with a cold and he was unable to see her, he was feeling very depressed. 'I have spent several very sad days,' he told her, 'full of worries, forebodings, bad dreams.' But he derived comfort from reading her book, which spoke to him of her 'great and noble soul'. 'Take care, my goddess,' he continued, 'and do not forget your poor poet, so lonely, so sad, so profoundly miserable. From a distance – even without seeing me – you can do so much for me, simply by remembering me, by sending me some of that *sabes?* of yours, which always reaches me.'[11] He continued to look for copies of *Esencias* and, a month later was glad to report that he had managed to find a few in some shops – and had even ordered one from another shop in an attempt to encourage sales. But he regretted that he had not yet fulfilled his promise of speaking to Cipriano Rivas Cherif, whose company was currently performing at the Español, about the possibility of staging a play called *El tercer mundo* that Valderrama had recently completed. Much as he wished to help her he clearly felt some reluctance to approach the celebrated theatrical manager. When he did eventually succeed in talking to him in a private room at the theatre, he found that the place was full of other authors who were competing for the impresario's attention. In such circumstances he was able to do little apart from handing the plays to Rivas Cherif for him to read.

Machado's diffidence had much to do with his fear of arousing suspicions about his relationship with Valderrama. This fear was always with him and especially so on those occasions when he and she found themselves in a public place at the same time. On one Friday evening in May, when they both attended the first performance of a play at the Español, Machado found it hard not to keep gazing at her across the auditorium, but she evidently took great care not to look in his direction. 'You must have felt I was looking at you', he later wrote to her a little reproachfully, 'although you did not manage to turn your head at all. What would my life be without these moments that, from time to time, you concede to me? Only it frightens me to think that I may perhaps have helped to make things difficult for you and cast a shadow over your life.'[12]

That summer, however, the chances of their accidentally bumping into each other were to become even more remote because Valderrama and her family were going to be out of town for some weeks. When she told him of their plans Machado was very upset:

> I am grief-stricken by the news of your absence
> during the summer. And as I am a lover without
> vanity or pride, as I love you religiously – although
> I am tormented – I have to say it all – because I am
> human, all too human – I am convinced that I am in
> love with a goddess, I fear that one day everything
> will vanish like a dream. And what will I do without

you, Pilar? But is it true that you will not forget me
as long as I live?

He told her that, although she had forbidden him to enter it, in
his imagination he often went to the 'Garden of the Fountain' where
in the past they used to meet. 'What a strange thing our past is!' he
wrote. 'It is defined as something that now *is not* or at any rate as
something that now does not operate. However, I believe that our
past not only exists in our memory but also continues to operate
and live outside us. In a word, I believe that we continue to go into
the Garden of the Fountain.' He also believed that they continued
to walk together along 'the esplanade of the Alcázar' in Segovia, as
they had done at their memorable first encounter two years before.[13]
    Not long before Valderrama left the heat of Madrid for the cooler
climate of Palencia, where her husband's family had a country house,
Machado wrote again to explain precisely why he felt such a sense of
desolation at her departure.

> If you could experience the total intensity of my
> passion and know how conscious I am of the barrier
> that fate has placed between us, you would have
> compassion on me. All my life I have been waiting
> for you without knowing you, because, although your
> mind may have been on other things, I have always
> been expecting you, imagining you, dreaming about
> you. And when at last, my goddess, you arrive...Yes, I
> do understand, it is not your fault that we are so often
> separated, and you are good and kind and merciful to
> your poet. Still, you must forgive me for more than
> once looking to death to cure me of my longing for
> the impossible.[14]

While Valderrama was away they continued to keep in touch
with each other by letter. Machado sent mail via her friend María
Estremera, who had a holiday home in Palencia. Early in August

he wrote to say that he lived in expectation of her visit to the *tercer mundo*. 'I devoted the whole night to waiting for it, and all this morning to conjuring up your image in our *rincón conventual*.'[15] Their accustomed café was a sad place without her, but his deprivation was short-lived. In mid-September Valderrama returned to Madrid and the couple resumed their clandestine encounters. Machado told her that in her absence his heart had been like a clock that had almost stopped. 'You have literally given my heart a spring. On many days I was suffering from moral and almost physiological exhaustion, but after seeing you I left our *rincón* feeling like a new man.'[16] In fact he felt energetic enough to walk all the way from Cuatro Caminos to the Plaza del Progreso (which today is called the Plaza de Tirso de Molina) – a considerable distance for a man with bad feet.

It was at this time that Machado's review of Valderrama's *Esencias* finally appeared in *Los Lunes de El Imparcial*. Preparing this had not been an easy task, for he could not write as freely as he would have wished for fear of arousing suspicions about his relationship with the authoress. It was frustrating not to be able to touch on personal aspects of her poetry that he knew more about than anyone. He could not reveal that it was he who had inspired one of the most memorable verses in the book:

> Love is always! always!
> the thirst that never ends
> for the water we never drink.[17]

When he came to discuss the specifically religious poems in her collection Machado had an opportunity to express his own view of Christ as 'the incarnation of love'. He was also able to make his rather more original observation that Jesus was the first man to treat women as persons rather than as objects. It goes without saying, however, that when he wrote to Valderrama about 'love' it had more to do with *eros* than with *agape* or *caritas*. In fact in a letter he sent her that October, following one of their encounters in the café, he confessed that he found her ever more attractive physically. He told her that treating love as 'anti-aphrodisiac' was 'a little cruel', for it obliged him to be blind to her beauty. 'How many times,' he protested, 'have I had to disavow my eyes!'[18]

Such frustration was clearly not good for his health. He had always had a tendency to hypochondria and in November he began to think he was mortally sick. Things became so bad that Valderrama recommended that he went to see her friend, the celebrated physician Carlos Jiménez Encina. 'I am not well, my goddess,' he told her. 'Only when I am with you do I feel that I am fully alive, having forgotten about everything. Yes, in those moments, I am happy, young, strong, healthy …Afterwards I begin to decline and to relapse into depression.' At such times, imagining that he was close to death, he felt the need to make haste to complete all the things he had planned to do. His most important task was to bring out the revised edition of his works that he proposed to dedicate to Valderrama – which he estimated would take him about two years. If he were able to do this, he told her, he would be content. But if he became very ill he hoped that she would not fail to come to see him. 'For me', he told her, 'that will be a great consolation, because you are, doubt it not, the great love of my life.'[19]

On his return to Segovia shortly after writing this he was delighted to find a letter from her waiting for him. With it she sent some verses she had recently composed, and reading them brought tears to his eyes. The poem was almost certainly the one entitled 'Testament of an impossible love' that she did not publish until after her husband's death many years afterwards. As she later pointed out, it was 'dominated by a great malaise and sad presentiments'.

> If I die first, you will return one evening
> to search among the trees of that old garden.
> You will sit again upon the stone seat
> by the fountain that will speak to you of me.

★ ★ ★

If I die first, I will come at night to visit you,
as I used to, in our *Tercer Mundo*.
It will feel the same as if I were still living,
I have to bring those nights alive for you!

If I die first, you will come to my grave
to weep and to pray for me in silence.
And you will pluck a blood-red rose from the stem
rising up from my heart towards you.

And one day you will be buried in the ground.
Near or far? Does it matter? For this our love
passed through life unstained, and when we meet again
I, with my hand in yours, shall bring you to God.[20]

Ian Gibson has suggested that Pilar, a great lover of Dante, saw herself as a new Beatrice 'charged with the mission of directing the erotic thirst that her person provoked in the poet towards the pure springs of Christianity.'[21] But, if so, her mission would prove to be a spectacular failure, for Machado's conclusion to his letter of thanks for her poem was as sensuous as ever: 'Tonight I hope to hold you very close to my breast, without saying anything to you, because there is nothing I can say to you that you do not know: my queen! my goddess! my life! my Pilar!'[22] And in the next of his surviving letters, written in mid-December 1930, he gave her an example of the sort of dreams he had when he lay in bed, imagining he was holding her in his arms. In a recent one he had dreamed that he was with her in Segovia, walking along the banks of the Eresma to the ancient monastery of Santa María del Parral, where they met Unamuno, 'clothed as a monk and singing the *Marseillaise*'.

> Afterwards he took us by the hand, led us to the high altar, gave us his blessing and disappeared. I cannot remember the rest of the dream very well, but it was immensely pleasurable and it was accompanied by

some marvellous music. Don't think I am inventing anything, my goddess.[23]

It is not surprising that, on reading this part of the letter, Valderrama decided to ink it out completely. What would her husband have had to say if he had seen it?

Because so few letters have survived from this period little is known about the lovers' relationship during the first half of 1931. This was a time of political upheaval in Madrid and it is likely that their encounters in the café were less frequent than previously. Early in July Valderrama, who had evidently been disturbed by these developments and distressed by the recent death of her mother, informed Machado that she was suffering from a nervous disorder. She had therefore decided to go to Hendaya, a town on the north coast near San Sebastian, to consult the country's leading psychiatrist, Gregorio Marañón. In her memoirs she said that the poet, greatly to her horror and surprise, had the temerity to follow her to the seaside resort. But she was at pains to point out that they did not meet on the beach, which she evidently thought would have been most improper, but in a road near her hotel. She vehemently denied the account of the meeting given by Justina Ruiz de Conde who, in her *Antonio Machado y Guiomar*, stated that the meeting took place at San Sebastian and that he had there made her a gift of a pair of gold earrings with mother-of-pearl pendants. At first, wrote Ruiz de Conde, 'she refuses to accept them, but at length the poet persuades her to do so and adorns her with the gift. (The scene opens in La Zurriola, on a hot summer night shortly before dawn, and afterwards the lovers go down to the beach.) He tries to kiss her, but she draws back, turns her head brusquely and, because an earring falls off, the kiss is aborted.'[24] Was this the experience that Machado was alluding to when, in 'Other songs for Guiomar', he spoke of 'the cold mother-of-pearl/of your earring in my mouth'?[25]

Next summer she went to San Sebastian, but this time he did not follow her. In a letter to her he said that from time to time he paid a visit to their *rincón* in Cuatro Caminos, a place that for them was 'blessed and unforgettable'. But he had some bad news for her: the proprietor, because of a shortage of customers, was planning to close the café. 'It is sad to think', he wrote, 'that a goddess and her poet are not enough to keep it going. But, if it does close, we will look for a similar one not far from there.' He concluded the letter by assuring her that he was continuing to follow her advice in everything. 'My health, however, depends on your not forgetting your poet, *sabes?* And as there are no *distancias* between us, I shall always, always! know when you are thinking about me.'[26] But were there really no *distancias* between them? Even when no geographical distance separated them and they met face to face, she was always careful to keep him physically *a distancia* – 'at arm's length'. Only once, perhaps, did his lips get close enough to her cheek to dislodge an earring.

Since this is the last of the surviving letters from the poet to his goddess not much is known about how things fared between them thereafter. Although in the event they did not lose their rendezvous in Cuatro Caminos, it became increasingly difficult to meet there. Valderrama records in her memoirs that in 1935, because the situation in Madrid was worsening from day to day and because the café was now so full of noisy people that conversation was becoming impossible, she decided to suspend their meetings. In April 1936 she wrote to Machado to tell him that her husband, thinking it was now too dangerous to remain in Madrid, had decided to move the family to Portugal. She said that she expected only to be away for a few months and suggested that he too should leave the city. She was bidding him farewell by letter because, she maintained, it would have been too painful for both of them to have done so by word of mouth.

Machado, however, had already said goodbye to her in 'Other songs for Guiomar', which ends with this verse:

> I know you will have to weep for me when I die,
> so as to forget me – and later,
> so as to remember me,
> to look on that time with dry eyes.

Beyond your tears
and your forgetfulness,
in your memory, I feel I'm taking a clear path:
a simple, tearless 'Goodbye, Guiomar.'[27]

This verse was in fact omitted from the version of the poem included in the fourth edition of the *Poesías completas*, published in the spring of 1936. But it is likely that it was included in the draft that he sent her prior to the book's publication.

Valderrama recorded that, after her arrival in Portugal, she sent one more letter to Machado. It was dated 13 June, San Antonio's day, and, in accordance with the customary Catholic practice, she wrote to congratulate him. Once again she urged him to leave Madrid, from whence she was daily receiving ever more alarming news. Hoping for a reply to her letter, she enquired at the post offices both in Lisbon and in Estoril, but none ever came. It may be that the poet never received this last letter from his goddess, for by this time the postal services, like so many other public institutions in Spain, were ceasing to function normally.

o o o

Machado's *aventura sentimental*, extending over eight years, cannot properly be called an 'affair'. Although it appears from his letters that he would have liked their relationship to be physical as well as spiritual, it is clear from the poems she inspired that his love for her was 'courtly'. As Willis Barnstone has observed, these verses 'have a compelling flow and the youthful courtliness of a medieval troubadour'. [28] As with the troubadours it was the very unavailability of the beloved that made her so attractive. It is significant that in 'Other songs for Guiomar' Machado should go so far as to say that 'all love is fantasy' – something that is 'invented' by the lover and his beloved.[29] What she thought about such a pessimistic assessment is not known; what is certain is that she remained determined to keep things cool. When he concluded a letter with the words: 'endless embraces, countless kisses', she promptly took up her pen and inked them out.

What then did she want from the relationship? Was this unhappy woman, married to a man who showed her no affection, looking for the good father that she had long since lost? It was, after all, the poet's 'very kind face' that had attracted her to him at their first meeting. Or did she have an ulterior motive for keeping up the connection for so long? She herself, it has to be remembered, had ambitions as a poet and she thought him to be in a good position to further them. It was evidently at her behest that, early in 1929, he had sent a copy of her *Huerto cerrado* to Unamuno, doubtless in the hope that he might give the book a favourable review. In the accompanying letter Machado said that she was 'a very intelligent and very good woman' and 'a fervent admirer' of the master's writings.[30] But, apart from telling him that he had once met her in Segovia, he was careful to say nothing about any other encounters he had had with her.

There must always have been an air of unreality about those encounters between two people from such different backgrounds with such contrasting outlooks on the world. What did they talk about in the long hours spent sitting over coffee in their *rincón*? If he had discussed the things that really most interested him – the philosophy of Heidegger or the spirituality of Tolstoy – she might have been either bewildered or bored. If he had tried to share with her his views on the current state of Spain she would probably have been shocked and horrified. In the event the likelihood is that she did most of the talking and he did most of the listening, just as they had done at their first meeting, when he could only gaze at her in silent admiration. She might have spoken to him about her current anxieties, while he, like a good counsellor, would have said little except the odd word of encouragement. She is known to have read him her poems, for he told her that nothing pleased him more than to hear them. Whatever their converse, its vacuity would have become ever more marked as the years passed and the condition of the country declined. With the widening gulf between their two worlds – his rabidly anticlerical republicanism and her devoutly Catholic monarchism – it must have become ever more difficult to maintain the *tercer mundo*, their private 'third world' in which nothing unpleasant could happen and where perfect love prevailed.

VII

Drama and Disruption in Madrid

Not long after Antonio had begun to meet Pilar regularly in their *rincón* at Cuatro Caminos, he and Manuel set to work on a new dramatic production entitled *La Lola se va a los Puertos*. In February 1929 they issued a press release about the play, but gave little information beyond saying that one of their purposes in writing it was to counter the increasing Americanization of Spanish life. They believed that the growing assertiveness of the United States that had led to Spain's humiliation in 1898 was now affecting the country adversely in other more subtle ways. That Antonio's students in Segovia could liken him to Charlie Chaplin indicates how much, since the arrival of the cinema, Spaniards had come under the influence of American films. And so the Machados' aim was to restore people's pride in their country's own culture.

It is likely that the idea of writing the play, whose title forms the opening lines of one of his best-known poems, came initially from Manuel; he was the one most deeply imbued with the particular culture that it celebrates. But there is no doubt that Antonio was as closely involved as his brother was with the actual writing of the drama, of which a first draft had been completed by mid-August. It was then that he sent Pilar the script of the last scene, to which he subsequently added some verses that she had composed. At the beginning of September it was reported that the authors were putting the final touches to the play and would finish the task by the end of the month. Then it was announced that the first performance would take place on the night of 8 November in the Fontalba theatre, a prestigious venue in Gran Via owned by the Marqués de Fontalba.

In interviews and press releases prior to the production Antonio and Manuel explained that the play's title had been taken from a well-known Andalusian folk-song. And when someone enquired whether the comedy should be classified as *andaluza* or *flamenco*, they replied that it was both. Southern Spain, they insisted, was composed of a great mixture of cultures, among which one of the most important was undoubtedly that of the *gitanos* or gypsies. 'Andalusia', they pointed out, 'which has known how to be so many things, to assimilate so many exotic elements, and where the grafts from so many races have produced so much fruit, has no need to be ashamed of being at times a little *gitana*.'[1] Lola, the play's heroine, may or may not have herself have been a *gitana*, but she is the embodiment of the *cante hondo*, the distinctive style of singing perfected by the gypsies of Andalusia. With the help of her guitarist and constant companion Heredia, she is able to withstand the amorous advances of a wealthy womanizer named Don Diego, who, to complicate matters, is competing for her favours with his son José Luis. It all ends happily with the triumph of the spirit of *flamenco* over the *donjuanismo* of Don Diego and his son.

It is not surprising that such a play, with its exaltation of something as distinctly Spanish as *flamenco*, should be popular with a patriotic Madrid audience. Its first performance was a huge success, the applause being more rapturous and prolonged than it had been for any of the Machados' previous plays. The critics, moreover, were unanimous in their praise of the production, the brothers being congratulated on their ability to write verse that approximated so closely to normal conversation. The 'extraordinary triumph' of the comedy was marked by a *homenaje* to its authors, which was celebrated on 27 November. It took the form of a special performance of the play, 'with the theatre full of a distinguished public', followed by a *fiesta flamenco* at the Ritz hotel. Among the important people who attended was the dictator Miguel Primo de Rivera, whose son José

Antonio made a fulsome speech and presented the brothers with a commemorative album containing the names of all those present. The *Heraldo de Madrid* reported that 'when the speaker announced to the splendid assembly that, with an Andalusian lavishness that was as truly *generoso* as its wines, the house was providing as much sherry as anyone wanted – or was able – to drink, great shouts of delight brought an end to his speech.'[2]

Not long after the last performance of *La Lola* on 5 January 1930 Madrid witnessed the first of a series of dramatic events off stage. Following the failure in December of a revolt at Jaca by two disaffected army captains, Fermín Galán and García Hernández, hostility to Primo de Rivera's oppressive regime had continued to grow and, at the end of January, Alfonso XIII, hoping to abort a rebellion, removed him and his ministers from office. The king replaced him as commander in chief of the army with the former High Commissioner for Morocco, the unpopular General Berenguer, who announced that he would form an 'apolitical' government in preparation for a meeting of the Cortes. At the same time he declared an amnesty for Unamuno and other exiled dissidents.

Change was in the air. Even monarchists began to talk about the removal of the unpopular king. On 11 February, the 56th anniversary of the establishment of the Republic, Machado attended a banquet in Segovia to commemorate the event and, according to a local newspaper, his arrival was greeted by loud applause. At the conclusion of the celebration a congratulatory telegram was sent to Unamuno, who two days earlier had staged a dramatic reentry into Spain. Machado was overjoyed at the return of his 'master' and contributed a laudatory piece about him to *La Gaceta Literaria*.

'Don Miguel de Unamuno', he wrote, 'is currently the most exalted figure on the Spanish political scene. He has initiated a fruitful civil war of the spirit, from which there must surely arise a new Spain.'[3] When a banquet in the great man's honour was held in Madrid in May, Machado was among those who attended to hear him speak about the current state of the country.

Machado shared Unamuno's despair at the failure of those dissatisfied with Berenguer's government to press for the establishment of a republic. When, early in 1931, following the suppression of a republican putsch, José Ortega y Gasset, Gregorio Marañón and Rámon Pérez de Ayala formed the Agrupación del Servicio de la República, the poet was among the first to join. He had long shared the group's conviction that only a republican regime would be capable of undertaking the all-important work of 'resuscitating the history of Spain' and of modernizing the country socially and technologically. He in fact presided at the first meeting of the republican campaign, which was held on 14 February in the Juan Bravo theatre in Segovia and addressed by its three founders. In introducing them to the audience, which filled the place to the rafters, he himself said a few words: 'The revolution will not go mad and put up barricades', he said; 'it is something less violent but more serious. Since the evolutionary continuity of our history has been broken, all we can do is to make a leap into the future. This necessitates the cooperation of creative minds, because without it the revolution will be a catastrophe. I salute these three men as true revolutionaries, as men of order, of a new order.'[4]

A few weeks later the Agrupación issued a proclamation in preparation for the municipal elections scheduled to take place on 12 April. When these produced a landslide victory for the republicans there was great rejoicing in the streets of Madrid. Machado was delighted with the result, but was well aware that Valderrama found it deeply upsetting. 'I too am worried by the news being circulated about political agitation,' he wrote diplomatically. 'Make sure, goddess of my soul, that at this time you do not go on foot into the centre of Madrid. As the anti-dynastic triumph has been overwhelming, I fear there will be serious disturbances. We shall see. For my part, as I now see that there may soon be a Republican victory, I think that those furthest removed from power will form parties.'[5] What he did not foresee was the swift reaction of Alfonso XIII, who fled the country two days later.

On 14 April, when news of the king's departure reached the city, a massive rally was organized in Segovia by the Agrupación and the Alianza Republicana. Machado participated and was one of a group of prominent people who later went to the Ayuntamiento to address the crowd from the balcony, where the republican flag now flew. After numerous speeches there was a minute's silence in memory of Galán and Hernández, the two officers who had been executed for their attempted putsch at Jaca. Next day Machado described what had happened in a letter to Valderrama. 'Some of us platonic republicans,' he reported, 'were charged with the task of maintaining order and exercising the interim government of the city. This,' he assured her, 'has been the sole involvement of your poet in the new regime.'[6]

Years later Machado was free to speak about the events of that day with rather greater enthusiasm than he had apparently thought it fit to show in his letter to Valderrama: 'Six years ago today saw the proclamation of the Second Spanish Republic', he recalled on 14 April 1937, and went on to record what it had felt like:

> Those hours, my God, all woven together with the purest flaxen thread of hope, when a few of us old republicans hoisted the tricolour flag at the Ayuntamiento in Segovia! ... Let us remember, let us again relive those hours in our hearts. With the first leaves of the poplars and the last blossom of the almonds, in came the spring, holding the Republic by her hand. Nature and history seemed to blend together into something that is the stuff of legend or children's balladry:
>
> > The spring has come
> > on a captain's arm.
> > Sing, children, in a ring:
> > Viva, Fermín Galán!

From the blood of the heroes of Jaca came forth the April flowers, and the name of the dead captain, buried like them under the winter snow, was evoked by a song that I sang – or dreamed that the children were singing – at that time:

> The spring has arrived
> and Don Alfonso departs.
> Many dukes accompany him
> on his journey to the sea.
> The storks on the towers
> are glad to see him go ...

And the song, monotonous and graceful, goes on. That was a day of rejoicing in Segovia. Soon we knew that it was the same throughout Spain. A day of peace that astonished the entire world.[7]

24 April, just eleven days after the proclamation of the Republic, saw the first performance of Antonio and Manuel's new play *La Prima Fernanda*. Its original sub-title of *Crisis total*, later replaced by the less sensational one of *Comedia de figurón*, indicated the political nature of its theme. In a press release issued prior to its production the authors were at pains to point out that the play had been written many months earlier, but that circumstances beyond their control had delayed its staging – and that, had it been performed before the overthrow of the monarchy, it might have appeared to be more polemical. 'We call it *scenes of the old regime*', they said, 'because we hope that that world has completed its *karma* in the days in which we now live.' They went on to say that they had called it a *comedia de figurón* 'because in it there is a ridiculous masked figure, a caricature of the kind of politician that has afflicted Spain for three quarters of a century. It is not an *obra de clave*: it does not allude directly or embarrassingly to anyone.' [8] Their insistence that the play had been conceived long before the inauguration of the Republic was

repeated in an interview they gave to the *Heraldo de Madrid* on the day of its opening performance. They said that its description of a political system that was on the verge of collapse represented a kind of foretaste of the future. 'Now that the *figurones* have been banished there would be no point in writing *La Prima Fernanda*,' they said, 'because we would not think it brave to thrust a spear into a dead body.'[9]

The first performance was a great success, with many calls for the authors to come on stage, and it was generally well received by the critics. A writer in *La Libertad* said it was 'a faithful reflection of the wretchedness of our life here in Spain, which until now was held in bondage by that aristocratic world where flourished the cunning financier, the chameleon-like politician, the "flirty" females, the subservient generals, all the rottenness that had to be swept away by the valiant endeavours of the people.'[10] Although some reviewers thought the play ought to have been in prose rather then verse, most were agreed that, in using poetry as a medium, the brothers were maintaining the great tradition of classical drama. Only one critic, a young poet named Antonio Espina, wrote disparagingly about the play. He said that the principal male characters – Bernardino, the clownish general, and Corbacho, the corrupt politician – were 'childish caricatures' that he likened to 'hoary old effigies that no author with a modicum of good taste ought to drag out of a mouldy back-stage wardrobe and deploy at this level'. He suggested that the Machados should give up writing plays and confine themselves to poetry. He said he admired Antonio's 'ardent melancholy' and Manuel's 'rhythmic jauntiness', and hoped they would continue to write the kind of verse for which they were famed. [11] What the brothers' reactions were can only be guessed. They were probably happy enough with their good reviews and delighted that *La Prima Fernanda* ran for 32 nights – a commendable achievement for a political satire that, unlike the popular and gutsy *La Lola*, might not have been expected to have a great appeal to the general run of theatre-goers.

Meanwhile, off stage, Spain's drama continued to unfold. On the day after the first performance of *La Prima Fernanda* the provisional government headed by Manuel Azaña began the process of dismantling the *viejo regimen* that had been so savagely ridiculed in the play. It issued a decree known as the Ley Azaña that forced some of the generals into retirement and effectively brought the Army under its control. Early in May there were other decrees that reformed the organization of public education. As Hugh Thomas has pointed out, many of the leading members of the new government had been educated at the Institución Libre de Enseñanza and it was 'the spirit of the Institute' that motivated them. [12] That the Machados were delighted by these reforms is clear from an interview they gave at the time. They were agreed that the 'most difficult and delicate problem' facing the new government was that of religion and, when asked how the problem might be solved, they replied:

> It is important to educate people so as to deepen and purify their religious feelings. The State must not subjugate the Church, but must guide and advise it lovingly, obliging the clergy to fulfil their mission more faithfully and to refrain from involvement in any sphere of activity that is not purely religious. It must also improve the economic situation of the Church and, above all, raise its cultural standards.[13]

It seems that here, unlike in some previous interviews, Antonio did not leave it to his elder brother to do all the talking. What was said on this occasion about the Church was precisely what he had been saying for years. Who but a man as idealistic as he could have conceived of a situation in which a struggling State could reform such a powerful institution as the Spanish Church? And who but a man that tutored his students so lovingly would ever have thought of describing the State's function as exercising *una tutela amorosa*?

Antonio was naturally delighted when, in May 1931, the provisional government set up an organization called Las Misiones

Pedagógicas under the presidency of his old friend and teacher Manuel
Bartolomé Cossío. It was designed to bring culture to those living
in the most remote regions of Spain – by means of theatre, cinema,
libraries and even the circulation of reproductions of paintings from
the Prado. One of its aims was to encourage an awareness of 'the
liberal and democratic principles that are the foundation of modern
civilization'. [14] Another was to provide educational opportunities for
the disadvantaged – a cause that had long been close to the poet's
heart. Writing under the nom-de-plume of Juan de Mairena he was
to speak with heavy irony about people who, as James Whiston puts
it, 'have a usurious ambition to be educated and are insolent enough
to seek ways of achieving it'.[15]

Meanwhile, back in Segovia, Machado was helping to establish
the city's branch of Acción Republicana, the political party (led by
Manuel Azaña) to which he had belonged since its formation in 1926,
and he became a founder member of its executive. At this critical
juncture in the affairs of the nation he clearly had no wish to stand
on the sidelines. He wanted to help build the Second Republic, as
his father and grandfather had helped to build the First. Eventually
an opportunity for him to make a practical contribution to the work
came in March 1932 when, at the instigation of the directorate of the
Misiones Pedagógicas, he was authorized to remain in Madrid until
the end of the academic year to oversee the organization of popular
theatre. What task could have been more congenial to him?

A week after the announcement of his appointment the Teatro
Español staged the first performance of a play that he and Manuel
had been working on since the previous summer. It was called *La
duquesa de Benamejí* and was set in the early part of the 19th century in
the reign of the unpopular Ferdinand VII. It told the story of a young
duchess, who fell in love with a highwayman named Lorenzo who
had ambushed her carriage in a mountainous region of Andalusia.
The other woman in the cast was a young gypsy called Rocío, who
was secretly in love with Lorenzo and, mad with jealousy, revealed
his hideout to the soldiers who were seeking him – and then, taking
advantage of the ensuing struggle, stabbed the duchess to death. That

the captain of the company of soldiers was a cousin of the duchess (and had long been enamoured of her) confirms the suspicion that the idea for the play, with 'impossible love' as its central theme, came more from Antonio than Manuel. Moreover, according to Manuel Guerra, some of the characters in the play, 'with their didactic manner and their intellectual attitude, their fatalism that reminds us of Seneca and their profound Christian sentiments', bear a strong resemblance to the younger of the two brothers.[16]

The play does not seem to have been particularly well received. Not all the critics approved of its novel mixture of poetry and prose, and some thought its plot was outmoded. Predictably enough, it was dismissed as 'a naïve and foolish kind of melodrama' by the waspish Antonio Espina. 'It is pointless to perpetuate old theatrical fashions', he wrote. 'Historical romanticism is now a museum piece. In our grandparents' day, when it was fresh and authentic, it had an emotive value... Today it has no appeal for those living in a moral and artistic climate far removed from the one that saw the genesis of the romantic in the realms of drama, the novel and journalism.'[17]

It is noticeable that the reception of La duquesa was much less enthusiastic than that of La Lola, which, by popular demand, was performed again on 25 May at the La Latina theatre.

La duquesa was the sixth play that the Machados had worked on together and it was to prove to be the last; a seventh one that they had begun to write some years previously was not to be performed until after Antonio's death. This was El hombre que murió en la guerra, a four act drama, written in prose, where the main character was one Juan de Zúñiga, who had enlisted in the Foreign Legion and had served throughout the 1914-18 war. Because they had heard nothing from him his family presumed that he had been killed and, when he did eventually re-appear, in disguise and with a false name, no-one at first recognized him. Eventually, however, everyone did so, with the single exception of a girl called Guadalupe, a friend of his childhood, who resisted his amorous advances and told him to go away. Unrequited love was one of Antonio's perennial preoccupations, but there are other clear indications of his influence on the plot. 'This work,' writes Bernard Sesé, 'illustrates once again many themes dear to Antonio Machado: the condemnation of war, deemed to be both stupid and mad; questions about the true identity of human beings, and the part played by reality and imagination in human relations.'[18]

Now that Machado was back in Madrid he was able to spend more time doing what he most enjoyed, which was talking with his friends in cafés. Among his favourite haunts was the *Café Español*, situated close to the Teatro Real, and it was here that the young poet Rafael Alberti once encountered him.

> It was a cold and rainy evening in January and from the street, through the illuminated lace curtains of the windows, I could see Machado's silhouette, and I went in to greet him. I was coming from a cozy little bookshop, whose proprietor, a great friend of the young writers of the day, had just secured for me a rare copy of Rimbaud's poems; and that evening I was feeling childishly happy as I clutched the book, which I kept under my overcoat to protect it from the rain. Machado greeted me very affectionately, at once offering me a seat beside him, while introducing me to his companions. I took off my coat and, with great pride, showed him my precious volume, which he looked at, grunted his approval and then placed it on the chair to his left on whose back the coats and scarves were hanging. Among those present I now remember only one: the old actor Ricardo Calvo, a great friend of the poet. That evening, unusually, his inseparable brother Manuel was absent...
>
> After some time I noticed that Machado was smoking and, as he was doing so, was absent-mindedly lowering his cigarette towards the place where I calculated that my precious Rimbaud was located. With ill-concealed consternation I wanted to look over Don

Antonio's shoulder and then under the table to make sure that the work of France's most outstanding poet was not serving as an ash tray for the great Spanish poet's cigarette stubs. But I did not dare to do so, because I felt that it would be a little indelicate and, furthermore, that my suspicions were exaggerated and unworthy...

But after that evening I was able — not without a kind of melancholy smile — to show the many people who came to my house my rare copy of Rimbaud, even more rare and valuable for the round burn marks that Machado's cigarettes had made on its rich brown binding.[19]

Another location for Machado's *tertulia was* the *Café de Varela* in the Calle de Preciados adjoining the Plaza de Santo Domingo. Pérez Ferrero described its appearance:

It is a spacious café and, although it has windows giving on to two streets, it is dark and gloomy, which results in its having a confidential atmosphere. It is very traditional and is much frequented by people who appear to want to keep themselves apart from the principal city streets on whose borders they are living. Surprisingly, among those sitting there are still to be seen the lady with a *mantilla*, the man with a cloak, the artisan with a knotted stick, the pawnbroker with an enormous *tumbaga* on his little finger... Through its revolving door pass a few young people and, if they are a couple, the girl has a saucy look and the boy invariably wears a shirt with a white *pañolito* on its collar. At the end of the evening, when the lamps have been lit, the vast room has an old-fashioned appearance.[20]

Among the regular attenders at the *tertulia* was Luis Álvarez Santullano, the friend who had been instrumental in securing Antonio's appointment as overseer of 'popular theatre'. Santullano long treasured the memory of their 'intimate and sensitive friendship'. 'Every evening, winter or summer, at about the time when it was getting dark', he recalled, 'the three brothers used to meet in a Madrid café and with them would be two or three friends, one of whom, inevitably, was the actor Ricardo Calvo. The Machados – the two poets and the painter – were at the centre of a circle into which were gradually drawn those who were, for the most part, friends and admirers of Antonio.'[21] They included Carlos Jiménez Encina, a distinguished white-bearded doctor, and the engraver Ricardo Baroja, brother of the novelist. Among the more occasional visitors was Unamuno, who was in the habit of dropping in at the café whenever he was in town. Another distinguished writer who sometimes attended was the Chilean poet Pablo Neruda, who at one period held a diplomatic appointment in Madrid. In his *Memoirs* he states: 'I saw Don Antonio Machado several times, sitting in his favourite café dressed in his black notary's suit, silent and withdrawn, as sweet and austere as an old Spanish tree.'[22] Not everyone, of course, was welcome to join the select company assembled in the *Café de Varela* In fact Santullano relates that, on some occasions when they felt that they were being crowded out by intruders, members of the group would secretly signal to each other and quietly decamp to another café nearby.

Santullano also used to see Machado regularly at the meetings of the management committee of Misiones Pedgagógicas, of which he was the secretary. The poet, he recalled, was 'one of the most assiduous members of the committee and, although he spoke little, what he said was always sound and to the point'.[23] He also gave a delightful description of what used to happen at the end of a meeting when Machado's friends tried to help him put on his coat, which was evidently made from some very thick and unyielding material. He said that they 'had the amusing task of getting his arms into the sleeves and tugging away until his whole body was accommodated – but never completely so, because of the resistance of the garment, which was as stiff as a board and rebelliously inflexible. Antonio used to endure the procedure with a smile on his face, saying between his teeth: 'That wretched coat... There is no-one who can make it see reason.'"[24] The coat was very similar to the 'coarse greatcoat' worn by his *alter ego*, Juan de Mairena, that provided the philosopher with a chance to allegorize 'something of what we call culture, which burdens so many without warming them':

> We zealously seek to defend it somehow against all those who, naked of culture themselves, would snatch it out of our grasp – or so we think. Bah! For my own part, if I have such a garment at all, I fear nothing from lurking coat-snatchers, nor do I think there will be many to challenge my right to wear it to the end of my days.[25]

When his temporary post at the Misiones came to an end Machado was appointed to the staff of one of the new secondary schools that the government, with its strong commitment to the advancement of education, had established in Madrid. And so in mid-September he became a teacher of French Language in the Instituto Calderón de la Barca, which now occupied the impressive buildings of the Instituto Católico de las Artes y las Industrias that had recently been confiscated from the Jesuits. Since most of the staff had been students at the Institución Libre de Enseñanza it is not surprising that the new school perpetuated many of the features of that pioneering establishment. In the Instituto Calderón, a pupil later recalled, 'there were no textbooks; we based what we wrote on the lessons given in class.' On one occasion, when a member of staff read out some of Machado's verses to his pupils, they were surprised to discover that their untidily attired French teacher, whose clothes were always speckled with cigarette ash and whose pockets were for ever bulging with bits of paper, was in reality a great poet. This led some of the boys to discover, in listening to him, 'a new attractiveness in his noble forehead and his great crop of greying hair'.[26] Machado stayed on the staff of the Instituto Calderón until March 1936, when he moved to the Instituto Cervantes, another recently established secondary school. He was appointed on the recommendation of an old friend from his Segovia days, Manuel Cardenal de Iracheta, who taught philosophy at the Instituto Cervantes and was most keen to have as a colleague the man he called 'the last great poet in the Castilian language'. [27]

Machado was glad to be once again living in Madrid after his long provincial exile. But although generally reluctant to leave the capital, he did so on one occasion that autumn to revisit Soria, where the city authorities wished to confer upon him the honorific title of 'adopted son'. His response to their invitation was overwhelmingly positive:

> I thank you with all my heart for the very great honour that I am receiving from that beloved city. I believe that Soria owes me nothing and, if it did owe me anything, it would be very little in comparison with what I owe to it; for it taught me how to experience Castile, which is the best and most direct way of experiencing Spain. Only one consideration has made me decide to accept such excessive homage: the adopted son has long ago adopted Soria as an ideal native city.[28]

Machado had not set foot in Soria for twenty years and, when he arrived there in October, he was disconcerted to discover how much the place had changed. 'He did not encounter any euonymus gardens, with their spider's webs', said his old friend José Tudela; 'the old gardens of the Dehesa park were not as they used to be, and the streets, being full of new buildings, looked very different. It was no longer a quiet, peaceful city … and his memory of the old Soria faded away.' But, as a press report of his visit recorded, he was delighted to find that one thing remained for ever the same; when he reached the bridge over the river he exclaimed to his brother José, who was accompanying him: 'Look, Pepe, this is my Duero, my Duero.'[29]

Surrounded by civic dignitaries the Machados walked along the old road to San Saturio that for Antonio held so many memories. In the little square in front of the hermitage a table and chairs had been set out. There were speeches: one by the mayor, another by the deputy mayor and a third by Soria's newly adopted son. Machado sang the city's praises, recalling how on one unforgettable evening in September 1907 he had first seen the moon rising behind Santa Ana. He talked about the beauty of the Castilian language as it was spoken in Soria and the influence that the city and its surrounding countryside had had on the literature of Spain. 'In words whose beauty was deeply moving', wrote the reporter from *El Avisador Numantino*, 'he said that Castile, diffused through all its parts, is the embodiment of Spain, and that the high Sorian tableland, this pure Soria, is the synthesis of Castile, which means that here is the very heart of Spain.' At the conclusion of the speeches the mayor uncovered a marble plaque with a bust of the poet and the inscription: 'Rincón del poeta Antonio Machado MCMXXXII'. The municipal band played a 'triumphal march', everyone applauded and shouted 'Viva Machado!' and 'Viva Soria!', and, after resting for a while in the Ayuntamiento, the brothers took the train back to Madrid. [30]

Little is known about Machado's movements in the course of the next six months. The only letter of his to survive from this time is the one he wrote early in March 1933 to his young friend Federico García Lorca to congratulate him on his new play, *Bodas de Sangre*. He had just been to see it performed at the Infanta Beatriz theatre and he judged it a 'magnificent tragedy'. 'Blood Wedding', set in a mountainous region of Andalusia and richly suffused with symbolism, was bound to appeal to Machado. Moreover, the 'impossible love' that a man could feel for someone else's wife, which was a central theme of the play, was something of which he himself had first hand experience. But it was perhaps Lorca's courageous exposure of the cultural and moral deficiencies of Spanish rural society that caused him to end his letter with a resounding 'Bravo!'[31]

Now that Machado was not himself engaged in the writing of plays he had time to turn his attention to other things, and he began work on a long poem called 'The Lamentations of Abel Martín'. The work, completed in July, begins with memories of his boyhood:

Today with the spring,
I dreamed of a slender body that trailed me
like a docile shadow. That thing
was my young body that easily
leapt three steps at a time up the stairs.

★ ★ ★

Absence and distance,
I dreamed again of the robes of dawn;
the arrow of tomorrow, set firm
in the tense bow, the terrifying sight
of flame moving in the fuse
of the grenade.

O Time, O Still Now
pregnant with imminence!
you walk with me on the cold path,
weaver of hope and impatience!

The poem concludes with a meditation that reveals much about the writer's current state of mind:
Today as once before on the broad violet sea
the dream sinks stone steps
and makes a way for a child's schooner
with bronze and gold dolphins leaping up.

Great actions and adventures
hover around a timid heart.
Mountains of hard stone – echo
upon echo – repeat my voice.

Oh, to linger in the blue of day
as the eagle lingers on the wind,
over cold summits,
sure of its wings and breath!

Nature, I ask you for august
confidence and peace,
a treaty with terror and hope,
a drop of joy, a sea of oblivion...[32]

It seems that the apocryphal writer soon came to believe that only in dying would he gain the reprieve for which he craved; for hard on the heels of his 'Lamentations' came another poem entitled 'The Death of Abel Martín'. It relates how one evening, just as it was getting dark and 'the last swifts were circling the bell-tower', Martín was alone in his *rincón* when a woman dressed in mourning entered his room and stood by his bed. It transpired that she was the personification of Death. That she took the form of one 'impossible to have as a lover, yet for ever loved' has led critics to see in her a representation of Guiomar; but there are similarities between the depiction of Death in this poem and that in one written soon after the loss of Leonor.[33]

Both 'The Lamentations' and 'The Death' of the apocryphal poet were included in the third edition of Machado's *Poesías completas*, which was published in the autumn of 1933. Also in the new collection was a short poem called 'Siesta: In memory of Abel Martín' and the one written in 1929 in adoration of Guiomar. Among the reviews of the book there was a very favourable one by Benjamin Jarnés in the Buenos Aires periodical, *La Nación*. 'Antonio Machado's poetry', he wrote, 'is circulating among what is called the general public with the slowness that is inevitable for all works of such importance, which have to act as leaven and not as dynamite.' He believed that Machado was the poet 'who elevated simplicity to the highest poetic level' and who consequently 'restricted his consciousness so as to seize from it the simplest sounds'.[34]

A further consequence of the publication of his book was an interview with the communist writer Rosario del Olmo, which was featured in *La Libertad* in January 1934. When asked about the duty of the artist in a world that was in crisis, Machado replied that his role was to be *actual*, that is, fully in touch with the contemporary situation. This meant, above all, being open to 'the other'. 'This is not the time', he insisted, 'for lyrical solipsism, in which the poet sings and listens to himself. The poet is beginning to believe in the existence of his neighbours and will end up by singing for them.' [35]

Machado's conviction that the poet's duty was to participate fully in the affairs of the world grew stronger as the political situation worsened not only in Spain but also, following the rise of Hitler and Mussolini, throughout Europe. In April he joined a new party, Izquierda Republicana, formed by the amalgamation of Azaña's Alianza Republicana with two other parties. At the same time his name appeared at the head of the list of signatories to a manifesto 'Against the Nazi terror' that was published in the *Heraldo de Madrid*:

> The cruel reprisals taken in Germany against all men and women opposed to the policies of Hitler have provoked the strongest protest from all liberal spirits, who regard it as fundamental to human solidarity, irrespective of whatever ideology an individual may have, to unite in demanding an immediate end to this intolerable form of persecution, which constitutes the greatest infringement of human rights that our age has seen.[36]

The letter went on to deplore the Nazis' hostility to communism, an ideology with which Machado had considerable sympathy – as is clear from an article that he contributed later that year, under the pseudonym of Juan de Mairena, to the Marxist publication *Octubre*. Here he states his belief that what was 'specifically Russian' in that country's pre-revolutionary literature exactly expressed 'the fraternal sensibility of Christianity' – and that the links between communism, in its authentic expression, and the Christian gospel were indissoluble. He was convinced that Moscow represented the heart and soul of Christianity, while Rome – which was only interested in power – had taken from Christ solely 'what was needed to defend itself against him'. In the world a battle was being fought between egoism and individualism on the one hand and a yearning for brotherhood on the other – and he believed that Russia was the country that stood for brotherhood. For Machado the *heart* of the Slavs was superior to the *intelligence* of Lenin, whom he dismissed as 'that German thinker'. Marxism at its best represented a new manifestation of the power and beauty of the Russian soul.[37]

The chances of Marxism making headway in Spain, however, were not great. In fact the influence of left-wing elements declined dramatically in October 1934, when the coalition headed by Azaña, which had ruled the country for the past two years, fell from power. Soon afterwards, when a reporter from *El Sol* encountered him in a café and asked him about the cultural consequences of the political crisis, Machado – a known supporter of Azaña – at first seemed reluctant to say very much. But the journalist was insistent. What did he think of 'the present turmoil, which is upsetting some people but providing others with a stimulus for visionary ideas and the actions consequent upon them'? The poet did not answer directly, but confined himself to generalities. He said that, since it was impossible for him to turn his back on the world, the artist was bound to be concerned about political and social issues – and therefore to experience a measure of 'disorientation'. When pressed to be more specific about his own position he made this significant statement:

> I am not a Marxist nor can I believe, in accordance with Marxist dogma, that economic factors are the most important things in life: they are important, although not the most important; but to be so mean as to be opposed to the masses having access to the realm of culture and to that which is their just due seems

to me to be an error that will always have disastrous
consequences.

When he went on to insist that the artist, and particularly the
poet, must not mix politics with his work, the reporter cut in with
a question. Were there not some great poets who, in their day, had
exercised a considerable influence on society? Machado did not deny
it, but said that the writers in question had not been placing their
pens at the service of explicitly political interests. When the journalist
suggested that this did not apply to the USSR, the poet replied rather
dismissively: 'All that I have read of the literature of the new Russia
is frankly superficial and in no way comparable with the work of the
old Russian masters.'[38]

At this time Machado had just begun, at the invitation of the
editor, to write a series of articles in a new paper called the *Diario de
Madrid*. He wrote thirty-three articles in total, the first published in
November 1934 and the last in October 1935. All appeared under
the pen-name of Juan de Mairena, the apocryphal philosopher
who had made his first appearance six years earlier in the second
edition of *Poesías completas*. He was now described as a teacher of
Rhetoric at an Andalusian *instituto* – an establishment that had many
features in common with the Institución Libre. The teaching method
was Socratic: dialogue was the order of the day, and pupils were
encouraged to disagree with their teacher if they felt moved to do
so. The views that Mairena expressed were often controversial. He
criticized his fellow Spaniards for being egotistical and unwilling to
learn from each other. 'In Spain', he said. 'there is no dialogue because
no-one asks a question, unless it be to answer it himself. We all wish
to return, without having been anywhere. We are essentially *paletos*,'
he concluded, using a word best translated as 'country bumpkins'.[39]
Nevertheless, Mairena had a high regard for country people and their
folklore. 'We have a people,' he wrote in language reminiscent of that
of *Demófilo*, 'who are wonderfully endowed with wisdom; a people
who continue to make the middle class look silly – a middle class that
in its turn has been rendered ridiculous by the scientific deficiencies

of our universities and by ecclesiastical pragmatism, always inimical to the highest activity of the spirit.' [40]

Writing these articles gave Machado an opportunity to bring together two aspects of himself – the poet and the philosopher – and to consider the difference between them.

> The day may yet come, Mairena says to his students, when the poets will change places with the philosophers. The poets will sing of their wonderment in the presence of the great metaphysical adventure, especially that most supreme of all marvels: the power of contemplating being untrammelled by time, essence disengaged from existence – the fish in his element and out of it, as it were, viewing the very waters of the river as an illusion of fish. They will deck their lutes with garlands and chant the old miracles of human meditation.

> The philosophers, on the other hand, pondering like poets the *fugit irreparabile tempus*, will gradually muffle their viols with veils. And out of that romantic deviation an existentialist metaphysics will emerge, deeply rooted in time: something, in fact, more poetical than philosophical in character. For the philosophers will speak to us of our anguish, the essentially poetical anguish of being face to face with nothingness (*la nada*); while the poets will appear drunken with radiance, reeling under the old Eleatic superlatives. Thus poet and philosopher will confront each other, no longer enemies, each carrying forward the great labour where it is relinquished by the other.

> So spoke Mairena, anticipating, albeit vaguely, the vision of a poet, á la Paul Valéry, and a philosopher, á la Martin Heidegger.[41]

Heidegger, a man a few years younger than himself, had a profound influence on Machado's thinking. He evidently warmed to the German philosopher's differentiation between an 'authentic existence', which acknowledged the reality of guilt and dread, and an 'inauthentic existence', which forgot about such things in its absorption with the day to day affairs of the world.

Machado's contributions to the *Diario* under the pseudonym of Juan de Mairena were the subject of a conversation that he had with Juan Guerrero Ruiz, the critic that Lorca had christened 'the Consul-General of Spanish Poetry', who, one day in February 1935, called on the poet at the apartment he shared with his mother and his brother José's family in General Arrando. Machado referred to the articles rather dismissively as' old material', to which he had added very little because he was now not producing much new work. He seemed to be in low spirits and his visitor later described his appearance as 'lamentable'. 'As on other occasions he is wearing a rather dirty dust jacket, which makes him look poor and shabby. As he seems to be exhausted I ask him about his health, and he tells me that he is not well, for he has a liver disorder and has some bad days.' Later, as he took his leave after an affectionate farewell Guerrero said he felt 'depressed by the sad impression left upon me by my meeting with the great poet of *Soledades*.' [42]

A month or so after this encounter Machado had another visitor: Rosario del Olmo came to interview him for a periodical called *El Tiempo Presente*. When she asked him to specify the causes of the troubles that were then threatening the peace of the world the poet replied:

> One of them is hunger, whose origin lies in the uneven
> distribution of resources and population. Another
> is man's limited ability to imagine the horrors of
> war, without having the most immediate experience
> of them. Another is the confused ideology of the
> bourgeoisie, with its activist dogma and its cult of the

struggle for life. A final one is the irremediable barbarity
and sadism of the urban masses. [43]

In his interviews with the press, as in his articles in the *Diario de Madrid*, he wanted to emphasize that the basic problem was, as ever, man's egocentricity and his lack of brotherly love. For him, as for his great Russian mentor Tolstoy, the prime need was for people to obey the Christian injunction to love their neighbours – and their enemies – as themselves.

In one of the last of his articles in the *Diario* Machado paid tribute to Cossío, the art historian famed for his rediscovery of El Greco, who had died at the beginning of September.

> The spiritual grace of the great Spaniard lost to us today deserves something more than a niche in the ethopoetic succession of ordinary Spanish accomplishment. Hardly a portrait is left us that does him justice. The most acceptable, the work of an artist from Valencia, faithfully transcribes the refinements of his physical person, but nothing more. The expression is blundering and ineffectual, as though the hand of the painter still groped for a means of resolutely engaging that inward authority – unmarred by the slightest suggestion of pretension – we all came to see in him. The closest we can come to a likeness, it may be, is the figure of the Marqués de Espínola, receiving the keys to a conquered city, in Velázquez' portrait by that name. For the general depicted there seems to have triumphed by a twofold exertion of spirit and intelligence – to have understood fully that yesterday's triumph may well prove tomorrow's defeat; and he would know how to lose everything with identical elegance of spirit. So much Velázquez, that prince among painters, caught with his brush: the chivalry of triumph unsullied by vainglory – something at

once Castilian and deep in the Spanish grain itself, part of the essence of the man whose passing we lament today. It is right and expedient that we mourn him without stint or reservation, in the spirit of Shakespeare's speech for the grieving Romans on the occasion of Caesar's death: '… you are not stones, but men.' And to our spirit's bereavement we may even add a touch of that forgetfulness which refines all we remember.[44]

The death of Cossío was largely ignored by the right-wing press but was announced on the front pages of all the left wing papers. For republicans the news came as a shock, and thousands of them joined the funeral procession to the Civil Cemetery, where the great man's body was interred next to the tombs of Francisco Giner de los Ríos and Julián Sanz del Río. The press reported the presence among the mourners of 'the Machado brothers', by which they presumably meant Antonio, José and Manuel. They would doubtless have been mindful of the occasion, nearly thirty years earlier, when they had been at that cemetery for their grandfather's funeral, at which his friend Cossío had also been present.

Some of those who gathered at Cossío's funeral may have felt like marching again in the following month – this time not in sorrow but in anger – when they heard the news of Mussolini's invasion of Abyssinia. Machado was one of the signatories of a strongly worded protest, published in the *Diario de Madrid*, against the outrageous Italian action. The ultra-conservative satirical review, *Gracia y Justicia*, having asked why such 'a true intellectual and unique poet' should have lent his support to the manifesto, mockingly suggested the answer he would give: 'In Abyssinia there is no Instituto and therefore no teachers of French,' they imagined Machado replying. 'Since, here in Spain, I have not been able to free myself from either of them after all these years, I look forward to Negus coming to suppress them with one stroke of a pen.' [45] The poet might have had difficulty in seeing the point of the intended joke. He would certainly have been puzzled by the suggestion that he would welcome the arrival of the former Emperor of Abyssinia, since he himself had condemned his deposition so strongly.

That the *Diario* had been the only Madrid paper to publish the denunciation of Mussolini was due to the stringent press censorship exercised by a government that, for the previous two years, had been predominantly right-wing. But change, once again, was in the air. Azaña and others on the left were hard at work setting up a Popular Front in preparation for the elections due to be held in February 1936. Early January saw Spain in the grip of pre-electoral fever, and Machado was inevitably infected. On the 19th, in the column that he was now writing regularly in *El Sol*, he asked the question: 'What would Juan de Mairena have thought of this second Republic, which does not appear in any of his prophecies?' And he replied: 'When it was inaugurated he would have said: "Beware of historic self-styled republicanism, that ghost of the first Republic! Because the enemies of this second one will have made use of it, as the Greeks made use of that wooden horse whose belly was filled with those planning to enter Troy, open its gates and capture its citadel."'[46] The allusion is to Alejandro Lerroux, the prime minister whom Machado called a traitor for having included in his cabinet men who had not been republicans in 1931 and who were in fact 'the worst enemies of the people'. He once referred pejoratively to this unpopular politician as a decrepit old man with 'the soul of a whore'.[47]

In the February elections, to Machado's delight, Lerroux's centrist Radical party was annihilated. Now Spanish politics became polarized between the left, who gained 4,838,449 votes, and the right, who gained 3,996,931 – which meant that the Popular Front had 257 seats in the Cortes and the rest 196. But although it had a clear majority the Front was gravely weakened by internal divisions. The Socialists were divided over whether or not to form part of a 'bourgeois' government and in the end decided not to do so. Consequently Azaña, the prime minister, ended up presiding over a cabinet drawn largely from the Izquierda Republicana, the party to which, as has already been noted, Machado himself belonged. The poet was doubtless overjoyed when, as one of its first measures, the new government ordered the release of the thousands of political prisoners who had been incarcerated in the *bienio negro* – the name given to the 'two black years' that had preceded the February elections.

At this time, however, what most worried Machado was the rapid growth of the Falange, the right-wing movement recently founded by José Antonio Primo de Rivera, whom he would have remembered for his eloquent speech in praise of *La Lola*. Now the former dictator's son was using his oratory to inspire university students in Madrid and other cities to share his vision of a Spain set free from socialism and democracy. Although the violence he stimulated was at first rhetorical, it soon became physical, and the streets of Madrid were turned into scenes of conflict between the Falangists and their Socialist opponents. Sometimes there were assassination attempts, as on 7 April, when members of the Falange tried to blow up the house of Eduardo Ortega y Gasset, the brother of Machado's friend José. When later that month Pilar de Valderrama told the poet that she and her family were leaving Madrid because it was no longer safe to live there, she would have been voicing the fears of those on the left as well as those who, like her, were on the right of the political spectrum.

For those on the right one of the safest places to be at this time, as Pilar's husband clearly realized, was Portugal, where Salazar had set up a fascist dictatorship. Machado was appalled by the reports of the brutality of this regime and in May he helped to found an organization called the Comité de Amigos de Portugal. Its aim was to disseminate information about what was happening in that unhappy country and to garner support for its people. Naturally, when this 'Committee of Portugal's Friends' sent a letter of protest to Salazar, the poet's signature was on it. But when, on 4 July, a copy of the letter was published in the *Heraldo de Madrid*, few were aware that, at this very time, final preparations were being made for a military rebellion that would lead to a bloody civil war and to the subsequent establishment in Spain of a regime even worse than the one in Portugal.

VIII

Fighting against Fascism

One Sunday afternoon in July 1936 Manuel Machado arrived at the Madrid apartment that Antonio shared with his mother and with José's family. He had come, as was his custom on Sundays, to compare notes with Antonio about their current literary projects. José later recalled that he and his two brothers had sat huddled together around a table. 'I do not exaggerate', he wrote, 'when I say that we had to remove, or at least reduce, the wall of books that prevented us seeing each other's faces once we were seated. And amidst the cigarette smoke and the inevitable cups of coffee, the two poets were working on the plots of their plays and I was reading to them the drafts of the scenes that had been completed.'[1]

Although of course they could not have been aware of it when they said goodbye to each other that summer evening, the two poets, whom their friends described as 'inseparable', were never to meet again. A day or two later Manuel and his wife left by train for Burgos to celebrate the saint's day of her sister Carmen, a nun in the convent of the Sacred Heart. They intended to stay for only a few days but, on 18 July, shortly after their arrival, a group of disaffected generals headed by Francisco Franco staged a major rebellion against the legitimate Republican government. Encouraged by the Falange, the rebels organized a series of uprisings in garrison towns across Spain and within a few days had succeeded in seizing control of several of them. One of these was Burgos, an ultra-conservative city where, as a local aristocrat proudly proclaimed, 'the very stones are Nationalist'. [2] The outbreak of civil war led to the severing of the rail link with Madrid and so the Machados, unable to hire a car, had no alternative but to stay where they were. Manuel, whose republican sympathies were known to the rebels who now ruled Burgos, was for a time kept in custody, but, thanks to the efforts of his wife and sister-in-law, he was eventually set free. He obtained work as a proof reader on a local newspaper, and from then on it seems that his sympathies changed rather abruptly. By the end of August he had been enrolled in the ranks of the Falange and soon afterwards, when Franco's headquarters was established in the city, he became one of the principal spokesmen of his regime.

What is the explanation for this dramatic *volte-face*? In his *Vida de Antonio Machado y Manuel* Miguel Pérez Ferrero suggests that it was merely the result of a 'geographical caprice'. 'Destiny,' he wrote, 'has definitively divided the two brothers, the one who goes on a journey and the one who stays behind. Their stars, hitherto bent on the same course, are now separated and in the end the distance between them is infinite.'[3] It should be pointed out that he wrote this in 1947, at a time when no-one in Spain could speak freely about the Civil War and writers were often obliged to bury the truth.

One would certainly have expected both brothers to be staunchly Republican. Both were sons of a man who had once proudly proclaimed that 'Machados are in the world to fight tyranny and obscurantism'. As schoolboys, they had both imbibed the liberal political views of Francisco Giner de los Ríos at the Institución Libre de Enseñanza. As young men, they had both been associated with the publication of *Electra*, the scourge of Spain's political and ecclesiastical establishment, and in middle age they had both been opposed to the reactionary dictatorship of Primo de Rivera. Not long before the outbreak of war they had both been seen marching shoulder to shoulder with other republicans in the procession to Cossío's funeral. In fact, prior to the summer of 1936 the two brothers seem to have been inseparable, drinking in the same cafés, discussing the issues of the day in the same *tertulias*, co-operating in the production of the (frequently subversive) plays that made *los Machado* the talk of the town. Indeed, so close was Antonio to his elder brother that, when Pérez Ferrero told him that he planned to write his biography, he apparently only agreed to it on condition that the book also featured Manuel.

Although Manuel's inability to escape from Burgos may account for his initial failure to maintain his allegiance to the Republic, it does not explain why he later proceeded to become such an enthusiastic supporter of its enemies. Had he really shared his brother's strong liberal convictions he could never have brought himself to write and broadcast on behalf of Franco's regime. Had it been Antonio who had found himself stranded in Burgos, Seville, Cadiz or one or other of the cities that had declared for the rebels, it is inconceivable that he could ever have been made to support the Nationalists. He might perhaps have thought it expedient to moderate his republican enthusiasm – as he had earlier done in his conversations with Valderrama – but he would surely have died rather than put his pen at the service of the contemptible Caudillo. But in fairness to Manuel it needs to be remembered that he was not a completely free agent. Because he was married to Eulalia Cáceres, a devout Catholic who, like her sister, was to end her life as a nun, there were pressures on him to side with those committed to defending the Church.

Fortunately for Antonio there was nothing in his life to prevent him maintaining his allegiance to the Republican cause. On 31 July he was one of thirteen well-known intellectuals who put their signatures to a statement published in *El Sol*: 'We the undersigned declare that, in the conflict that is engulfing Spain, we are on the side of the Government, of the Republic and of the people, who with exemplary heroism are fighting for its freedom.'[4] As it turned out, five of the thirteen signatories – Ramón Menéndez Pidal, Ramón Pérez de Ayala, Juan Ramón Jiménez, José Ortega y Gasset and Gregorio Marañón – had so little confidence in the government that they left the country soon afterwards, with Ortega asserting that he had only signed the document under duress, 'with a pistol at my head.'[5] These men went into exile because they believed that their lives were in danger. Madrid was now in the grip of what came to be known as the Red Terror, with left-wing extremists attacking the homes of those suspected of disloyalty to the Republic. Since they operated on the principle that 'all those not for us are against us' many moderate republicans were unjustly accused of belonging to a 'fifth column' of fascist sympathizers.

'At the outbreak of the Civil War', writes the historian Raymond Carr, 'the middle classes were divided in their loyalties. The flower of middle-class civilization, the intellectuals, were uncertain in their allegiance: of the older generation only the great poet Machado was a convinced Republican.'[6] Machado, who abhorred any kind of violence, was unhappy about the activities of the militant Marxists, but what most upset him were the atrocities committed by Franco's rebels. He was profoundly distressed and greatly angered by the news, confirmed by the Madrid press on 8 September, that the fascists in Granada had assassinated his young friend and disciple García Lorca. 'Poor Granada!' he wrote in his diary that day. 'But poorer still if you are in any way to blame for his death. Because he is your Federico, your own Federico, and time will not dry his blood.' 'Yes, Granada,' he continued, 'Federico García Lorca was your poet. He was so much part of you that he had come to be your very heart – a heart pulsating through the length and breadth of Spain.'[7] In memory of him Machado wrote a poem, 'The crime was in Granada', published in October in the international journal *Ayuda: Semanario de la Solidaridad*. It was a long poem but the verse that the world would come to remember ran:

> Federico fell dead
> – blood on his face and lead in his guts –
> …Know that the crime was in Granada –
> poor Granada! –in his Granada.[8]

In the meantime Franco's troops continued their march towards Madrid and by early November they had reached Móstoles–on its southern outskirts. To provide air cover Germany and Italy had supplied fleets of planes that daily flew over the city dropping bombs or, alternatively, leaflets urging the citizens to surrender. It was at this critical time that Machado penned one of his most memorable verses:

Madrid! Madrid! How good your name sounds,
strong bulwark of all the lands of Spain!
The ground is churned up, the sky thunders,
yet you smile with lead in your guts![9]

Is it surprising, writing at a time when so many were being shot, that the poet should find himself repeating the evocative phrase, *plomo en las entrañas* – 'lead in the guts'?

In the course of November the aerial bombardment of Madrid continued apace and several buildings of major importance, including the Prado museum, the Biblioteca Nacional and the palace of the Duke of Alba, were damaged. Machado expressed his horror and detestation in a pamphlet entitled *El fascismo intenta destruir el Museo del Prado*. 'The love shown by the communist soldiers who are guarding the Duke of Alba's palace,' he wrote, 'is in sharp contrast to the fury of the fascists who are destroying it.'[10] On 19 November a periodical called *El Mono Azul*, the organ of the Alianza de Intelectuales Antifascistos para la Defensa de Cultura, published a manifesto condemning 'the pathological cruelty of the fascists'. It was addressed to intellectuals throughout the world – 'to all whose vision has not been impaired by egoism, cowardice and hypocrisy.'[11] The document was signed by Antonio Machado, María Teresa León, Rafael Alberti, León Felipe and several other well known writers.

On 21 November Machado was deeply saddened by the news that the celebrated sculptor Emiliano Barral, a friend from his Segovia days, had been killed in action on the outskirts of Madrid. His body was buried in the Civil Cemetery not far from the magnificent mausoleum of Pablo Iglesias that he himself had designed some years earlier. Machado later paid a fine tribute to him:

Emiliano Barral, captain of the Segovia militia, fell at
the gates of Madrid, defending his country against an
army of traitors, mercenaries and foreigners. He was
such a great sculptor that even his death left us with
an immortal engraving of his face.

> *And although his life ended*
> *his memory left us*
> *full of consolation.*

(Jorge Manrique)[12]

It was at this time that the men of the Quinto Regimiento, who
were defending Madrid, decided to evacuate those who, in their
judgment, represented the 'living culture' of Spain. Accordingly
Alberti and Felipe, wishing to persuade Machado to leave Madrid,
called at his apartment.

Out came Machado, tall and slow-moving, and behind
him, like the merest shadow of a branch, his ancient
mother. It was hard to understand how that fragile
little woman could have brought forth such a tall tree.
The house, like all houses, rich or poor, in Madrid in
those days, was freezing. Machado, preoccupied and
sad, heard what we had to say. Eventually he told us
that he did not believe the time had come for him to
abandon the capital. But what about the shortages and
the severity of the approaching winter? Such things,
he replied, he had endured all his life in Soria and
other towns and villages in Castile. He resisted the
idea of leaving. We had to pay him a second visit, this
time speaking with urgency. Now there was fighting
in the streets of Madrid and we did not wish to expose
him to the same fate as Federico.[13]

Whether it was the reference to the death of Lorca or some other
consideration that influenced him, in the end Machado reluctantly

agreed to go – provided that his *familia* was allowed to accompany him. Since this comprised not only his mother and his brother José and his wife and children but also the wife and children of Francisco (who, with Joaquín, had already moved with the government to Valencia) it constituted a party numbering eleven.

On 24 November, the day appointed for their departure, the Machados and the other families that were travelling with them were invited to a farewell lunch at the headquarters of the Quinto Regimiento and, at its conclusion, Antonio gave a vote of thanks. 'I might not have gone away,' he said; 'I am old and ill. But I wanted to fight alongside you. I wanted to die, as I have lived, with dignity. And that could only mean falling at your side, fighting like you for a just cause.'[14] At the end of his speech, according to the report in the *Heraldo de Madrid*, Tomás Navarro Tomás, director of the Biblioteca Nacional, shouted 'Viva el Quinto Regimiento!' 'It was a moment of great emotion. Many of those present were weeping, and men who had been in tough fights, in difficult situations, were visibly overwhelmed with grief.'[15] In the photograph taken on this occasion Machado is to be seen sitting in a place of honour next to the presiding *consejero*, the expression on his face one of sadness and quiet resignation. How else would a man look who had just been forcibly uprooted from his home, leaving behind him a fine library of books and other treasured possessions, and about to embark on a journey from which, as he may have foreseen, he would never return?

As soon as lunch was over the guests bade farewell to their hosts and prepared to depart from the city. They travelled in two large buses, escorted by a contingent of soldiers and four tanks. As José recalled, it was an uncomfortable journey.

> At dusk we departed for Tarancón, where we arrived at night and in time for supper, so to speak, before going to bed. Almost all of us on the expedition slept, or rather tried to sleep, in one very large unfurnished bedroom, on mattresses on the bare floor. Our attempt

to get a good night's rest was rendered impossible by some picturesque little incidents.[16]

José gave no clue as to the nature of these 'incidents' that he, with his artist's eye, deemed 'picturesque'.

Next day the party set off again, but they had only got as far as Contreras when the bus the Machados were travelling in, which seems to have lagged behind the other one, came to a sudden halt. 'Our vehicle,' Francisco's daughter Leonor remembered, 'had a breakdown; its engine began to get overheated or something; there was a great hole in the road, and we were unable to continue. Hours passed and no-one picked us up. We tried to halt a car, but it didn't stop and, as we later discovered, subsequently crashed. There was no food and there were no restaurants, nothing. We were quite stupefied. There were six of us girls altogether: I and my sisters Ana and Mercedes, and our cousins Eulalia, Carmen and María, the daughters of Uncle José and Aunt Matea.'[17] But it turned out all right in the end, as José recalled. 'We were able to commandeer a small private car in Utiel, a nearby village, and go back to pick up my mother and the poet, who, ill and worn out by travelling, were in a very weak state.'[18] It is not clear what happened thereafter, but eventually they were all able to get safely to Valencia, where they were installed in the Palace Hotel, which had been renamed the Casa de la Cultura in their honour.

At a press conference soon after their arrival in Valencia, Machado spoke about the aerial bombardment of Madrid. He pointed to the damage done – deliberately, in his judgment – to buildings of great cultural significance. He made the same point in an article on the subject that he wrote in English – a language of which he clearly had a good (if not entirely faultless) command:

> The fascist army appears to pursue with special insistance (*sic*) the systematic destruction of our glorious tradition (*sic*) culture. Without the efforts made by our Government and the vigilance to (*sic*)

the people, the artistic wealth of the Prado Museum would have disappeared already many months ago. The Titian's, the Greco's, the Ruben's, the Velásquez's, all the treasures of our admirable picture-galleries would have been devoured by fire. The teutonic cruelty, the stupidity of our phalangists, the impetuous insolence of degraded Italy under the orders of a deified porter, give themselves up entirely, united in a stream of savageness, brutality and cowardice, to dangerless (*sic*) crime and irreparable damage, and at the same time destroy part of the spiritual patrimony of the entire humanity.[19]

If this article, which was probably written in June 1936, had ever come to the notice of people in Britain, it would have upset lovers of art but it would almost certainly not have caused as much distress as the reports of the numbers of civilians who were being killed or wounded in the bombing in Spain.

It was partly because it was thought that in due course the bombing would be extended to Valencia that the Machados were moved out to the village of Rocafort, where they were lodged in the Villa Amparo. Since it was close to the station, which was a mere twenty-minute train ride from the centre of the city, it was easy for Francisco and Joaquín to commute to work daily. The large house was surmounted by a turret that commanded a fine view of the surrounding countryside. Antonio would sometimes climb up to admire the view, but what he most loved was the garden, where there were orange and lemon trees that reminded him of his boyhood in Seville. He was also delighted by the little watercourse that ran past the garden: 'since childhood', as José commented, 'he had been enthralled by water and it continued to feature prominently in his poetry.'[20]

Only on rare occasions did he go into Valencia, but he did so on 11 December, when the government staged a grand *tribuna* or 'public speech-making' in a square in the centre of the city. A huge crowd gathered, the band of the Quinto Regimiento played martial music and a film depicting scenes of the civil war was projected on to a large screen. Following the speeches Machado went to the podium and recited 'The crime was in Granada'. Among those listening was José Bergamín, Lorca's friend and publisher, who later recorded his impression of the occasion:

> At midday I saw the poet go up to a little platform erected in the middle of the largest *plaza* in Valencia. Around him there was a great throng of people. It looked as if he were standing on a scaffold. But his voice did not choke; on the contrary he spoke from up there with such power that his habitual reticence deserted him, or rather, he became so fired with emotion that he was able to express the intense feelings that were being experienced by everyone in Spain. The poet spoke of the death of Federico García Lorca. And those of us who were listening to that voice, which we had so often heard speak in the language of intimacy and solitude, now heard it for the first time ringing out with perfect precision and absolute truthfulness. His voice was charged with anger, for he was in touch with something much deeper than his own invisible personal life – the collective life, now made visible by his words, of a whole nation. The multitude became manifest in one man; when he spoke, he did so not only as a single individual but on behalf of a single people.[21]

The citizens of Valencia were never again to hear Machado's voice ringing out in this way. In the following March, when he was asked to speak at a festival arranged by a left-wing relief organization called Socorro Rojo Internacional in aid of the victims of fascism, he declined the invitation but he sent a new poem to be read out by someone else. It was entitled 'Today's meditation'

In front the palm tree of fire,
which the setting sun is leaving,
on a silent late afternoon,
in this garden of peace,
while flowery Valencia
drinks the Guadalaviar waters –
Valencia of slender towers,
in the lyrical sky of Ausias March,
changing its river into roses
before it gets to the sea –
I think of the war. The war
comes like a hurricane
through the barren lands of the upper Duero,
through the fields of standing wheat,
from fertile Extremadura
to these gardens with tribes of lemon trees,
from grey skies of the north
to the marshes of light and salt.
I think of Spain, all of it sold out,
from river to river, mountain to mountain, sea to
sea.[22]

The poem was followed by a long passage of prose in which he drew a comparison between those who had 'sold the whole of Spain to Europe's reactionaries' and the treacherous Judas Iscariot, who had betrayed Christ in return for thirty pieces of silver.[23]

Not long afterwards *El Pueblo*, the Valencian daily, published a manifesto that Machado and four others had addressed to 'the students, artists, scientists and writers of rebellious Spain' and which, it reported, had been widely distributed throughout the regions controlled by the fascists. 'We call on your Spanish conscience', they wrote. 'Do not betray us who have been betrayed. Do not betray Spain's past or its future. Do not, by your complicity, assist the enemies of our native land – those who want to turn it into a foreign country's colony.'[24] It is possible that the manifesto, printed in the form of leaflets, had been dropped from the air on towns and cities in western and north-western Spain. In this way people may have come to realize, if they did not already know it, that the nation's greatest living poet remained a strong supporter of its legitimate Republican government.

This was a matter of great importance since another Machado, who was also a famous poet, was becoming well known as a fascist propagandist. In January 1937 Manuel had published a poem entitled 'Spain!' in the *ABC* of Seville, where he spoke of 'the elegance/ with which Seville "fought" Death', employing the verb *"toreó"* to indicate the bloody similarities between this fight and one staged in a bull ring. In the same poem he went so far as to hail Franco's Spain as a 'bulwark/ against Europe's Asiatic plague'.[25] As well as writing, Manuel made regular radio broadcasts from Burgos, in which he sang the praises of the man he called the 'Caudillo of the new *Reconquista*', thus likening the dictator to those who, four centuries earlier, had driven the heathen out of Spain. It is not known whether Antonio heard his brother's voice on the wireless, but he certainly read what he wrote in the press. Indications of how he felt about this can be found in a poem, which is evidently addressed to Manuel, published towards the end of his time at Rocafort in *Hora de España*:

> Yesterday again. Behind the blinds,
> music and sun; in the nearby garden,
> within a hand's reach, the golden fruit;
> and pure blue slumbering in the fountain.
>
> The Seville of my childhood! so Sevillian!
> How time gnaws at your memory in vain!
> So much our own! Just remember that, brother.
> We don't know whose it will be tomorrow.
>
> Somebody sold the sacred hearthstone
> to the weighty Teuton, to the ravenous Moor,
> and the gates of the sea to the Italian.

Hate and fear to the redeeming race
that grinds the fruit of the olive groves
and fasts and tills and sows and sings and weeps! [26]

The final tercet of the sonnet, as James Whiston has pointed out, echoes the memorable words spoken in Valencia in July 1937 by Manuel Azaña, the President of the Republic: 'Hate and fear, the causes of pain's misfortune, are men's worst advisers in private and, above all, in public affairs.'[27]

Machado's feelings about his brother Manuel's defection, as expressed in this poem, help to explain why visitors to Rocafort found him looking so weak and sad. One young man, the philosopher Vicente Gaos, was shocked by his appearance:

> My immediate impression on meeting Don Antonio was of a man much older than I had imagined, judging by recent pictures of him. His back was bent and he dragged his feet as he walked. His appearance was exactly as it has been described – 'clumsy and awkwardly attired'. Here was a man who did not care what he looked like. His weariness and exhaustion were apparent from the unsteadiness of his hand as he autographed our books. I remember that, in order to write, he put on spectacles, while explaining to us that his sight was now not good enough for him to be able to work without them.[28]

Another young visitor, the Valencian writer Juan Gil-Albert, also remarked on the poet's unkempt appearance. He noted 'the unbuttoned collar, the untied shoelaces, the drooping lips, the greying hair. In the slanting rays of sunlight coming through the window there could be seen on his shoulder a sprinkling of white dust that, deposited at this altitude around the head from which so much creativity had flowed, made one think metaphorically of lava from a volcano.'[29] The dust, of course, was the ash from the cigarettes that he was continuously smoking. 'In the last days of the war,' José recalled, 'he used to puff away more than ever. And on days when he had no tobacco he used to search eagerly for his own half-smoked cigarettes, so that he could finish them off.' He said that, when he was working, 'tobacco was so essential that he had hardly finished one cigarette before he was lighting another, even though it was bad for his health'.[30] He was also addicted to coffee, often drinking eight or ten cups a day.

Among all those who called at the Villa Amparo the one who provided the fullest account of his visit was Pascual Pla y Beltrán, a young writer from Alicante, who came to see the poet in August 1937 and found him sitting with his brother José at a little table in front of the house. He recalled that when Antonio spoke – 'in his clear resonant voice and with a slight Andalusian accent' – he kept turning for confirmation to his brother, who indicated his agreement with a word or a gesture or a smile. 'This place is beautiful', he said, 'very beautiful. It is like a little piece of paradise. The gardens are aflame with reds and greens and yellows. The irrigation channels, with their reddish water, flow gracefully – like veins bringing life-blood to the body of this land. How men must have laboured to achieve this! The Valencians are proud of their land, which they don't treat roughly but tenderly, as though caressing a little child. But this blessed land, which I love and admire, is not like that of Castile – broad, hard, ascetic and combative. Castile made Spain what it is! It is possible that without Castile these orange trees would not now be shedding their blossom beneath these skies.' And he went on to meditate aloud, in language more akin to poetry than prose, about the contrast between these two regions of Spain. 'Castile', he concluded. 'is conquest, expansion, faith, the absolute. Valencia is labour, constancy and the conservation of what it was conquered for. Castile is the spirit of Spain!'[31]

Machado then continued at some length to consider how and why Spain had got into its present predicament:

> The betrayed and slandered generation of '98, in
> which I am included, has surpassed everyone in its love
> for Spain and has grieved for it ...as no-one has ever
> before grieved for any country. But we Spaniards have
> dreamed too much of superabundance and have been
> living on the seemingly miraculous achievements
> of our forebears. Our dreams were shattered by the
> bankruptcy of our remaining overseas enterprises.
> The overwhelming reality of our failures showed
> us that, with toy swords, one could fight but never
> conquer. We recalled our ships, the few battered ones
> that still remained to us, and headed back to port. At
> this point we had to come to terms with our situation.
> Our universality, the universality of Spain, cannot
> now be a physical universality, but a spiritual one. Let
> us not deceive ourselves.[32]

After listening to the poet's views on the current state of Spain,
Pla y Beltrán sought to turn the conversation to more personal
matters. 'What news of your brother Manuel?' he asked. Machado's
face lit up, but he did not answer the question directly. 'It is for me
a tremendous misfortune to be separated from Manuel', he replied.
'He is a great poet. And, besides being my brother, he has been my
faithful collaborator in a series of theatrical works; without his drive
those works would not have been written.' He paused briefly before
continuing: 'Life is sometimes cruel; sometimes it is extremely hard.
But this suffering of ours, deep though it is, is as nothing compared
with the catastrophe that is about to fall upon mankind. However,
when I think about the possibility of being banished to some country
other than this tortured land of Spain, my heart is troubled and
stricken with grief. I am certain that, for me, exile would mean
death.'[33]

Because of his increasingly poor health the poet rarely left
Rocafort, but that summer he did agree to go into Valencia to attend
the second International Congress of Writers for the Defence of

Culture. Here he rubbed shoulders with distinguished literary figures from several other countries, including André Malraux and Julien Benda from France, Mijail Koltsov and Alexis Tolstoy from Russia, W. H. Auden and Stephen Spender from England, Pablo Neruda from Chile and Malcolm Cowley from the United States. In his own contribution – the concluding address of the congress – he strongly criticized the custom of referring to the people as 'the masses'. With Ortega y Gasset's recently published book, *The Revolt of the Masses*, clearly in mind, he said that the term was used in good faith by 'many of our good friends' who did not realize that it came from 'the enemy camp'. It was beloved of the capitalist bourgeoisie, who exploited and degraded humanity, and by the Church, which was only interested in power but claimed to exist 'for the salvation of the masses'. And in language reminiscent of that of his father, whose nom de plume was *Demófilo* ('friend of the people'), he made this passionate declaration:

> If you address the masses, the individual man will not listen to you nor feel that you are referring to him, and will therefore turn his back on you. This is the evil implicit in a false catch-phrase that we, being incorrigible *demófilos* and enemies of all cultural snobbery, should never willingly employ, out of a respect and love for the people that our adversaries will never feel.[34]

In the photograph taken of those attending the congress Machado looked old, ill, tired and diminished in size. As his brother José recalled, he seemed to be shrinking:

> Each day his coat seemed bigger and he smaller. It was on account of the cold, which made him shrink into himself, and because his body was wasting away, not so much under the weight of the years – he was now sixty – as through the depletion of his physical energy. We have to bear in mind that he used to be

the tallest of all the brothers and that, when he was younger, he cut a fine figure. But if his body had been so perceptibly worn away by infirmity, his brain, by contrast, continued to function lucidly until the last days of his life.[35]

In spite of his physical decline Machado continued to dedicate his remaining energy and skill to supporting the Republican cause. In the autumn of 1937 he was a principal contributor to a booklet published by the government's information office entitled *Madrid: Baluarte de nuestra Guerra de Independencia*, designed to demonstrate that, as during the war of independence from the French in Napoleonic times, in the current conflict Madrid remained the country's chief bulwark against alien invaders. Here the poet reproduced his famous little 'Madrid, Madrid' poem and wrote a new article expressing his contempt for the fascist traitors and their allies – 'the Italians, magnificently equipped militarily in the service of a jumped-up errand boy' and 'the sagacious executioners of the human race in the pay of ambitious Germans'.[36] He said that Spain was now fighting not only for its own salvation but for that of all humanity.

The end of the year saw the publication of Machado's book, *La Guerra (1936-1937)*, containing reprints of all the poems and articles that he had published in newspapers and reviews since the outbreak of war. In addition to 'Today's meditation' there was a beautiful poem, simply entitled 'Song':

> Now the moon is climbing
> over the orange grove.
> Venus shines like
> a tiny glass bird.
>
> Behind the far range
> the sky amber and beryl,
> and purple porcelain
> on the quiet sea.

Now night is in the garden,
water in its stone gutters!
Only a smell of jasmine,
nightingale of perfumes.

How the war seems
asleep from sea to sea,
while blossoming Valencia
drinks the Guadalaviar!

Valencia of slender towers
and tender nights, Valencia,
I shall be with you,
when I cannot see you,
where sand grows on the land
and gone is the violet sea.[37]

The book was handsomely illustrated with pen and ink sketches by José Machado, including six of Villa Amparo and its surrounding countryside. Since it had great propaganda value it may have been published with financial support from the government. It was well received. The young María Zambrano, daughter of Antonio's old Segovia friend and colleague Blas Zambrano, wrote a glowing review in *Hora de España* in which she said that the terrible circumstances in which the Spanish were now living had given a new and powerful relevance to the poet's words. 'In Machado's fatherly words we find a parental wisdom that is both acute and consolatory, and can at times be profoundly melancholy; in giving us certainty they provide us with security'. She went on to say that the man whom she described as 'both ancient and modern' was 'the poet of a whole nation' – a nation that stood wholly behind him.[38]

Machado was deeply moved by the article and sent her a letter of thanks, asking her to remember him warmly to her father. 'Tell him that, a few nights ago, I dreamed that we met again in Segovia, free from fascists and reactionaries, as in the good times when he

and I, with other old friends, were working for the future Republic.'
They had bumped into each other at the Roman aqueduct, where
Zambrano, pointing to the arches, had shouted: 'You see, friend
Machado, how important it is to love things that are big and beautiful,
because that aqueduct is the only friend we have left in Segovia.' [39]
Zambrano had left Segovia when war broke out and was now living
in Barcelona, where the Republican government had been located
since October. By Christmas 1937 Machado suspected that he too
would soon have to move there. At the beginning of February, as the
Nationalist army was advancing triumphantly on Teruel, he was told
that he and his family must get ready to go to Barcelona. Machado's
reaction was negative. 'Although I am always at the government's
disposal,' he wrote, 'I prefer to stay in these surroundings, which are
more peaceful than those of Barcelona.' [40] But now there was not
much peace at night when there were air raids on Valencia.

It was Machado's custom to stay up much of the night writing
and one noisy night in March 1938 he wrote no fewer than four
sonnets. The first sonnet was 'Spring', in which the beauty of the
season is contrasted with the ugliness of war. The second one, 'The
poet recalls the land of Soria' is occasioned by the thought that one of
the planes bombing Valencia might be on its way to Soria. Although
the third one, 'Dawn in Valencia' makes no mention of the war, it
is followed by a fourth that tells of its tragedies. 'The death of the
wounded child' is the most poignant of all Machado's war poems:

> It's night time again... It's the hammering
> of the fever in the bandaged temples
> of the boy. 'Mother! The yellow bird!
> The butterflies are black and purple!'
>
> 'Sleep, my son.' The mother at the bedside
> squeezes the little hand. 'Oh, fiery flower!
> Flower of my blood, who is making you shiver?'
> There is a scent of lavender in the tiny sick-room,

and, outside, the rounded moon is whitening
the towers and cupolas of the darkened city.
An aeroplane, invisible, buzzes like a fly.

'Are you sleeping, sweet flower of my blood?'
The balcony window is rattling.
'Oh, cold, cold, cold, cold, cold.' [41]

Machado used the sonnet form for all the nine poems he wrote
in 1938. As Willis Barnstone points out, he 'made of the sonnet a
complete vehicle for his final poetic expression, using it in sequence
for his fields of Spain, his woman in open-eyed dream and his
fields of war.'[42] Why did he adopt the form? The reason may be, as
James Whiston has suggested, that what the poet termed its 'baroque
mould' enabled him to 'avoid the emotional rhetoric that the war
demanded'. 'Machado', he says, 'was able to use the sonnet form
to express a wide range of emotions and ideas, personal and civic,
and was able to achieve an overall clarity in his view of the deepest
circumstances of the war and its highest aims.' [43]

In mid-April, soon after he penned these sonnets, Machado
received a telegram from the government informing him that he
must move forthwith to the Catalan capital and that an official car
had been made available for the purpose. Since there was a danger
of the road being blocked by the enemy he had no alternative but to
obey instructions and leave the house and garden at Rocafort that he
had come to love so dearly. And so, without further ado, the party
of four adults and three children made ready to depart for Barcelona,
where Francisco and Joaquín were already living. On their journey
to the city, as José recalled, the poet was in contemplative mood:

That evening, in spite of the atrocious conditions in
which the journey was undertaken and of the poor
state of his health, he seemed to be absorbed in the
contemplation of the twilight. It was just another
sunset, but this one seemed to weigh on his spirit.

Now it was his life that was approaching its end. After
the sun had set he began to feel the cold that heralded
the night. The first shadows fell on the road ahead.
We caught our first glimpse of the lights of the city.
Barcelona at last![44]

It is understandable that, because of war-time restrictions, the
poet's second arrival in the Catalan capital did not receive the same
attention from the local press as his first visit, ten years earlier, had
done. But shortly before his arrival the city's principal newspaper,
La Vanguardia, welcomed him as a contributor to its columns. In an
introduction to his first article the editor wrote:

> *La Vanguardia* is greatly honoured to publish this
> article by Don Antonio Machado, which marks
> the beginning of its association with this most
> glorious of contemporary Spanish poets. This brief
> announcement would normally suffice as a welcome
> to a new contributor, but, besides being a great
> writer, Don Antonio is one of the most distinguished
> examples of what the Spanish tragedy has produced.
> Don Antonio, weighed down by age and infirmity,
> and loaded with honours, has renounced his right to
> rest, maintains the youthful vigour and heroism of the
> liberal spirit that has informed his life and, to his own
> surprise, his pen retains the elegance and grace of his
> finest hours. With Don Antonio Machado a writer
> and a man have arrived. We bid them both welcome.[45]

On their arrival Antonio, his mother, José, Matea and the three
girls were accommodated in the Majestic Hotel, but the place was
not to the poet's liking. According to José the hotel was as crowded
and noisy as a railway station, with all kinds of people perpetually
coming and going. For Antonio the only consolation was that he
now had many opportunities of speaking with some of the more

congenial guests, who included León Felipe and José Bergamín, whom he had got to know well in Valencia, and with the American hispanist, Waldo Frank.

After a month in the hotel the Machados were provided with what the authorities considered to be more suitable and secure accommodation in La Torre Castañer, an 18th century palace on the outskirts of the city that had been confiscated from the Marquesa de Moragas. But they were depressed rather than impressed by the mansion's baroque splendour. Its vast reception rooms were festooned with cornucopias, mirrors in gilded frames, ancestral portraits and lithographs that had turned yellow with age. The only signs of life were provided by huge spiders, which were everywhere spinning their webs. The palace was set in spacious grounds, but its ornamental gardens, so long neglected, were a sorry sight. The patios lacked the charm of those that Machado remembered from his childhood at Las Dueñas. It seems that what pleased him most about the palace was a glazed *galería* where he would often sit and enjoy the sun.

In July 1938, on the second anniversary of the fascist rebellion, he wrote an article for a weekly called *Voz de Madrid*, which was published in Paris. Its aim was to tell the outside world what was actually happening in Spain and to muster French and British support for the Republican cause.

> We are fighting against traitors from within and robbers from outside our country; against scattered groups of soldiers who, because of their treason and cruelty, have forfeited the right to call themselves Spaniards, and against armed forces (no less vile, but much more powerful) that German racism, Italian fascism and Moorish avidity have introduced into Spain, with the help of a servile little nation and the diplomatic hypocrisy of conservative elements in the democracies of western Europe. [46]

In this article, and in others that he wrote at this time, Machado had many harsh things to say about foreign countries. The worst, of course, were Germany and Italy, who had invaded the sovereign territory of Spain, and Portugal, the 'servile little nation' that was supporting them. But almost as reprehensible were the two leading democracies of western Europe that had decided not to intervene in the war and, in so doing, were lending tacit support to the fascists. The poet was especially critical of France, which had a Popular Front government and was geographically well placed to come to Spain's aid. But he was also very disappointed that no help was forthcoming from Britain, 'a democracy from whom we have learned something and could learn much more'. [47] He placed the blame on Neville Chamberlain who, he contended, resembled a character in a Dickens novel – 'not the honourable and ingenuous Mr Pickwick, but Penknife' (which was presumably a reference to the arch-hypocrite Pecksniff in *Martin Chuzzlewit*).[48] Alternatively, he suggested, the British premier might have walked off the stage of a Shakespeare play. 'Beyond the boundaries of Spain, in fogbound Albion', wrote Machado, 'there is someone who does not sleep because, like Macbeth, he has murdered a dream – this time not in a Scottish castle but in the heart of the City.'[49] In citing Dickens and Shakespeare, whose works he was then re-reading, his memory (or a faulty Spanish translation) sometimes let him down. What Macbeth had actually murdered was not 'a dream' (*un sueño*) but 'sleep' (*el sueño*); but for the poet, who believed that Chamberlain had destroyed people's *dreams* of a better world, the mistake was understandable and excusable. It is to be noted that he wrote 'the City' in English and with a capital 'C', thus making it clear that, in his view, the British prime minister was in hock to London's influential moneymen.

Chamberlain, who featured in many of his articles in *La Vanguardia*, could be described as Machado's *bête noire*. It is significant that, in his final contribution to the Barcelona daily, published on 6 January 1939 – the last words he ever wrote for publication – he should have taken a swipe at him:

> Chamberlain's politics are characterized by an
> unflagging determination to navigate muddy waters,
> by the constant concealment of his motives and by his
> total blindness regarding the future of Europe and,
> primarily, the future of England.[50]

Here he was writing more as a prophet than a poet. He clearly
foresaw that, by trying to appease Hitler, the British government was
storing up a multitude of troubles for itself.

Machado was equally scathing about the attitude of 'the so-
called League of Nations', whose members at a recent meeting in
Geneva had ignored the pleas of the Spanish delegate, Julio Álvarez
del Vayo, for help in the fight against European fascism. Instead
they had listened to the advice of Georges Bonnet, who represented
France, and Lord Halifax, who spoke for Britain, and voted for
non-intervention. The poet dismissed these statesmen's speeches as
'two pieces of the most vulgar diplomatic oratory, which did not
even try to convince anyone'. He said it was unfortunate that the
voices of two such great nations should have come through 'the
mouths of the *homunculos* that are professing to represent them'. He
reflected that, in the 1914-18 War, Britain and France had eventually
been victorious because they had 'moral reason' on their side. But
the League of Nations, which had come into existence in order to
prevent the outbreak of any more such wars, had no regard for ethical
considerations. 'Wherever reason and morality are pensioned off', he
concluded, 'only bestiality retains its employment.'[51]

Meanwhile the war against bestiality continued relentlessly
and Machado, who read the newspapers and listened to the radio
broadcasts put out by both sides, was following events very closely.
Towards the end of July he was greatly encouraged by the news
of the battle of the Ebro, where the Republicans had succeeded
in halting the Nationalist advance on Valencia. 'Whatever is the
final result of the contest,' he wrote, '– and I have never had any
doubt of our victory – the battle of the Ebro is a magnificent and
universally significant event, consoling us with the possibility that

justice will triumph over iniquity.' [52] Writing pieces for the press that were designed to raise its readers' morale he had to appear to be confident of victory, but he clearly did have doubts. As has been seen, even before he moved to Barcelona he had been talking about the possibility of being driven into exile.

In an article in *Hora de España* written in August 1938 he criticized those Spanish intellectuals who were at best only half-hearted in their support for the Republican cause. He had some sympathy with 'the philosopher who, in order to meditate about the war, requires a measure of detachment' from it, but it could be argued, on the contrary, that 'all deep insight involves (and we apologize for the horrid jargon) the existential'.

> And perhaps there is something frivolous about the position of the philosopher who thinks that war is an intrusion, coming by surprise to disturb the rhythm of his meditations. Because we have all caused the war to happen (and it is right that we all should suffer) it is an episode in the great controversy that constitutes the life of our society; and no-one with a modicum of moral sense can believe himself to be completely free from responsibility. And if we regard the war as an unexpected irruption in the flow of our meditations, if the war takes us so completely by surprise that we have to revise our way of thinking about it, this indicates that our thinking is shoddy and in need of improvement, and that we should throw some of our useless academic papers into the wastepaper basket.[53]

As Ian Gibson points out, 'the philosopher' in question was almost certainly José Ortega y Gasset, 'whose silence is creating a serious dilemma for our poet'.[54] Now living in exile in Paris, the distinguished scholar, whose two sons were serving in Franco's army, had abandoned his support for the Republican cause and had adopted a neutral stance that some perceived to be pro-fascist.

In addition to writing regularly for *Hora de España* and *La Vanguardia* the poet on one occasion gave an interview to a reporter from *La Voz de Madrid*. In the course of the meeting, which took place in La Torre Castañer at the beginning of October 1938, he talked about his schooldays at the Institución Libre and the influence of Giner de los Ríos and other outstanding teachers. 'It is therefore not difficult to deduce', he said, 'that my education had to be liberal and republican and therefore had to be in line with my family's political history, seeing that my father and my grandfather were fervent republicans.' When asked about his time in Soria he spoke of his wife, 'whom I loved passionately and whose death shattered me', and of his walks in the countryside. 'I went up Urbión, to the source of the Duero', he recalled. 'I made excursions to Salas, scene of the tragic legend of the Infants. And that led to my writing the poem about Alvargonzález.' The journalist reported that the poet's reminiscences were then brought to a close by the sudden appearance of his mother, 'an ancient and venerable lady, who crept in silently and remained very still, with the weightlessness of a bird', and was followed by 'some happy and unruly little girls, who reminded the master that it was lunchtime'.[55] But the girls, who were the daughters of José and Matea, were not to remain happy and unruly for long; their parents had regretfully decided to send them to safety in France in the company of some old and trusted friends, who were to arrange for them to take refuge in Russia. It appears that the choice of Russia was Antonio's: even if he had any awareness of what was happening in that country under Stalin he evidently continued to believe that things could not go far wrong in the land of Dostoevsky, Turgenev and Tolstoy.

After the departure of his three boisterous nieces the poet must have found La Torre Castañer eerily quiet. At this stage he rarely left the house and kept out of the political controversies that were then raging in Barcelona. There is no truth in the report, circulated in the city at this time, that he had attended a great banquet organized by local communists and had there and then been signed up as a member of their party. But the rumour was evidently believed by Enrique

Castro Delgado, the fanatical ex-communist author of *Hombres made in Moscú*, who called on Machado in order to protest that he had been made 'the prisoner of a great lie' and to point out that Moscow did not care two hoots about Spain or democracy. 'The lie had done its work', Castro wrote later. 'It had stupefied a man who, that apart, was one of Spain's greatest poets and had made him so blind that he could not see what was really happening.' Machado, he contended, 'had been incarcerated in an invisible prison where he spoke only with his gaolers, lived only with his gaolers, listened only to his gaolers who brought food and tobacco to him in that house that was far too grand for people who were so old and so accustomed to plain living.'[56] That Castro should have included the poet among 'the men made in Moscow' shows how little he really knew about Machado. It was clear from his writings and from his radio broadcast 'Calling all Spaniards' made in November 1938 that, although a great admirer of Russia and of some aspects of Marxism, Machado was not – and could never be – a card-carrying member of the Communist Party.

Other visitors to La Torre Castañer, however, were more agreeable than the cantankerous Castro. They included Machado's old friend Tomás Navarro Tomás, the celebrated phonologist, who brought recordings from his collection of folk-songs, and the philosopher Joaquín Xirau, rector of the University of Barcelona, who played Catalan dance tunes on an old piano belonging to the *marchesa*. But, because of the poet's poor health, the most frequent visitor seems to have been José Puche Álvarez, the government's *Director General de Sanidad*, who was also his personal physician. Years later the doctor shared his memories of Machado. 'I felt for him the great admiration that all Spaniards had for him. It was perhaps because of this admiration that I had imagined him to be a strong, powerful man. I soon realized that what I had in front of me was a worn-out machine... I was helping Don Antonio more as a friend than as a doctor, since he possessed the understanding of an intelligent patient and I had such a tolerant attitude to him that I reached an agreement with him that he could sometimes disobey my instructions.' Puche never forgot Machado's affection for his family and his extraordinary dignity in the face of suffering. He also recalled that his mother looked after him 'like a very young child, preferring him to her other sons, because he was the *sick son*'.[57]

Looking back on his time in Barcelona, Puche recalled that he had made professional visits to three illustrious people. He described the first, whom he did not name, as being 'restless, impatient, giving clear indications that he wanted to escape quickly from the beleaguered city'. The second, also not identified, who was physically stronger and in better health, had lost his habitual confidence, 'although nobly pulling himself out of his momentary bouts of depression'. The third was Antonio Machado, who remained so serene and calm in that time of crisis that he seemed to embody 'the most authentic expression of the Spanish soul'.[58]

Another impression of Machado's state at this time was provided by the Russian writer and journalist Ilya Ehrenburg, who visited him towards the end of 1938. He had not seen him since the summer and was shocked by his appearance. 'Machado did not look well: his back was bent and his face unshaven, which made him appear to be even older. He was 63 and he walked very slowly. The only part of him that was fully alive were his eyes, which were bright and sparkling.' He read some verses to his visitor – those famous lines of Jorge Manrique that liken life to a river running down to 'the sea that is our dying' – and said that foreigners were wrong to regard the Spanish as 'fatalists who accept death with resignation'; on the contrary, he insisted, 'we Spaniards know how to fight against death.' Reflecting on the current fight against fascism he recalled that, during the battle of the Ebro, a Republican officer had recited one of his poems to his men: 'The Spain of El Cid, the Spain of 1808, acknowledges you as her sons.'

When the journalist was about to leave. Machado turned to him and gave him his verdict on the war which, as he was now well aware, would soon be ending:

> Perhaps, after all, we never learned how to fight a
> war. Apart from that, we were lacking armaments.

> But we must not judge Spaniards too harshly. This
> is the end, whenever it is that Barcelona falls. For
> strategists, for politicians, for historians, it will all be
> clear: we have lost the war. But, in human terms, I
> am not so sure... Perhaps we have won it.

He then accompanied his visitor to the front door: 'I turned round,' wrote Ehrenburg, 'and looked at this sad stooping man, as old as Spain, this gentle poet. And I saw his eyes, set so deep that they never gave an answer, but on the contrary were perpetually asking something, only God alone knows what...I looked at him for the last time. A siren was sounding. The bombing began again.'[59]

A few weeks later, when the bombing of Barcelona reached an unprecedented level of intensity and the Nationalists were advancing rapidly on the city, the Machados were told to be prepared to leave for France at a moment's notice.

IX

Exile and Death

At midnight on 22 January 1939 an official car, which had been placed at the Machados' disposal, arrived at La Torre Castañer. Soon afterwards it was joined by another, in which Dr Puche and Joaquín Xirau and his wife were travelling, and also by an ambulance full of intellectuals and professionals. At 3 am the caravan moved off and followed the coast road as far as Malgrate de Mar, where it turned inland and proceeded to Girona. As Xirau later recalled, the city was jammed with vehicles of every description belonging to people fleeing towards France. 'Enormous lorries carrying crates, armchairs, wheels and propellers, filing cabinets, typewriters … blocked the way. In spite of the traffic jam the silence was impressive. We were held up there for some hours. It was impossible to move. There was an atmosphere of weariness and fear.'[1]

Eventually the caravan was able to set off again and in due course reached Cervià del Ter, about ten kilometers beyond Girona. Here the mayor welcomed the refugees and provided them with a hot meal before conducting them to a commodious farmhouse called Can Santamaria in the nearby village of Raset. Soon they were joined by other evacuees from Barcelona, including Machado's friend Tomás Navarro Tomás, the poet Carles Riba and his wife, the novelist Josep Pous i Pagés and the journalist Andrés Garcia de Barga, better known by his nom de plume of Corpus Barga. In addition to the literary celebrities there was a naturalist, a geologist, an astronomer, a neurologist and a psychiatrist. According to Xirau, some of these people actually enjoyed their stay. 'Such was the peace of the countryside,' he recalled, 'that it seemed impossible to believe that there was a war on.' [2]He said that, while some of the party engaged in serious intellectual discussion, Machado spent most of the time gazing out of the window at the Catalan countryside, which he had never before had an opportunity to visit. It was thought that he was contemplating the landscape in preparation for celebrating it in a poem.

After four days the cavalcade was on the move again. Before he left the farmhouse Machado asked Llúcia Teixidó, who was in charge of the place, whether he could leave a briefcase with her for safekeeping, but she told him that she could not assume such a responsibility. Did it contain manuscripts and other papers, including a file of Valderrama's letters? If so, it is understandable that he should have wanted to leave them with a stranger, who would probably not have been shocked – as members of his own family might have been – to read what the letters revealed about his relationship with Valderrama. It was clear that the briefcase contained some of his most treasured personal possessions, and to part with them would have been a natural part of the process of 'letting go'. Sensing that he was nearing the end of his life he may have felt a need to discard all the emotional baggage that was still weighing him down. As he embarked on this late stage of his journey he may have wanted – to borrow one of his own favourite phrases – to 'travel light'.

Before the refugees left Can Santamaria someone photographed a group of them. On the far right stands José and to his left is Antonio, who is sitting, stick in hand, with downcast eyes, looking far older than 63 and far more battered than his brother, who was only four years his junior. Years later, with the photo in front of him, one of those in the group, the naturalist Enrique Rioja, recalled the circumstances in which it had been taken. In spite of everything, he said, 'Don Antonio's mood was one of humour that was indicative of his stoicism and of the total serenity of his spirit. Most of us were shattered. Without a doubt he was the one who had most self-control.'[3] Their departure from Raset took place at midnight on 26 January, the very day that Barcelona fell and the civil war effectively ended. Thinking that they might still be exposed to aerial attack, the party travelled under cover of darkness. Because the road was so clogged with traffic, progress was painfully slow, but eventually the caravan reached a farmhouse called Mas Faixat, situated between Orriols and Viladasens. The house had a capacious kitchen, with a huge wood fire burning in the grate, and here the refugees spent an uncomfortable night. Rioja recalled that Machado sat on an old settee, chatting with Navarro Tomás, Corpus Barga and others. But, if his brother's recollection is accurate, he did not do much of the talking.

> On this nightmarish occasion, in the midst of that restless multitude, the poet seemed a veritable soul in torment. He gazed in silence at the various groups of people huddling together here and there, in the midst of the general disorder and the cigarette smoke (there was always someone smoking) he caught a glimpse of some familiar faces among others which, in these chaotic surroundings, he was seeing for the first time… In the course of that terrible night soldiers came and went, carrying blankets, rifles, and great branches to put on the fire that had almost gone out. We felt the cold of dawn in the marrow of our bones, when, before our bleary eyes, faint lines of light began to appear in hitherto invisible windows. The poet, numbed and exhausted, maintained the most profound silence, while surrounded by all these people who, as in the last movement of an informal dance and in a final spasm of activity, were collecting their wretched suitcases and bags and bundles of the strangest shapes before taking the sad road into exile.[4]

The party resumed their journey at dawn on 27 January. Another passenger in the crowded truck-ambulance, the philosopher Juan Roura-Parella, later described the scene:

> There was scarcely room for all the passengers in the vehicle. Again personal belongings had to be left behind. When all were boarding, Machado insisted on being the last to find a seat. While his friends and relatives urged him to take a place, he remained in the courtyard and then insisted on being the last to board the ambulance, saying, '*Yo tengo tiempo, yo tengo tiempo*': I have time, I have time.'[5]

When all were aboard the caravan moved off and drove along secondary roads as far as Torroella de Montgrí, where it was hoped they would be able to buy engine oil. Since none was available there they went on to L'Escala, but the local police refused to supply any without instructions from the authorities in Figueres. While they were waiting there enemy warplanes suddenly appeared. Most of the party sought refuge in crevices in the rocks, but Machado and his mother and some others remained in the ambulances. When the immediate danger was past the caravan continued on its way to Figueres. Xirau, who wrote an account of the journey, said that they did not enter the severely damaged city; but, according to Machado family tradition, it was here they had an unexpected encounter with Joaquín, who had just arrived with his wife in another vehicle.

After leaving Figueres the party proceeded to Perefita and thence to Port de la Selva. After passing through Llançà the caravan was halted by a group of soldiers but, when informed of the importance of the people in the ambulances, they saluted respectfully and let the caravan carry on. They were now only 25 kilometres from the border, because so many people were fleeing towards it either on foot or in cars, carts and lorries, they could not move very quickly. Moreover, there was always the risk of an attack from the air or a bombardment from the sea. Whenever planes were heard approaching, the caravan stopped and people threw themselves into ditches. When that happened, as José recalled, Antonio was always the last to leave the ambulance. On one occasion he was heard to remark that there was no point in being in a hurry because, if a bomb should descend on them, 'it would provide a definitive solution to life's problems'.[6] Such a remark was characteristic of the man who, a few days earlier, had confessed to Navarro Tomás: 'I ought not to leave Spain; it would be better for me to remain and die in a ditch.'[7]

The last stage of the journey to the frontier, as Navarro Tomás recalled, was horrendous.

> Machado sat opposite me in the crowded vehicle. We were all so numbed from the last sleepless nights and the most painful conditions of our travelling that none of us was able to utter a coherent sentence. During the trip Machado sat with his head lowered, lost in deep reflection and a tremendous sadness. Occasionally, he mumbled a word to his brother José, who sat crammed next to him in the ambulance. When we reached the border at Port Bou it was already night, cold and raining heavily. The French police were preventing people crossing the border between Port Bou and Cerbère. The accumulation of people and vehicles was so great that we had to get down from the ambulance and walk half a mile by foot, in the rain, with hordes of terrified women and children, until we reached the immigration office. There Machado walked with difficulty. I had to help him, supporting his arm.[8]

Among the luggage that the refugees had been obliged to leave in the ambulances was the briefcase that Machado had tried to deposit with Llúci Teixidó at Can Santamaria. Any hope he might have had of being able to retrieve it later was not to be fulfilled, and its precious contents, which may have included unpublished poems, were lost to him – and to posterity – for ever.

At the frontier they found, crowded together, thousands of people who, despite lacking documentation, were hoping to be allowed into France. Happily, however, the Machados' papers were in order and, according to Navarro Tomás, the French authorities were friendly. 'I spoke to the chief customs officer and explained to him who Machado was', he recalled. 'Fortunately, the officer remembered his name from a Spanish textbook when he was studying the Spanish language, and was a man of understanding.'[9] It is possible that he was also impressed by Corpus Barga's remark that Machado was 'a Spanish Paul Valéry'.[10] Be that as it may, the gendarmes provided the hungry travellers with bread and cheese, and gave Antonio and his mother a lift in a prison van to the railway station at Cerbère, four kilometres further on. But when they arrived and went into the restaurant they found that the waiters were discourteous and would not accept Spanish money.

They were soon joined by José and Matea, and were eventually given permission to spend the night in a railway carriage. It was bitterly cold and the noise of the rain beating on the roof made it almost impossible to sleep. At six o'clock, when the train in which they had taken refuge was due to depart, carrying less fortunate refugees to a concentration camp, they found shelter in the hall of the station restaurant. Ana Ruiz, who by this time was losing her mind, kept repeating: 'We must go and greet these gentlemen who have been kind enough to invite us.' Once she succeeded in escaping and got lost in the crowds waiting on the platform. 'We managed to find her,' Xirau recalled, 'and relieve Don Antonio's exasperation. He told her off gently and after that she did not leave his side.'[11]

In the evening Navarro Tomás and Corpus Barga, who had been to the Spanish consulate at Perpignan, arrived at the station, bringing with them a supply of French currency and a letter in which Julio Álvarez del Vayo, the Republican minister of state, informed Machado that the Spanish embassy in Paris would be responsible for his and his family's expenses. Corpus Barga advised the Machados to stay for a while at Collioure, the picturesque fishing village frequented by Henri Matisse, André Derain and other well-known painters. When they arrived there they encountered a young railway clerk called Jacques Baills and asked him if he could recommend a cheap hotel. Baills suggested the Bougnol-Quintana, where he himself was living. Since there were no taxis at the station the party had to walk to the hotel in the pouring rain. Corpus Barga lifted up Ana Ruiz, who now weighed no more than a child, and carried her along in his arms. While they were walking she whispered in his ear: 'Will we be in Seville soon?' As he later recalled, he did not know if it was a joke or if 'she had returned in her imagination to her youth, when she was a happy mother in the capital of Andalusia'.[12]

When they reached the centre of the village they stopped at a shop and asked if they could rest there a while. The proprietress, Juliette Figuères, later recalled what happened next:

> I said 'yes', made them sit down and, to revive them a little, gave them *café au lait*. The mother was very tired, could not say anything because her mouth was so dry and, as I say, was being carried because she could not walk. That gentleman [Corpus Barga], who spoke good French, asked if there were any taxis and if there were a hotel. I told him, 'The hotel is in front of you', but, as the water in the river was so high, it was not possible to cross at the ford and they would have to go round by the cemetery. My husband said to him: 'Go and see if the proprietor of the garage can come to get them.' That gentleman went off and we chatted for a bit, because Antonio spoke very good French, while the others hardly said anything. Well, I know Spanish and was able to chat a little to José's wife. When the taxi arrived they went away and thanked me. They stayed in the house for a good half hour and afterwards went off to the Quintana hotel.[13]

The proprietress of the hotel, Pauline Quintana, was a kindly person who was sympathetic to the Spanish Republican cause and happy to welcome the bedraggled refugees. She allocated two first floor rooms to them – one for José and Matea, and one for Antonio and his mother. They were all exhausted after their ordeal and later that evening, when Jacques Baills returned home from his job at the station, he found that the Spaniards had gone to bed without supper.

Some days later Baills, who worked part-time at the hotel, discovered the names of the new guests in the register and was excited to see that they included Antonio Machado, whose poems he had learned at night school. He soon found an opportunity to talk with the poet, whom he found to be very friendly and willing to chat. In due course he took to joining the Machados each evening after supper. 'We used to talk about trivial things,' he said, 'because I felt I was dealing with someone whose level of understanding was far above mine and that [if he asked me anything] I would find it very difficult to answer him.' But Baills still had in his possession the exercise book that he had used at night school, in which he had copied out some of Machado's poems; he showed it to the poet, who was evidently deeply moved. He was also delighted when the young man lent him two books by Pio Baroja and a little book about the life, work and death of Vicente Blasco Ibáñez. 'Was it a premonition?' Baills wondered. 'I don't know. What is certain is that he read this along with the others and returned them to me. And now I would almost say that I regret having lent it to him because it perhaps made him think that his own life might soon come to an end.'

Baills recalled that Machado, who was anxious to keep up to date with events in Spain, spent a lot of time reading newspapers and listening to the radio. He used to sit in a little room next to the kitchen and tended to avoid the dining room, which was often full of noisy Spanish army officers who had taken refuge in the village. 'They all used to talk loudly about their exploits, while Machado thought only about one thing: the loss that the disaster represented for the freedom of Spain, and his having been obliged to abandon as much as he had.'[14]

The poet rarely left the hotel, but he did once or twice visit the shop kept by Juliette Figuères, where he would talk with her and her husband about the current situation in Spain. He told them that, in the course of their journey, he had lost the books he had brought with him and also revealed to them that he suffered from asthma. But what he was most worried about were his brother's three little girls, of whom they had had no news. 'One day,' Juliette recalled, 'José said to me: "We have no news of the girls because we do not have the money to write to them." Then my husband exclaimed: "Why didn't you tell us this before?" Then he gave them the money to buy stamps and they wrote. Afterwards they received news.'[15]

The Machados were deeply appreciative of the kindness and generosity of Juliette and her husband. She used to provide Antonio with cigarettes and also, as she later remembered, with more essential supplies:

> One day José said to me, 'My brother cannot come down.' I said to him, 'Why aren't you all coming down together to eat?' And he replied, 'Because we have no change of clothes. On the day when one of the two of us washes his shirt, he waits until the other one has finished eating and has come up – and then he, in his turn, comes down. Sometimes it was José who remained upstairs and at other times it was Antonio. I said to him, 'If you are willing to accept it, I will give each of you a shirt, so that you can have one to change into and then you can come down together.' He replied, 'I wouldn't dare. Previously we had a great deal of money, and now we possess nothing of any value.' He brought out a packet of banknotes, high value banknotes, and said to me, 'These are all due to be burned because they are worth nothing.' I replied, 'Keep them, because you don't know what might happen. Maybe, some day …'

Well, we gave him underwear, shirts, and also some clothes for his mother, and they were delighted.' [16]

Other friends were also concerned for the Machados' welfare. Not long after their arrival at Collioure Antonio received a letter from José Bergamin, who was now in Paris, enquiring about his financial situation. The poet replied, saying that the government had supplied him and his family with the means to stay at their hotel until the end of February, but that thereafter they would need further assistance from somewhere. Although he wanted eventually to emigrate to Russia, his immediate plan was to 'move to some nearby locality where they could live in a small furnished apartment in very modest circumstances'.[17] That he specified a 'nearby locality' is an indication that he liked being in Collioure, where people were so friendly and supportive and where he was in easy reach of the sea that he loved.

Although the sea was only about 300 metres from the hotel it seems that Antonio, who now found walking very difficult, only went to see it twice. José recalled that on the last occasion that they walked there together his brother sat in one of the boats beached on the sand:

> It was very windy, but he took off his hat that he fastened with one hand to his knee while his other hand rested, in its own way, on his cane. So he remained absorbed, silent, before the constant coming and going of the waves, untiring, stirring as under a curse that would never let it rest. After a long while of contemplation, he told me, pointing to one of the small humble houses of the fishermen, 'If only I could live there behind one of those windows, freed at last from worry.' Then he got up with a great effort and, walking laboriously over the slipping sand in which his feet were almost completely sinking, we went back in the most profound silence.[18]

As he sat in that boat listening to the waves beating on the shore might he not have remembered the words that, long years before, he had written in a little poem called 'Advice'?

> Be content to wait, watch for the turning tide
> as a beached boat waits, in no rush to float away.
> Whoever waits can be sure he'll win in the end
> since life is long and art only a toy.
> And if life is short
> and the sea never reaches your skiff,
> still wait and don't depart, go right on hoping,
> for art is long and, besides, it doesn't matter.[19]

On that last walk down to the sea along the river bank did Machado reflect on those lines of the medieval poet Jorge Manrique that he often quoted, where life is likened to a river and death to the sea into which it flows? Be that as it may it is certain that by now Machado sensed that he did not have long to live. One day he came into the sitting room of the hotel with a little wooden jewel box in his hand and gave it to Pauline Quintana, saying, 'It contains Spanish soil. If I die in this village, I want it to be buried with me.' When she tried to make him banish all such thoughts, he shook his head and said, 'My days, señora, are numbered.'[20]

One night not long afterwards Matea went into the bedroom that Antonio shared with his mother to see how they were and was shocked by the poet's appearance. She awakened her husband and told him that Antonio was very ill. José got up, saw the situation and decided that, as soon as it was morning, they should send for a doctor. Soon after 6 am Matea called at Juliette's house to tell her the news, whereupon she said that she would go with her to the house of Dr Cazaban, her own physician, and pay his fees. The doctor came at once and confirmed that Antonio was gravely ill, giving his opinion that his asthma had been aggravated by catching cold at Cerbère. He prescribed some medicine, but said there was nothing more he could do.

Not long after the doctor's visit Machado mustered the energy to dictate a letter to his old friend Santullano, now secretary of the Spanish embassy in Paris. He told him that he was well enough to travel to the French capital and hoped to see him there soon. 'This is what the letter said,' Santullano commented, 'but his shaky signature showed that the life of the poet was ebbing away.'[21] He died two days later, on 22 February, with José and Matea at his bedside. The last words they heard him say were, 'Goodbye, mother; goodbye, mother.' But, according to Matea, Ana Ruiz, who was in the next bed, heard nothing, because she had fallen into a deep coma.

At some point, after they had laid out Antonio's body under a sheet, his mother awoke suddenly and turned her head to look at him, but could not see him. 'Where is Antonio?', she asked. 'What has happened?' José did not tell her the truth, but said he was ill and had gone to hospital. 'There he will get better', he tried to assure her. But, as Matea later recalled, 'Mama Ana gave him a look that indicated that she didn't believe anything he had said ... I am sure that in those few lucid moments she realized that her son had died.'[22] Years afterwards José acknowledged that he had tried to conceal Antonio's death from her, but in vain. 'A mother is never deceived,' he wrote, 'and she burst into tears like an unhappy little girl.'[23]

Some days later José found a crumpled sheet of paper in a pocket of Antonio's old overcoat. On it, written in pencil, were three separate notes. The first recorded the opening words of Hamlet's famous monologue, 'To be or not to be', which he had so often written in his notebooks. The second was a single line of his own composition: 'These blue days and this sun of my infancy.'[24] The last consisted of four lines from 'Other songs to Guiomar (after the manner of Abel Martín and Juan de Mairena)':

> I will send you my song:
> 'One sings what is lost,'
> and a green parrot
> to say it on your balcony.[25]

The news of the poet's death, as Baille expressed it, 'spread like wildfire'.[26] Soon telegrams of condolence began to arrive, including an especially affectionate one from Manuel Azaña, the former president of the Republic, who was now in exile in France. José also received a letter from a representative of a group of French writers proposing that his brother's body should be interred with due solemnity in Paris, but he decided to decline the honour. The mayor of Collioure had already arranged for a burial in the local cemetery, where a friend of Pauline Quintana had generously made available a place in her family's vault.

For the funeral, which took place on the afternoon of 23 February, the simple coffin was draped in a Spanish Republican flag that had been hastily sewn together the night before by the ever-attentive Juliette. It was carried from the hotel to the cemetery on the shoulders of Spanish soldiers from the Second Cavalry Brigade, who at the time were interned in the castle of Collioure, and had been temporarily released for this purpose by the French authorities in recognition of the poet's importance. It is said that among the onlookers were some Spaniards who had recently succeeded in escaping from the nearby concentration camps at Argolès and Saint Cyprien.

The funeral was attended by two very distinguished Spaniards – Vicente Rojo and Julián Zugazagoita. Rojo, the general who had commanded the Republican forces at the battles of Teruel and the Ebro, was a man that Machado had greatly admired and had been the subject of one of the last articles that he wrote. Zugazagoita, a pioneering socialist and a former member of the Republican government, had also been a regular contributor to *La Vanguardia*. It fell to this good friend, who himself was soon to die – not in his bed but in front of a fascist firing squad in Madrid – to give the funeral oration. Its tone was highly emotional and it concluded with three lines from one of Machado's poems:

> O heart, beating yesterday,
> isn't your little gold coin
> sounding today?[27]

Those familiar with the rest of the poem would have known that the poet was likening the sound of a heart beating to the rattle of a coin in a moneybox.

On the day after the funeral José answered a letter addressed to Antonio that had just reached Collioure: it was from Professor J. B. Trend, offering the poet a lectureship in the department of Spanish in the University of Cambridge. Trend, who was in the process of editing a second edition of the *Oxford Book of Spanish Verse*, in which he had included extracts from *Campos de Castilla* and *Galerías* as well as five other poems, was a great admirer of Machado's work. José replied promptly, giving him the news of his brother's death. 'Given the deep and devout admiration that he always felt for England,' he wrote, 'to visit that country had, all his life, been one of his greatest ambitions. Indeed, it was the masterpieces of English literature that he was reading and re-reading in these last few months. But the dream did not come true! We buried him yesterday in this unpretentious little fishing village in a simple cemetery close to the sea. There he will remain until such time as a less cruel and barbarous group of people permit him to return to the land of Castile that was so dear to him.'[28]

On 25 February, which was in fact her 85th birthday, Machado's mother also died. Following those few moments of lucidity after her son's death she had never regained consciousness. But she had kept the promise she had once made at Rocafort: 'I am prepared to live as long as my son Antonio.'[29]

O O O

Not long afterwards a moving elegy on Machado's death was penned (not in poetry but in prose) by his close friend Juan Ramón Jiménez, now living in exile in Puerto Rico:

Even as a child Antonio Machado sought death, the dead and decay in every recess of his soul and body. He always held within himself as much of death as of life, half fused together by ingenuous artistry. When I met him early in the morning I had the impression that he had just arisen from the grave…

A poet of death, Antonio Machado spent hour after hour meditating upon, perceiving, and preparing for death; I have never known anyone else who so balanced these levels, equal in height or depth, as he did, and who by his living-dying overcame the gap between these existences, paradoxically opposed yet the only ones known to us; existences strongly united even though we others persist in separating, contrasting, and pitting them against each other. All our life is usually given over to fearing death and keeping it away from us, or rather, keeping ourselves away from it. Antonio Machado apprehended it in itself, yielded to it in large measure. Possibly, more than a man who was born, he was a man reborn…

When bodily death came he died humbly, miserably, collectively, the lead animal of a persecuted human flock, driven out of Spain – where he as Antonio Machado had had everything, his dovecots, his sheepfolds of love – through the back gate. In this condition he crossed the high mountains of the frozen frontier, because such was the way his best friends, the poorest and most worthy, made the crossing. And if he still lies under the ground with those buried there away from his love, it is for the comfort of being with them, for I am certain that he who knew the rough uneven path of death has been able to return to Spain through the sky below the ground.

All this night of high moon – moon that comes from Spain and returns to Spain, with its mountains and its

Antonio Machado reflected in its melancholy mirror,
moon of sad diamond, blue and green, in the palm
tree of violet grassy plush by my little door of the
true exile – I have heard in the depths of my waking-
sleeping the ballad 'Night Rainbow', one of Antonio
Machado's most profound poems and one of the most
beautiful that I have ever read:

> And you, Lord, through whom
> we all see and who sees our souls,
> tell us whether one day
> we are all to look upon your face. [30]

Epilogue

On 26 February 1939 the *Diario de Burgos* carried the news that 'the distinguished poet Don Manuel Machado, resident in this city since the beginning of the *Glorioso Movimiento Salvador*, was receiving innumerable expressions of sympathy and messages of condolence following the recent death of his brother Don Antonio, which occurred last Thursday in Paris'.[1] Equally inaccurate was the report in *El Pueblo: Diario del Partido Sindicalista* of Valencia, the first news of Machado's death to appear in a Republican paper: it stated that the poet had died in a camp for Spanish refugees near Toulouse. In fact the Spanish press continued to report that Machado had died in a French concentration camp and it was the London *Times*, whose correspondent (together with one from the *Daily Telegraph*) had attended his funeral, that was among the first to provide an accurate account of events. The obituary, published on 2 March, which stated that Machado had died in 'a small hotel at Collioure', was doubtless contributed by J. B. Trend, who would have just received José's letter. 'Unlike many Spanish intellectuals who, after having first supported the Republic, gradually transferred their sympathies to the Nationalists' he wrote, 'Machado remained devoted to the Republican cause to the end.' He reported that Antonio's brother José was with him at his death, but that Manuel, who now 'served the Nationalist ideal', was not.[2]

What the writer of this obituary did not know was that Manuel and his wife Eulalia, as soon as they heard the news of Antonio's death, had been given permission to travel to France in an official car. The only information about what happened after they reached Collioure comes from Machado's first biographer Pérez Ferrero, whose account, although evidently based on conversations with Manuel, is very brief:

In the two days that Manuel spends at Collioure he does not leave the little seaside cemetery where his loved ones lie. The grief is too strong to be made bearable by the reunion with his brother José. He does not want to talk – he finds it impossible! – or to hear anything; he does not wish to know anything at all. All he wants to do is to go to sleep as well in that place and never wake up again. Eulalia Cáceres, who is equally upset, tries to intervene in order to ease her husband's pain at leaving and make his return home more bearable. They must hit the road again. They must get back to Burgos. Their destiny is not to remain there but, no matter how much grief it gives them, to go on their way. They have to go on living!

And, when the two days are up, the couple return home. [3]

It is significant that in his memoirs José, who may have found it difficult to forgive Manuel's treachery, made no mention whatsoever of his visit.

After this José and Matea did not stay long in Collioure. In May 1939 they were living in a village in the department of Aube, where they were joined by Joaquín and his wife Carmen. At the end of the year the four of them took ship to Buenos Aires, from where they crossed the continent to Santiago, the capital of Chile. After the second World War they were joined by two of the three girls who had been evacuated to Russia. Both brothers were to die in Chile – Joaquín in 1956 and José in 1958 – having been denied the opportunity to return to Spain. Meanwhile Francisco, who was evidently less opposed to fascism than they were and had returned with his family to his home country at the conclusion of the Civil War, went back to his old job as director of Madrid's prison for women. After his death in 1950 his three daughters remained in Madrid, where in 2005 the youngest, Leonor, shared with Ian

Gibson her recollections of her family's flight from the city nearly 70 years previously.

Francisco probably owed his reinstatement to Manuel who, as soon as he was free to do so, had returned with Eulalia to their old apartment in Madrid. When they called at the former family home in General Arrando they found everything, including the extensive library of poetry and philosophy, in good order. These were sad times for Manuel, whose bond with Antonio had once been so strong He sought comfort in things that would have been anathema to other members of his family and became, like his wife, a devout Catholic. After his death in 1947 his body was clothed in the habit of a Franciscan friar and lay in state for a time in the vestibule of the Royal Academy, of which he had been made a member in 1938. Unlike Antonio, whose appointment to this prestigious body eleven years earlier had been richly deserved, Manuel's elevation had probably been due more to his political activities than to his latest literary achievements. Poems and prose in praise of Franco could hardly be regarded as significant contributions to his country's culture.

While Manuel's posthumous reputation declined Antonio's flourished. Because of his loyalty to the cause of freedom and democracy, his memory continued to be revered by countless numbers of Spaniards, who saw him as the embodiment of all that was noblest and best in Spain. This became evident in 1966, when it was announced that a monument to Machado that had been erected just outside Baeza, on the route of one his favourite walks, was to be unveiled. On 20 February thousands of people from all over Spain converged on the town, but armed police (known from the colour of their uniforms as 'the Greys') tried to stop them entering it. Abandoning their buses and cars, however, some 2,500 people succeeded in making their way on foot to the vicinity of the monument, only to discover that the way had been blocked. After a lieutenant had read the Riot Act and the crowd had disobeyed his order to disperse, he drew his pistol and shouted 'Charge! Charge!' 'From then on', recorded an eye-witness, 'it was brutality and violence. The crowd cried "Murderer! Murderer!" Many fell down under the blows. Groans, cries; young people sobbed with fear. The Greys savagely pursued the few people who ran in the first moments and continued to beat those who remained standing.' Those who escaped to the town took shelter in bars and cafés, from which they were forcibly expelled by police. In all they arrested twenty-seven people, of whom eleven were kept in prison until they had paid a heavy fine. There would be no more public acts of homage to Machado as long as Franco ruled. [4]

After the dictator's death in 1975 the commemoration of opponents of his regime was no longer forbidden and Spaniards were now free to pay proper respect to the poet's memory. In Madrid a monument to him was erected in a street bearing his name and plaques were placed on the house where he had lived in General Arrando and also in the Instituto Cervantes, where he had briefly been a *catedrático*. The schoolroom where he had taught in Baeza and the house where he had lodged in Segovia both became museums devoted to preserving mementos of his life. But perhaps the most frequently visited place on the Machado pilgrimage trail is not in any of these cities nor in Soria, where the memorial set up in his lifetime still stands, nor yet anywhere in Spain, but in the village just over the border in France where he spent his last days. It is to Collioure that visitors come from all over the world to place flowers on his grave or, strange to relate, post letters to him in the adjoining pillar box. There have been suggestions that his remains should be disinterred and reburied in Spain, but this seems unlikely to happen. It is probable that his bones will continue to lie in that *rincón* of a foreign field that, as a patriotic poet might put it, remains for ever Spain.

Conclusion

In the Conclusion to his study of Machado's *Campos de Castilla,* the celebrated English hispanist Arthur Terry had this to say about the poet's work:

> Literary critics are perhaps too prone to speak of a poet's 'development'. Where Machado is concerned, one is aware, not of any outstripping of earlier selves, but of a core of integrity which can be recognized at every stage in his work. It is this which ensures the consistency with which he is able to assimilate a great many kinds of experience and which keeps the balance between the personal and the social. As Machado himself realized, to keep such a balance is never easy, least of all when one is writing in a consciously subjective tradition. This explains why, at several points in his career, he appears quite deliberately to change direction. The obvious example of this is the search for greater 'objectivity' which begins after *Soledades.* Yet this only partly accounts for the differences between the early poems and *Campos de Castilla...* There are differences, but there is also continuity, the continuity of a temperament which remains clear-sighted even at moments of personal crisis.[1]

Something similar might be said in a Conclusion to a book that concentrates on Machado's 'development', not so much as a poet, but as a person. In the course of his life he never 'outstripped his earlier self' but seems to have integrated every stage of his past into his present. There was part of him that never left the magical garden of his childhood with its fountains, cobblestones, cypresses and orange and lemon trees. As his brother José expressed it, he 'retained in the depths of his consciousness the unsullied world-view of his infancy'. He never seems to have lost contact with his own 'inner child'; indeed 'These blue days and this sun of my infancy' were the last words he wrote down before he died. In his desire to keep in touch with – and celebrate – his childhood, he had more in common with Wordsworth or Thomas Traherne than with T. S. Eliot, who once wrote rather chillingly that 'the reminiscence of childhood is something to be buried and done with, though its corpse will from time to time find its way up to the surface.' [2] Far from wishing to bury the memories of his infancy, Machado wanted to continue to reflect upon them. He confessed to having 'an incorrigible desire to give utterance to the spirit of whatever lies buried in the memory'. Just as he was always eager to trace a river back to its source, so he wished to reflect upon the whole course of his life without neglecting any stretch of it.

Throughout his life his early relationships remained vitally important to him. At the age of 40 he addressed a moving poem to his father, whom he had lost at the age of 17: 'I am older than you were, my father, when you used to kiss me/ but in my memory I am still the child that you held by the hand'.[3] However, although he was fond of his father his closest bond was always with his mother. It has been observed that a woman often has a special bond with her second child – particularly if he it is a boy – and Ana Ruiz was no exception to this. All her life she watched over Antonio with marked solicitude. It was only during his years in Soria that he seems to have been able to escape entirely from her constant attention. After Leonor died and her beloved son was restored to her, Ana hardly let him out of her sight. She kept house for him for some years in Baeza and, while he was working in Segovia, provided a home for him in Madrid at weekends. From 1932, when he moved back to the capital, until his death in 1939, mother and son seem to have slept every night under the same roof – and in their last days in the same room. She said she was 'prepared to live as long as my son Antonio' and, three days after his death, she also died. The poet's closeness to his mother may help to account for the strength of his 'feminine side' which, in the macho culture of Spain, was quite remarkable. But, at the same time, it may go some way towards explaining the difficulties he had in his relationships with the opposite sex. If there was already such a formidable woman in his life, could there ever be room for another? Is it surprising that he chose a teenager as a wife and a 'goddess' as a paramour?

How did the strength of his bond with his mother affect Antonio's relationships with his brothers? Although José was his faithful companion in his final years, it was from his elder brother Manuel that he was said to be 'inseparable', until the Civil War came between them. When Antonio was born it would have been only natural for Manuel to resent the advent of a rival for his mother's affection, but at 11 months he was perhaps too young to harbour such feelings. Had he been older he might have reacted like the jealous little boy who, on first seeing another baby in his mother's arms, urged her promptly to 'get rid of it'. As far as is known, Manuel and Antonio always got on well together and, because the elder was at first so much more successful than the younger, no envy or jealousy appears to have marred their youthful relationship. Even when the roles were reversed and Antonio became more celebrated than Manuel, they seem to have remained the best of friends.

At a deeper level, however, Antonio may have harboured doubts about his relationship with Manuel. What is the explanation for his fascination with the biblical account of a man who was so upset by the favours shown to his younger brother that he had to kill him? His interest in the story of Cain and Abel almost amounted to an obsession, for in his writings he referred to it again and again. Was it an accident that, in searching for a pseudonym, he adopted the name of *Abel* Martín? So strong was Machado's antipathy to Cain that he coined the word *cainismo* to denote all that was most harmful and destructive in the Spanish national character. It was *cainismo*, he contended, that had caused a war that tore families asunder and pitted brother against brother in the fight. For Antonio the saddest consequence of that conflict was that his elder brother was, by association, guilty of fratricide.

In happier times the two brothers had worked well together – and this may be because they were so very different in character. The difference is clear from surviving photographs of the two of them: on the one hand there is Antonio, inward-looking, unsmiling and anxious; and on the other is Manuel, bright-eyed and cheerful, sporting a stylish moustache and a bowler hat worn at a debonair angle. The journalist who interviewed them together in 1928 drew a sharp contrast between the one, 'a man searching for God among the clouds, finding his bearings by the promptings of his heart', and the other, 'nimble, lively and elegant', resembling a gypsy bullfighter or 'a dandy dressed up as a matador'. There is no doubt that the extravert Manuel and the introvert Antonio represent two contrasting attitudinal types. While the one was primarily interested in what was experienced in the external world, the other's consciousness was directed inwards. In terms of Jungian typology the brothers were polar opposites. The smartly dressed Manuel, whose appearance resembled that of 'a man on his way to an assignation with a *flamenco* dancer', might be classified as a 'sensation' type – one acutely aware of things that he could see and hear and touch. He had some of the attributes of what his brother called 'tambourine Andalusians' – people who were 'boastful, prone to exaggeration, loving things that were noisy and gaudy'. The quietly spoken, carelessly dressed Antonio, by contrast, who said he had 'a profound belief in a spiritual reality that is set against the world of the senses', was clearly an 'intuitive' type.

According to the Jungian analyst Marie-Louise von Franz, introverted intuitive types have a capacity for 'smelling out the future, having the right guess or the right hunch about the not-yet-seen future possibilities of a situation' and among them are to be found prophets and poets. Antonio often wrote and spoke like a prophet. As with Amos and Isaiah of old he was wont to lambast the political and ecclesiastical establishment of his day; he hated cruelty and corruption and injustice; he championed the rights of the poor and the oppressed. But his inspiration came more from the New Testament than the Old. It was to Christ, who proclaimed the universal brotherhood of man, that he looked for directions about how he should conduct his life. It could be said that he, like the great Spanish mystics, believed in the 'indwelling Christ' and looked inwards rather than outwards for the seat of authority in religion. What a contrast to Manuel! When, towards the close of his life, he eventually turned to religion, he was inevitably drawn, because of his strong sensation function, to an institution that offered the most spectacular trappings.

There is, however, a downside to being an introverted intuitive. Von Franz says that such people generally have problems with their 'inferior function', which is extraverted sensation. 'The inferior sensation of an introverted intuitive is extremely intense, but it breaks through only here and there and then fades again from the field of awareness. The introverted intuitive has particular trouble in approaching sex, because it involves his inferior extraverted sensation.' [4] This may throw light on Antonio's marriage to Leonor which, in view of his promise that he would never forget that she was 'still a child', may possibly never have been consummated. It may also help to explain the nature of his relationship with Valderrama, whom he went to bed with every night in his imagination but never once in reality. It may have a bearing, too, on his decision to adopt the alter ego of Abel Martín, the side of himself that he described as 'extremely erotic'. This suggests that, unlike less self-aware people, he did not despise his inferior function, but recognized the need to relate to his 'shadow side'. 'I talk with the man who is always at my side', he wrote in the poem he entitled 'Portrait'.[5] And in the 'Proverbs and Songs' that he dedicated to Ortega y Gasset he explained why he did so:

> Look for your counterpart
> who's always alongside you
> and is usually your opposite.[6]

This clearly indicates that Machado had taken seriously the saying of the ancient Greek philosopher, 'Know thyself and thou shalt know all things', and, in the course of his musings, had attained a quite remarkable measure of self-awareness. He had come to understand the mechanism of what depth psychologists call 'projection' and what Christ talked about in terms of 'motes' and 'beams'. In his self-analytical survey of 1913 he had said: 'I look inwards rather than outwards and recognize the injustice of criticizing in my neighbour what I am aware of in myself.' He knew that, without such self-understanding, it was impossible to obey the Gospel injunction to 'love thy neighbour as thyself'. And although he doubted whether anyone would ever 'be able to know our souls better than the old religions',[7] he was evidently prepared to acknowledge the contribution to self-understanding of what a character in *Las adelfas* called the 'new science of psychoanalysis'.

What would the founder of psychoanalysis have made of Machado, if he had analyzed him on his couch in Vienna? Sigmund Freud would have noticed that, as the poet Don Paterson has observed, Machado was 'obsessed with the suppression of his own ego'.[8] Freud would also have been impressed by his patient's ability to recall his dreams in minute detail and, in the one in which he imagined himself marrying Pilar de Valderrama, he would have found confirmation of his theory that dreams have much to do with wish-fulfilment. He would probably have taken particular note of the episode that stood out so clearly in Antonio's memories of childhood, when an authoritative female figure (corresponding to his 'superego') rebuked him severely for saying that his stick of sugar cane was larger than another boy's. Could the analyst have refrained from pointing out the phallic symbolism of the stick and the sexually inhibiting effects of the rebuke? It is unlikely, however, that Freud would have found indications of the classic 'oedipal complex' that might lead a son to want to kill his father. Parricide, as described in *La Tierra de Alvargonzález*, his longest poem, may have held for him a certain fascination, but here the motivation for the murder was clearly covetousness rather than jealousy.

In analyzing Machado, a psychotherapist might have been surprised by his apparent inability to get angry. It is astonishing that, after the antics of hooligans had wrecked his wedding day, he felt no outrage, but only sadness and shame. Feelings of hostility long lay buried deep in his unconscious and only seem to have surfaced in his dreams – like the one in which, beside himself with rage, he threw an obstructive ticket inspector off the Barcelona train. In the revelatory piece he wrote about himself in 1913 he referred to 'aggressive impulses' of which he had later felt ashamed. His inability to express feelings of anger may have led to them being turned inward against himself and made manifest in melancholy and depression.

After the outbreak of the Civil War, however, everything changed Faced with the destruction of all that he held dear, he could no longer suppress his anger. Now he had a legitimate target for his hostility and part of him clearly relished the prospect of a fight. He announced that, although too old and ill to draw a sword, he would put his pen at the disposal of the Republic and he then proceeded, in article after article, to hit out at the crooks and cowards who he felt had betrayed it. Confronted by the excesses of foreign invaders, the disciple of Tolstoy abandoned his pacifism. In Valencia he overcame his natural timidity to address a huge crowd in a public square, and his hearers were astonished. Those who had so often heard him speak in 'the language of intimacy and solitude' now heard his voice ringing out with power. His voice, as José Bergamín expressed it, 'was charged with anger' – because he was now 'in touch with something much deeper than his own invisible personal life'. Bergamín concluded by saying that on this occasion 'the multitude became manifest in one man; when he spoke, he did so not only as a single individual, but on behalf of a single people'.

The last time that people heard Antonio Machado's resounding voice was in the radio broadcast he made for *La Voz de España* at the end of November 1938. It was not long before he died. On this occasion, like members of his family before him, he was upholding the cause of democracy, insisting that the Republic was 'an unmistakable expression of the political will of the people'. He was also, like them, making a passionate plea for freedom; but now there was a new note of urgency. The freedom that was in danger was not just the right, so important to liberals and republicans, to speak and act without fear of retribution. It was the right, precious to Spaniards of all classes and parties, to be free from foreign oppression. Now that Germany and Italy had sent their planes to bomb Spanish cities this was no longer just a *civil* war. 'The day has come,' Machado said, 'when we must acknowledge this incontrovertible truth: our most urgent duty is to fight for our liberty, which is under terrible threat.' Now it was time for all Spaniards to recognize that, in the face of a foreign foe, nothing could be allowed to 'break the fraternal bonds that unite the sons of a common fatherland'.[9]

On this, as on other occasions, he was speaking to and for what he called *todas las Españas* – all the lands of Spain. Machado, who had been born and raised in Andalusia, had spent formative years in Castile and had ended up in Valencia and Catalonia, appreciated what each land contributed to the totality of Spain. While delighting in the beauty of Valencia he could assert – in his Andalusian accent – that 'Castile is the spirit of Spain'. He loved the distinctive qualities of every region, but had no time for provincial particularism. He recognized that Madrid, the capital created at the geographical centre of the peninsula for the specific purpose of countering such particularism, was – as his celebrated poem expressed it – the 'bulwark of all the lands of Spain'. The role of the *madrileños*, who generally had broader horizons than people in the provinces, was to provide a defence against the divisive elements that were threatening the integrity of the nation.

It is likely that most of those who listened on the radio to the two Machado brothers – the one urging Spaniards to support Franco and the other to oppose him – would have realized that it was Antonio who spoke, not for a faction or a region, but for the nation as a whole. They would have recognized that the one broadcast by *La Voz de España* was the authentic voice of Spain.

Appendix

'Calling all Spaniards'

The text of a broadcast by Antonio Machado for
La Voz de España, *22 November 1938*

To all Spaniards: I have said more than once, and I am not tired of repeating it, that my only political ideology is acceptance of the sole legitimacy of the Government that represents the freely expressed will of the people. I must add that for me 'the people' does not signify a particular social class: all Spaniards form part of what I call 'the people'. Therefore I have always been on the side of the Spanish Republic, for whose coming into being I worked, to the best of my ability, in ways that I deemed to be legal. When the Republic was established in Spain as an unmistakable expression of the political will of the people, I welcomed it gladly and I prepared to serve it without expecting any material advantage from so doing. If it had come into being as a result of a sudden uprising, accompanied by trickery or violence, I would always have been opposed to it.

I know very well that a Republic has to deal with problems that are much more deep-rooted than those that are strictly political – there are, for instance, those of an economic, social, religious or cultural nature – and that within that Republic are to be found ideologies that are not only different but even conflicting. But, no matter how bitter the struggle, the Republic retains its legitimacy so long as the freely expressed will of the people does not condemn it. Therefore, when part of the military turned against the legitimate government of the Republic the very arms that they had been given to defend it from wrongful oppression, I was, without hesitation, on the side of the government that had thus been disarmed. Without hesitation, I say, and also without the any boasting: because I believed it was my duty. Since the professional soldiers were no longer the army of Spain, thenceforth, in my opinion, the army of Spain was the one that the people had improvised from the best of her sons; an army as weakly and insufficiently armed on the outside as it was strongly and abundantly equipped on the inside with the energy of moral righteousness. Improvised, I say, from the best of her sons and, I do not hesitate to add, from a small group of genuine volunteers – selfless and generous-hearted men who came to Spain with no trace of a materialistic motive, to shed their blood in defence of a just cause.

With all these considerations – and persuaded of the blindness, the errors and the unjust behaviour of our adversaries, whose seditious nature I did not doubt for a moment – I confess that I could never hate them: with all their faults, with all their sins, they are Spaniards; and not even the bitterest civil war could break the fraternal bonds that unite the sons of a common fatherland.

But then came the monstrous eventuality of the foreign invasion. The invasion took place in a cowardly and surreptitious fashion, and, as time went on, became an undeniable fact. Two foreign nations had penetrated into Spain to shape its future and, by force and calumny, to obliterate its past. In the tragic and decisive times in which we are now living, no Spaniard can have any doubts or hesitations. It is no longer a case of his choosing a party or a faction: he has to be *for* Spain and *against* the invaders. Let us leave aside the part of the blame for the invasion that the Spanish themselves have incurred. If there is such a crime, and if anyone committed it consciously, it is of a kind that is beyond the jurisdiction of any human tribunal.

Note too that I have not spoken of either fascism or Marxism. I do not think there is anyone in Spain who has a greater aversion than I have to the ideology of fascism. I have always believed, however, that it is theoretically possible to be a fascist without thereby ceasing to be a Spaniard. But I have said too that it is not possible to be a Spaniard and to surrender the lands and destinies of Spain to the greedy imperialism of Italian fascism or German racism. I do not think that today anyone in Spain can believe that this is possible.

240

We have been slandered inside and outside Spain by those who say that we also serve a foreign cause – that we are working on behalf of Russia. The calumny is doubly perfidious, but it so gross that it has not been able to fool anyone who is not a complete imbecile. Because everyone knows very well that Russia, that admirable nation which gave up its empire in order to liberate its people, never assailed anyone else's liberty and never had any designs on the territory of Spain. Everyone knows this, although many pretend not to.

Men of Spain, of *all* Spain – which means all the Hispanic peoples whose land has been invaded – the day has come when we must acknowledge this incontrovertible truth: our most urgent duty is to fight for our liberty, which is under terrible threat. And Spain is strong, much stronger than our enemies think, because, as I have said once, and I don't mind repeating it, Spain is not an invention of foreign diplomacy or the consequence of more or less ineffective peace treaties. Having existed as a distinct entity for centuries, it is perfectly defined by its ethnicity, by its language, by its geography, by its history and by its contribution to universal culture. Do not doubt for a moment that he who refuses to defend it against foreign invasion is a traitor to his country.

Chronological Table

1875   Birth in the Palace of Las Dueñas, Seville (26 July)

1879   Departure from Las Dueñas

1883   Move to Madrid. Admitted to Institución Libre de Enzeñanza

1889   Admitted to Instituto Cisneros

1893   Death of Antonio Machado Álvarez (*father*) Publication of articles in *La Caricatura*

1896   Death of Antonio Machado Núñez (*grandfather*)

1899   First stay in Paris

1900   Passed baccalaureate. Admitted to University of Madrid

1901   Publication of first poems (in *Electra*)

1902   Second stay in Paris

1903   Publication of *Soledades*

1904   Death of Cypriana Álvarez Durán (*grandmother*)

1907   Publication of *Soledades. Galerías. Otros Poemas*. Move to Soria

1909   Marriage to Leonor Izquierdo Cuevas

1911   Third stay in Paris

1912   Publication of *Campos de Castilla*. Death of Leonor. Move to Baeza

1915   Admitted to University of Madrid as external student

1917   Publication of *Poesías completas (1899-1917)*

1918   Awarded Licentiate

1919   Awarded Doctorate in Philosophy. Move to Segovia

1924   Publication of *Nuevas canciones*

1925   First performance of *Hernani*

1926   First performance of *Desdichas de la fortuna o Juanillo Valcárcel*

1927   First performance of *Juan de Mañara*. Election to Spanish Royal Academy

1928   First performance of *Las adelfas*. Publication of *Poesías completas* (2nd edn).

First encounter with Pilar de Valderrama.

1929   First performance of *La Lola se va a los Puertos*

1931   Proclamation of the Second Republic (14 April)

First performance of *La Primera Fernanda*

1932   First performance of *La duquesa de Benameji*

Appointed to post at the Instituto Calderón de la Barca in Madrid

1933   Publication of *Poesías completas* (3rd edn)

1936   Appointed to post at the Instituto Cervantes in Madrid (10 March). Outbreak of Civil War (18 July). Departure from Madrid (24 November). Public oration in Valencia (11 December)

1937   Conference of Writers for the Defence of Culture in Valencia

Publication of *La Guerra (1936-1937)*

1938   Move to Barcelona (April). Broadcast for *Voz de España* (22 November)

1939   Departure from Barcelona (23 January). Fall of Barcelona (26 January).

Arrival at Collioure (28 January). Death (22 February)

Bibliography

A. WRITINGS OF ANTONIO MACHADO

LC Los Complementarios, ed. Domingo Ynduráin (Madrid, 1971)

PC Poesías completas, ed. Manuel Alvar (Madrid, 2008)

PD Prosas dispersas (1893-1936), ed. Jordi Doménech (Madrid, 2001)

PP Poesía y prosa, III Prosas completas (1893-1936); IV Prosas completas (1936-1939), ed. Oreste Macri (Madrid, 1988)

B. WRITINGS OF ANTONIO MACHADO IN TRANSLATION

BARNSTONE, Willis, *Border of a Dream: Selected Poems of Antonio Machado*, (Washington, 2004)

BELITT, Ben, *Juan de Mairena* (Berkeley and Los Angeles, 1963)

BLY, Robert, *Times Alone: Selected Poems of Antonio Machado* (Middletown, Connecticut, 1983)

TRUEBLOOD, Alan S., *Antonio Machado, Selected Poems* (Cambridge, Massachusetts, 1982)

C. OTHER WORKS CITED

BAKER, Armand J., 'Antonio Machado's "Profession of Faith"', *BHS*, lxiv (1987), 119-26. [*BHS = Bulletin of Hispanic Studies*]

BARNSTONE, Willis, *Six Masters of the Spanish Sonnet* (Carbondale, Illinois, 1993)

BROTHERSTON, J. G., 'Antonio Machado y Álvarez and Positivism', *BHS*, xli (1964), 223-29.

CARR, Raymond Carr, *Spain 1808-1939* (Oxford, 1966).

CERNUDA, Luis, 'Antonio Machado y la actual generación de poetas', *Bulletin of Spanish Studies*, xvii (1940), 139-43.

COLLIER, L. D., 'Giner de los Ríos and his contribution to education in Spain', *Bulletin of Spanish Studies*, xi (1934), 73-85.

GALÁN, Pilar, *Antonio Machado: Biografía poética de una soledad* (San Vicente, 2013)

GIBSON, Ian, *Ligero de equipaje: La vida de Antonio Machado* (Madrid, 2006).

GONZÁLEZ, Gloria and TALAVERA, Begoña, *El instituto del Cardenal Sisneros: Crónica de la enseñanza secundaria en España* (Madrid, 2014)

GRANT, Helen, review of Segundo Serrano Poncela, *Antonio Machado:su mundo y su obra* in *Bulletin of Hispanic Studies,* xxxiv (1957), 48.

KAMEN, Henry, *The Disinherited: The exiles who created Spanish culture* (London, 2007).

LÓPEZ-MORILLAS, *The Krausist Movement & Ideological Change in Spain 1854-1874*, trans. Frances M. López-Morillas (Cambridge, 1981).

MACHADO, José, *Últimas soledades del poeta Antonio Machado* (Madrid,1999).

MARCO, José María, *Francisco Giner de los Ríos: Pedagogía y poder* (Barcelona, 2002).

MARTÍNEZ, Manuela Villalpando, *La Universidad Popular Segoviana 1919-1936* (Segovia, 1999).

NERUDA, Pablo, *Memoirs*, trans. Hardie St Martin (London, 2004).

PASCUAL PIQUÉ, Antoni, *El diálogo con el inconsciente: Antonio Machado*, trans. Ricard Fernández Aguilà (Barcelona, 2009).

PEERS, E. Allison, *Spain; A Companion to Spanish Studies*, (4th edn. London, 1948).

PÉREZ FERRERO, Miguel, *Vida de Antonio Machado y Manuel* (Buenos Aires, 1952).

RIBBANS, Geoffrey, 'Unamuno and Antonio Machado', *BHS*, xxxiv (1957), 10-28.

--------------------------, 'Recaptured Memory in Juan Ramón Jiménez and Antonio Machado', *Studies in Modern Spanish Literature and Art presented to Helen Grant*, ed. Nigel Glendinning (London, 1972), 149-161.

ROMERA-NAVARRO, M., *Historia de la Literatura Española* (Boston, Massachusetts, 1928).

ROSALES, Luis, 'Muerte y resurrección de Antonio Machado', *Cuadernos Hispoamericanos*, nos. 11-12 (1949), 435-79.

SÁNCHEZ, Alberto, 'Antonio Machado, funcionario docente y educador de la juventud', *Instituto de Bachillerato Cervantes: miscellanea en su cincuentenario 1931-1981* (Madrid, 1982), 307-27.

SESÉ, Bernard, *Antonio Machado (1875-1939): El hombre. El poeta. El pensador*, trans. Soledad García Mouton (Madrid, 1980).

TERRY, Arthur, *Antonio Machado: Campos de Castilla* (London, 1973).

THOMAS, Hugh, *The Spanish Civil War* (4th edn. London, 2003).

TREND, J. B., *Antonio Machado* (Oxford, 1953).

---------------- *The Origins of Modern Spain* (Cambridge, 1934).

VILA-BELDA, Reyes, *Antonio Machado, poeta de lo nimio* (Madrid, 2004)

WHISTON, James, *Antonio Machado's Writings and the Spanish Civil War* (Liverpool, 1996).

References

INTRODUCTION

1   Barnstone, *Border of a Dream,* xix.

2   Pérez Ferrero, 203.

3   Grant, review article in *Bulletin of Hispanic Studies,* xxxiv (1957), 48.

I THE THREE ANTONIOS

1   Gibson, 32.

2   *Ibid.,* 35.

3   López–Morillas, 134.

4   The first twelve of Krause's 23 Commandments are set out in Marco, 48-9.

5   Brotherston, 225.

6   *PP,* 2106.

7   Pérez Ferrero, 21

8   *PC,* XCVII.

9   Gibson, 52.

10 *Ibid.,* 53.

[11] *Ibid.*

[12] *Ibid.*, 55.

[13] *PC*, XXXI S.

[14] *PP*, 1168-9.

[15] *Ibid.*, 2106.

[16] *PC*, V (trans. Barnstone, 15).

II THE MAKING OF A POET

[1] Marco, 205.

[2] Gibson, 63.

[3] Trend, *Origins of Modern Spain*, 77. In actual fact the first soccer match in Spain was organized by English mine technicians and took place in Huelva in the 1880s.

[4] *Ibid.*, 67

[5] Gibson, 64.

[6] *PP*, 1575.

[7] *Ibid.*

[8] Collier, 80.

[9] *PP*, 1576.

[10] *Ibid.*

[11] Trueblood, 9.

12 Pérez Ferrero, 29–30.

13 Gibson, 74.

14 *Ibid.*

15 González and Talavera, 378.

16 *PP*, 1524.

17 *PC*, CXXXVI xlviii; cf. *Hamlet*, V i 191–92.

18 Gibson, 83.

19 *PP*, 1083.

20 *PC*, I.

21 Sesé, 39.

22 *PP*, 1449.

23 *PD*, 209n.

24 *PP*, 2061 (trans. Belitt, 84).

25 Cited in Sesé, 47.

26 Gibson, 106.

27 Cited in *ibid.*, 120.

28 This extract from the poem as it first appeared in *Electra* is in Gibson, 119–20. A slightly revised version is to be found in *PC,* I S.

29 Cited in Gibson, 140–41.

[30]   *PC*, XLII, verse 2.

[31]   Sesé, 57.

[32]   Cited in *ibid.*, 53.

[33]   *PP*, 1464.

[34]   Gibson, 151.

[35]   *PP*, 1458.

[36]   Gibson, 154.

[37]   *Ibid.*, 154–55.

[38]   *PC*, VII (trans. Barnstone, 19).

[39]   *Ibid.*, LVII i (trans. Barnstone, 83).

[40]   *PP*, 1474.

[41]   Gibbans, 'Unamuno and Antonio Machado', 20, 27-28.

[42]   *Ibid.*, 13.

[43]   *PD*, 175–80.

[44]   Geoffrey Gibbans, in a review of J.M. Aguirre, *Antonio Machado, poeta simbolista* (Madrid 1973) in *Bulletin of Hispanic Studies*, liv (1977), 76.

[45]   *PP*, 1474.

[46]   Gibson, 166.

III JOY AND SORROW IN SORIA

1   Pérez Ferrero, 75-6.

2   *PC*, LXII (trans. Trend, 14-15).

3   Pascual Piqué, 21-24.

4   Barnstone, xx.

5   *PC*, IX.

6   Pascual Piqué, 83

7   Vila-Belda, 69.

8   Gibson, 216-17.

9   Sesé, 167.

10   *PP*, 1483-84.

11   *PC*, XCVII.

12   Gibson, 209.

13   *Ibid.*

14   *Ibid.*, 210.

15   *PC*, CXII.

16   Gibson, 213.

17   *PC*, XCVIII (trans. Trueblood, 103, 105).

18   Pérez Ferrero, 81-2.

[19]   *PP*, 1487.

[20]   *Ibid.,* 1489.

[21]   *Ibid.,* 1490.

[22]   *PC,* XCIX.

[23]   Gibson, 227.

[24]   *PD*, 255.

[25]   *LC,* 7r; *PP,* 1159.

[26]   Gibson, 236.

[27]   *PC,* LIX (trans. Barnstone, 87).

[28]   Trueblood, 281-2, citing articles by Fernando Lázaro and R.A. Molina.

[29]   *PC,* CXXXVI iii.

[30]   Pascual Piqué, 66-7.

[31]   Cited in Sesé, 195.

[32]   *PC,* CXIII (trans. Trueblood, 113, 117).

[33]   *Ibid.,* CXIV (trans. Barnstone, 189, 191).

[34]   *PD,* 418.

[35]   Terry, 52

[36]   Cited in *ibid.,* 39.

37 Cited in Sesé, 358.

38 Gibson, 253-54.

39 *PC*, CXXIII (trans. Bly, 105).

40 Gibson, 255-57.

IV SEVEN LONG YEARS IN THE SOUTH

1 *PD*, 319-20.

2 *PC*, CXXXVII v (trans. Trueblood, 149). This translator renders *en el mar* as 'of the sea', but points out in a note (p. 288) that it actually means both *in* and *on* the sea.

3 Baker, 120.

4 Gibson, 264.

5 *PC*, CXXI (trans. Barnstone, 237).

6 *Ibid.,* CXXXI.

7 *Ibid.,* CXXXV (trans. Trend, 24-25). Frascuelo was a celebrated matador.

8 Gibbans, 'Unamuno and Antonio Machado', 20-21.

9 *PP,* 1954 (trans. Belitt, 26-7).

10 *PP,* 1519.

11 *PC*, CXXVI (trans. Barnstone, 247).

12 *PP,* 1531.

[13] *PC*, CXXVIII (trans. Trueblood, 131).

[14] Terry, 89-90.

[15] *PP*, 1531.

[16] *Ibid.*, 1524-5.

[17] *Ibid.*, 1537.

[18] *PD*, 327, n.12.

[19] *Ibid.*, 327.

[20] *PC*, CXLIII.

[21] Cited by Romera-Navarro, 627.

[22] *LC*, 8*v*-9*r*, 10*r*, 11*r* -13*r*; *PP*, 1161-62, 1163-64, 1165-68.

[23] Gibson, 303-04.

[24] *PC*, CXXXII (trans. Trueblood, 139, 141)

[25] Trueblood, 287.

[26] Pérez Ferrero, 114.

[27] *PC*, CLXVI iv (trans. Trueblood, 221).

[28] *PP*, 1558.

[29] *PD*, 381.

[30] *Ibid.*, 352.

[31] *Ibid.*, 408.

[32]   Gibson, 326.

[33]   Sesé, 179.

[34]   *PC*, CXXXIX (trans. Bly, 115).

[35]   Barnstone, xxx–xxxi.

[36]   *PC,* CXLVIII.

[37]   *Ibid.,* CLXV iv (trans. Trueblood, 217).

[38]   *PP*, 1595.

[39]   Gibson, 325.

[40]   *Ibid.,* 341.

[41]   *PC*, p.73 (trans. Trueblood, 7).

[42]   *Ibid.,* p.74 (trans. Bly, 79–80).

[43]   *Ibid.,* CXXXVI xxix (trans. Barnstone, 281)

[44]   *Ibid.,* II.

[45]   *PP,* 1600–1.

[46]   *PC,* CXXXVII vii (trans. Trueblood, 151)

[47]   *PD,* 383.

[48]   Gibson, 342.

V IN AND OUT OF SEGOVIA

[1]   Pérez Ferrero, 145–6.

2   Gibson, 345.

3   *Ibid.*

4   Sesé, 408.

5   *Ibid.*, 411–12.

6   *Ibid.*, 417.

7   Barnstone, xiii.

8   *PP*, 2410.

9   *PC*, CLXIV (trans. Barnstone, 385)

10   *Ibid.,* CX.

11   *PD*, 445–49.

12   *PC,* LV S.

13   *PD*, 452–53.

14   *PP*, 1621–22.

15   *LC*, 54r–55r; *PP*, 1221–22.

16   Martínez, 58, 60.

17   *PP,* 1234–38.

18   *Ibid.*, 1632.

19   *LC*, 127v; *PP*, 1289.

20   *LC*, 151v; *PP*, 1316.

21 *PD*, 512.

22 Cited in Sesé, 458.

23 *PC*, CLXII (trans. Trueblood, 205-7).

24 Ribbans, 'Recaptured Memory', 157-61

25 Sesé, 466-67.

26 Gibson, 373.

27 *Ibid.*, 374.

28 *Ibid.*, 375.

29 *Ibid.*, 378.

30 *Ibid.*, 389.

31 *PC,* CLXVII (trans. Bly, 155); cf. Sesé, 699-70.

32 *PC*, 324.

33 *Ibid.*, 329.

34 *PD*, 494-5.

35 Sesé, 601, citing an unpublished article by J. P. Bernard.

36 Belitt, xviii-xix.

37 Gibson, 395-7.

38 *PD*, 543-57.

39 Manuel and Antonio Machado, *Las adelfas* (Madrid, 1928), 8-9.

[40] Gibson, 411.

[41] *Ibid.*, 429–30; for 'searching for God among the clouds', see *PC.*, LXXVII.

[42] Gibson, 432.

[43] The whole poem is translated in Trueblood, 227–39.

[44] Rosales, 435.

[45] *Ibid,* 462, 469–70, 478–79.

[46] Barnstone, xv.

[47] Gibson, 409.

VI THE COURTLY LOVER

[1] Gibson, 420

[2] *PP,* 1703–06.

[3] *Ibid.*, 1735–36.

[4] *PD,* 577.

[5] *Ibid.,* 585.

[6] Gibson, 444.

[7] *PP,* 1678–79.

[8] *PC,* CLXXIII ii (trans. Barnstone, 435, 437).

[9] Sesé, 567.

10 P. de Valderrama, *Esencias* (cited in Gibson, 457).

11 *PP*, 1706-08.

12 *Ibid.*, 1695.

13 *Ibid.*, 1695-96.

14 *Ibid.*, 1746.

15 *Ibid.*, 1703.

16 *Ibid.*, 1719.

17 Valderrama, *Esencias* (cited in Gibson, 467).

18 *PP*, 1726.

19 *Ibid.*, 1728-9.

20 Valderrama published the poem in her book, *Sí, soy Guiomar*. See Gibson, 470.

21 Gibson, 470.

22 *PP*, 1755.

23 *PD*, 665.

24 Gibson, 484.

25 *PC*, CLXXIV (trans. Barnstone, 441).

26 *PP*, 1744-45.

27 Gibson, 532.

28 Barnstone, xxxviii.

29 *PC, CLXXIV*, ii.

30 *PD*, 570.

VII DRAMA AND DISRUPTION IN MADRID

1 *PD*, 614.

2 Gibson, 454–5.

3 *PD*, 617.

4 Gibson, 473–4.

5 *PP*, 1743.

6 *Ibid.*,1739.

7 *Ibid.*, 2332–33.

8 *PD*, 682–83.

9 *Ibid.*, 683.

10 Gibson, 479.

11 *Ibid.*, 480.

12 Thomas, 34–5.

13 *PD*, 687–88.

14 Whiston, 16.

15 *Ibid.*

[16] Cited in Sesé, 439.

[17] Gibson, 488.

[18] Sesé, 441.

[19] *Ibid.*, 581-2,

[20] Pérez Ferrero, 193.

[21] Gibson, 493.

[22] Neruda, 119.

[23] Whiston, 16.

[24] Gibson, 525.

[25] *PP*, 2099-2100 (trans. Belitt, 106).

[26] Gibson, 513.

[27] Sánchez, 308.

[28] *PD*, 727.

[29] *Ibid.*, 733.

[30] *Ibid.*

[31] *Ibid.*,736.

[32] *PC*, CLXIX (trans. Barnstone, 427, 429).

[33] *PC*, CLXXV.

[34] *PD*, 745, n.2.

35 *Ibid.*, 743-44.

36 Gibson, 509.

37 *PD,* 749-51.

38 *Ibid.,* 762-65.

39 *PP,* 2088.

40 *Ibid.,* 2054.

41 *Ibid.,* 2050 (trans. Belitt, 78-9).

42 Gibson, 513-14; Sesé, 590.

43 *PD,* 773-4.

44 *PP,* 2049 (trans. Belitt, 77-78). Belitt suggested that Machado may here have been writing about Giner de los Ríos, but he died long before the adoption of the pseudonym of Juan de Mairena.

45 Gibson, 527.

46 *PP,* 2085.

47 Gibson, 528-9.

VIII FIGHTING AGAINST FASCISM

1 José Machado, 122.

2 Thomas, 227.

3 Pérez Ferrero, 203-4.

4 Gibson, 541.

[5]   Kamen, 272.

[6]   Carr, 437.

[7]   Gibson, 542.

[8]   *PC,* LXXXIV S.

[9]   *Ibid.,* LXXXIX S.

[10] Gibson, 551.

[11] *Ibid.,* 552.

[12] *Ibid.*

[13] Sesé, 812.

[14] *PP,* 2166.

[15] Gibson, 555.

[16] José Machado, 123.

[17] Gibson, 559.

[18] José Machado, 124.

[19] *PP,* 2175.

[20] José Machado, 124.

[21] Gibson, 564.

[22] *PC,* LXXXV S (trans. Barnstone, 495). Ausias March was a 14th century Valencian poet.

23   *PP*, 2177-9.

24   Gibson, 572.

25   *Ibid.*, 575.

26   *PC*, LXXVIII S.

27   Whiston, 172-3.

28   Gibson, 575.

29   *Ibid.*, 577.

30   José Machado, 31.

31   *PP*, 2208-9.

32   *Ibid.*, 2209.

33   *Ibid.*, 2211.

34   Gibson, 580-81

35   José Machado, 125

36   Gibson, 587-8.

37   *PC*, LXXXIII S (trans. Barnstone, 489).

38   Gibson, 589.

39   *PP*, 2228.

40   Gibson, 590.

41   *PC*, LXXVI S (trans. Bly, 163).

42 Barnstone, *Six Masters*, 120.

43 Whiston, 150-51.

44 José Machado, 128.

45 Gibson, 592.

46 *Ibid.,* 596-7.

47 *PP*, 2485.

48 *Ibid.*, 2247, 2529.

49 *Ibid.*, 2483.

50 Whiston, 239.

51 *PP*, 2449-51.

52 Gibson, 599.

53 *PP*, 2394.

54 Gibson, 600.

55 *PP*, 2276-80.

56 Gibson, 604.

57 *Ibid.*, 605.

58 *Ibid.*, 606.

59 *PP*, 2299-300.

IX EXILE AND DEATH

1   Gibson, 612-13.

2   *Ibid.*, 613.

3   *Ibid.*, 614.

4   José Machado, 137.

5   Barnstone, xlv.

6   José Machado, 137.

7   Gibson, 615.

8   Barnstone, xlvi.

9   *Ibid.*, xlvi-xlvii.

10   Gibson, 619.

11   *Ibid.*, 620.

12   *Ibid.*, 621.

13   *Ibid.*

14   *Ibid.*, 622-3.

15   *Ibid.*, 624.

16   *Ibid.*, 626-7.

17   *PP*, 2302-3.

18   José Machado, 142.

[19] *PC*, CXXXVII iv (trans. Trueblood, 149).

[20] Gibson, 627.

[21] *Ibid.*, 628.

[22] *Ibid.,* 630.

[23] José Machado, 144.

[24] *PC*, XCII S.

[25] *Ibid.*, CLXXIV vi (trans. Barnstone, 443).

[26] Gibson, 630.

[27] *PC*, CXXXVI xxxi.

[28] Gibson, 633-4.

[29] *Ibid.*, 634.

[30] Jiménez, 'Antonio Machado: A Reminiscence' in Barnstone, xvi-xvii.

EPILOGUE

[1] Gibson, 635.

[2] *The Times*, 2 March 1939, 19.

[3] Pérez Ferrero, 209-10.

[4] A translation of the full text of the report is in Bly, 169-72.

CONCLUSION

[1]   Terry, 92.

[2]   Cited in Margaret Drabble, *The Pattern on the Carpet* (2009), 56.

[3]   *PC*, XXXI S.

[4]   Marie-Louise von Franz and James Hillman, *Lectures on Jung's Typology* (Irving, Texas, 1979), 33, 35.

[5]   *PC*, XCVII (trans. Trueblood, 101).

[6]   *Ibid*, CLXI xv (trans. Trueblood, 179).

[7]   *PP*, 2107.

[8]   Don Paterson, *The Eyes: a version of Antonio Machado* (1999), 55.

[9]   *PP*, 2291-5; see Appendix.

Genealogical Table

Francisco Machado Rodríguez *m.* Mariana Núñez Domínguez

Manuel Machado Núñez   Francisco Machado Núñez   Antonio Machado Núñez *m.* Cipriana Álvarez Durán
1827-1904

Antonio Machado Álvarez *m.* Ana Ruiz Hernández
1846-93   *1854-1939*

Manuel	Antonio	Rafael	José	Joaquín	Francisco	Cipriana	Ana
1874-1947	*1875-1939*	*1876/7-8*	*1879-1958*	*1881-1955*	*1884-1950*	*1885-1900*	*1890-91(?)*
m. Eulalia Cáceres	*m.* Leonor Izquierdo		*m.* Matea Monedero	*m.* Carmen Lopéz	*m.* Mercedes Martínez		

Manuel   Antonio   José   Joaquín   Francisco

Index of Names

Index of First Lines of Poems

★ Indicates that this is the first line of only part *of a poem*

Ingram Content Group UK Ltd.
Milton Keynes UK
UKHW042025220623
423898UK00002B/379

9 781984 595386